A.G. Tyapin

SOIL-STRUCTURE INTERACTION IN SEISMIC ANALYSIS

ASV Construction
Stockholm, Sweden
2019

Readers:

Professor of the Department of Mechanics and Strength of Materials and Structures of the St. Petersburg State University of Railway Transport, member of the European Association for Earthquake Engineering (EAEE), member of Earthquake Engineering Research Institute (EERI), USA, member of the Russian Society for Soil Mechanics, Geotechnics and Foundation Engineering, Senior doctorate in Engineering, Full Professor **Aleksandr M. Uzdin** (Russia);

Chief Scientific Officer of the Scientific and Production Association SCAD Soft, full member of the Academy of Construction of Ukraine, a foreign member of the Russian Academy of Architecture and Construction Sciences, a member of the Ukrainian Association for Metal Structures, Senior doctorate in Engineering **Anatoliy V. Perelmuter** (Ukraine).

Tyapin A.G.
Soil-structure interaction in seismic analysis / ASV Construction, 2019. – 200 p.

ISBN 978-91-982223-7-1

Soil-structure interaction (SSI) is an important phenomenon in the seismic response analysis. As seismologists describe seismic excitation in terms of the seismic motion of certain control point at the free surface of the initial site, the question is whether the same point of the structure (after structure appears) will have the same seismic response motion in case of the same seismic event. If yes, then seismic motion from seismologists is directly applied to the base of the structure (it is called "fixed-base analysis"), and they say that "no SSI occurs'" (though literally speaking soil is forcing structure to move, so interaction is always present). This is a conventional approach in the field of civil engineering. However, if heavy and rigid structure (sometimes embedded) is erected on medium or soft soil site, this structure changes the seismic response motion of the soil as compared to the initial free-field picture. Such a situation is typical for Nuclear Power Plants (NPPs), deeply embedded structures, etc. The book describes different approaches to SSI analysis and different SSI effects. Special attention is paid to the Combined Asymptotic Method (CAM) developed by the author and used for the design of NPPs in seismic regions. Nowadays, some civil structures have parameters comparable to those of NPPs (e.g., masses and embedment), so these approaches become useful for the civil structural engineers as well.

ISBN 978-91-982223-7-1   © ASV Construction, 2019
                                © Tyapin A.G., 2019

CONTENT

INTRODUCTION 6

1. SEISMIC WAVE FIELD IN THE SOIL WITHOUT STRUCTURE 11

1.1. Waves in the horizontally-layered linear medium 11
1.2. 1D wave problem. Outcropped motion and motion in depth 16
1.3. Equivalent linear approach to the non-linear soil behaviour. Degradation curves 20
1.4. Site response analysis with SHAKE. Convolutions and deconvolutions 24
1.5. Half-space tuning method 30

2. PRIMARY AND SECONDARY SUPERPOSITIONS – COMMON STARTING POINT FOR ALL SSI METHODS 37

2.1. Primary superposition. Substitution of the initial SSI problem with a new problem 37
2.2. Secondary superposition — initial and reflected waves in the free field 38

3. DIRECT APPROACH 42

3.1. Elementary boundaries 43
3.2. Acoustic boundaries 46
3.3. Surface waves in layered soil. Analytical transmitting boundaries in the frequency domain 50
3.4. Semi-analytical transmitting boundaries in the frequency domain 64
3.5. Flexible half-space 72

4. SUB-STRUCTURING APPROACH 79

4.1. Winkler models 79
4.2. Impedance approach as a particular case of simplified approach 82
    4.2.1. The simplest case: surface basement, horizontally-layered soil, vertical seismic wave 82

4.2.2. Embedded rigid basement. Vertical wave
   in horizontally-layered soil 84
4.2.3. Complicated soil environment for rigid base 86
4.2.4. Multiple rigid basements 86
4.3. Problems with damping in modal and linear-spectral
   approach to SSI analysis 87
   4.3.1. Conventional modal and spectral analysis 87
   4.3.2. Inhomogeneous damping 90

5. COMBINED ASYMPTOTIC METHOD (CAM) 101

5.1. General remarks 101
5.2. The basic scheme of the first step of CAM 102
5.3. Illustration of the CAM methodology 104
5.4. Dynamic inertia condensation procedure 107
5.5. Soil impedances and seismic loads: possible sources 109
5.6. Comparison of SASSI impedances obtained using
   condensation with CLASSI results 119
5.7. Comparison of SASSI impedances obtained using
   condensation with ASCE4 results for almost
   homogeneous half-space 121
5.8. CAM and some of the SSI effects 127
   5.8.1. Two types of soil profiles 127
   5.8.2. Role of the embedment 130

6. APPLICATION OF CAM 131

6.1. Stiff structure 131
   6.1.1. Site response analysis 131
   6.1.2. Soil impedances 140
   6.1.3. Dynamic inertia 142
   6.1.4. Transfer functions 144
   6.1.5. Response spectra 147
6.2. High-rise building 148
   6.2.1. Model description 151
   6.2.2. Soil impedances 152
   6.2.3. Dynamic inertia 153
   6.2.4. Transfer functions 156
   6.2.5. Response spectra 158
   6.2.6. The criterion for the SSI importance 161
   6.2.7. Specific of the low-frequency building in SSI 166

7. COMPLICATED SOIL ENVIRONMENT 172
   7.1. Impedance/load calculation.. 172
   7.2. Application to the soil upgrade case 179
      7.2.1. Demonstration of the protective effect......................... 180
      7.2.2. Role of kinematical interaction in the seismic
             protective effect of the soil pillow 183
      7.2.3. 1D modelling of the soil pillow.................................. 187
      7.2.4. Effect of the soil pillow stiffness................................ 191
      7.2.5. Conclusions about soil upgrade.................................. 194

CONCLUSIONS 196
REFERENCES.. 198

INTRODUCTION

The more sophisticated human civilization becomes the more risks it faces in all fields. This is true for seismic events as well — they can be extremely disastrous, and almost every year it is proven again and again. Shaking of the ground itself is unpleasant, but in fact, it is not so dangerous for human beings. In old times the main risk was secondary natural effects like earth slides and tsunami. When a man started to create massive structures, the collapse of structures became the important reason of human and material losses. In twentieth century secondary disasters caused by earthquakes (mainly in the engineering communication lines) became also important. One can remember fires, breaks of gas tubes and electrical lines leading to great losses. Chemical facilities are generally vulnerable to earthquakes as well. In the last eighty years, nuclear power plants and other nuclear facilities added to the overall seismic risk. General trend is the extension of the scope of dangerous effects potentially caused by earthquakes.

Nowadays mankind is not able to prevent the occurrence of seismic events. So, the only possible way is to prevent disastrous consequences of these events – starting from collapse of structures and up to malfunction of the safety-related equipment. To achieve this goal one should be able to predict structural response to the seismic loads. This is important both as 1) an issue for structural strength and stability (to prevent collapse), and 2) input for the safety-related equipment design (to prevent dangerous malfunction).

Seismic analysis is an important part of earthquake engineering. Historically, it started at the beginning of the XX century from the simple structural models subjected to the excitation given by seismologists. Later they recognized that soil can play the important role being not only the path for seismic waves but also a part of the "soil-structure" system responding to the seismic excitation. So, "soil-structure interaction" (SSI) was recognized as an important part of the whole picture. This book is about soil-structure interaction in seismic analysis.

Seismologists almost always come out with seismic motion of the certain point in the free field (i.e. without structures, usually at the surface of the soil). This point is called "control point". Most often there is an additional assumption that all other points at the horizontal surface of the free soil during seismic event move similarly. Sometimes the control point is placed in the depth (e.g., at the surface of the underlying rock). But anyhow seismologists never deal with structures.

On the other hand, structural engineers usually start from the seismic motion of the base and study the response of the upper structure. The question is whether the first motion coincides with the second one, i.e. whether one can apply seismic motion obtained from seismologists directly to the base of the structure (in case the control point in the free soil is set up on the future base).

The answer to this question depends on several physical factors. If soil is stiff, if structure is light and flexible, if it is not embedded, if soil is not changed during the construction works, then the structure does not significantly change the motion of the base as compared to the free-field motion. In this case they often say about the "absence of the soil-structure interaction". It means that instead of "interaction" one has just an impact of the soil motion on the structure without back impact of the structure on the soil motion (in terms of the interaction forces there is surely a back impact, but these interaction forces do not change the soil motion significantly). So, one can indeed apply the soil seismic motion obtained from seismologists as a kinematical excitation on the base mat. That was a common assumption for seismic analysis during the first sixty years of the XX century. Now it is called "fixed-base seismic analysis" and is still widely used for civil structures.

However, this simple situation may be spoiled in different ways. First, the initial soil may be changed somehow before the upper structure is constructed. For example, piles can be implemented; soil improvement by different technologies may be used (e.g., jet grouting or deep soil mixing popular nowadays); the embedded part of the structure may substitute part of the initial soil. As a result, seismic motion of the basement will differ from the free-field motion of the soil even before the upper structure appears. This part of the soil-structure interaction is often called "kinematical interaction" (further rigorous definition will follow). It is not always manifested: if the structure has a surface basement, and if the free-field seismic motion of the soil is "rigid" within a spot under this basement (before the basement appears), then nothing is changed before the upper structure appears – in such case they say that "no kinematical SSI occurs".

After the upper structure appears, the basement motion is further changed. The heavier is the upper structure, and the softer is the soil, the more pronounced is this additional change. It is often called "inertial soil-structure interaction". Historically, the SSI field started the intensive development when heavy rigid structures with dangerous technologies appeared – namely nuclear power plants.

So, these two changes in the basement motion as compared to the free-field motion of the soil (i.e., kinematical and inertial SSI) compose total soil-structure interaction effect. There are numerous methods to analyze SSI. In this text the author tries to provide a systematic classification of all these methods, stressing key choices and additional assumptions. The first attempt to tell this story (see Tyapin (2012)) was a success – over 10,000 readers registered and loaded the text since then. So, the author decided to prepare the extended version including some recent achievements.

The book consists of seven chapters.

In the first chapter the preliminary stage of soil-structure interaction (SSI) analysis is discussed – this is site response analysis (SRA), i.e. analysis of soil seismic response without structure. Site response analysis provides two sets of data for the further calculations. First of all, as the subsequent SSI analysis is nowadays mostly linear, all physical non-linearity in the soil behavior is "packed" into the equivalent linear characteristics of the soil. The more intensive is seismic excitation and the greater are dynamic shear strains in the soil, the lower is the effective soil stiffness and the greater is the effective soil material damping. This is called the "degradation of the soil properties". The result is certain shift of soil characteristics from those measured in the field tests. Surely, in the soil-structure system this shift is caused both by seismic waves in soil without structure (this is called "primary non-linearity"), and by the impact of the structure (this is called "secondary non-linearity"). Modern standards allow accounting for the primary non-linearity only. That means that the first result of SRA is set of effective soil characteristics compatible with particular seismic excitation. The author in the first chapter proposes special technique for the approximate accounting for the secondary non-linearity as well. Another author's technique described in the first chapter is "half-space tuning method".

The second result of SRA is seismic response motion at different elevations of the site (calculated without structure). As the initial excitation is given in the certain point, one has to calculate motions in other points. Besides, very often the initial motion is given for the initial soil profile, and during the construction process this initial soil profile is somehow modified before the structure appears (e.g., upper layers of the initial soil are withdrawn to certain depth). So, one cannot simply apply the excitation given for one soil profile directly to another soil profile.

The second chapter presents basic concept of the SSI analysis. This is "primary superposition". In fact, the initial SSI problem is substituted by some other problem, leading to the same results, but only inside certain limited physical volume (this volume includes structure and, optionally, some part of surrounding soil). This substitution helps to localize seismic loads within finite volume (unlike the initial problem where seismic source is usually far away from the site). One has to understand additional assumptions and limitations implicitly used in this substitution.

Then there is "secondary superposition", linking seismic loads to the free-field wave picture. This is also an important issue, because in the SSI problem the structure modifies the free-field wave picture, and one generally cannot point out the node in the soil-structure system keeping the free-field seismic motion. These two superpositions (i.e. "basic" one and "secondary" one) form a basis for all subsequent SSI calculations. Two main approaches to the SSI analysis – direct and impedance calculations – are just particular cases of the general approach described in the second chapter.

The third chapter describes the so-called "direct" approach to SSI. The selected finite volume in this approach includes not only the structure but also the considerable part of soil surrounding the structure. Soil and structure inside this volume are modeled physically (i.e., mathematical model is representing physical prototypes). The key issues here are boundary conditions and seismic loads set there. As generally there are no physical boundaries from all sides (i.e. selected volume is chosen and boundaries are set up by analyst, at least partly), any finite model is artificial and not physical. These boundaries should not create artificial effects spoiling physical solution. Several types of such boundaries (elementary boundaries, acoustic viscous boundaries, transmitting boundaries in the frequency domain) are discussed in the third chapter.

The fourth chapter describes alternative approach to SSI, usually called "impedance" approach. Unlike direct approach, here the selected finite volume in the model includes only structure. Soil is modeled not physically, but artificially – to reproduce main parameters controlling SSI. This approach is simpler in implementation; therefore the author prefers to call it "simplified approach", leaving the conventional term "impedance approach" for the particular case of rigid soil-structure contact surface. However, this popular approach has a number of underlying additional assumptions. They are discussed in the fourth chapter.

The fifth chapter describes special technology of the SSI analysis developed by the author and called "combined asymptotic method" (CAM). This technology, in fact, is a sub-structuring technology developed for the case of a fully linear soil-structure system. The so-called "first option" of CAM presented in this book refers to the case with rigid soil-structure contact surface – so, it is a particular case of the impedance approach. Soil in CAM is modeled without structure (in SASSI, CLASSI or using approximate analytical formulae). Structure is modeled without soil (i.e. fixed-base structural model is used) in any general code – e.g., the author uses ABAQUS. The results of both calculations (for soil and for structure) are condensed to the format of 6×6 complex frequency-dependent matrices and combined. The result of this combination is seismic response of the rigid soil-structure contact surface. In the further calculations of structural response the fixed-base structural model can be used without soil, but the input motion of the base is taken from the combined calculation described above, and not directly from seismologists. The approach is called "combined" as it combines modal analysis for fixed-base structural model, calculations in the frequency domain and calculations in the time domain.

In the sixth chapter the author present two cases from his practice of the last decade. CAM was used (i) for the typical nuclear structure, (ii) for the high-rise building. Though certain civil structures are already comparable to the nuclear structures in mass, their natural fixed-base frequencies are completely different. Effects of "dynamic inertia" discussed in the fifth chapter were manifested in these cases differently, and the response is different. The author hopes this comparison is interesting for those who try to understand SSI effects.

In the seventh chapter the author presents another interesting example — SSI analysis of the comparatively stiff heavy structure resting on soft soil upgraded under the base. It turns out that such finite "soil pillow" under the base can work as a certain seismic isolation, decreasing structural response. CAM helps to understand drivers of this effect.

The author will be grateful for the response. E-mail of the author is atyapin@bvcp.ru.

December 2018

Chapter 1. SEISMIC WAVE FIELD IN THE SOIL WITHOUT STRUCTURE

Even if one is going to perform structural analysis applying the free-field seismic motion from the soil surface directly to the base of the structure (this is called "fixed-base model"), he still should know this soil motion over the whole spot under the future base before the structure appears. This is, in fact, a small fragment for the whole wave field in the initial soil without structure. Hereafter we will use the term "free-field motion" not only for the free surface of the initial soil but also for the whole wave field in the initial soil free from structures.

To perform soil-structure interaction (SSI) analysis, one should know much about this wave field in advance. Traditionally this part of structural mechanics is called "engineering seismology". In practice seismologists, geotechnical specialists and structural engineers (responsible for the further SSI analysis) work here together or in parallel. As this stage (it is called "site response analysis" – SRA) is a preliminary part of the SSI analysis, the first chapter will discuss it in detail.

1.1. Waves in the horizontally-layered linear medium

Real soil is a very complicated medium. First, it is a mixture of several different components: solid part (called "soil skeleton"), porous water and porous air. Second, the soil is heterogeneous – both with sharp internal boundaries (e.g., sand resting on rock) and with smooth changes in properties (e.g., sand in the deep soil site has properties varying with depth). Besides, there may be internal cracks in the rock, inclusions of one soil type into another soil type, etc. Third, some types of soil may demonstrate anisotropy. Fourth, soil behaviour is a non-linear one.

Keeping all that in mind, engineers try to use simplified models of soil, enabling reasonable predictions. Applicability of simplified models is limited and should be carefully checked on case by case basis.

In the soil-structure interaction analysis engineers usually use soil models composed of horizontal layers of homogeneous isotropic materials with linear behaviour (including hysteretic internal damping). The reasons for such simplified geometry will be discussed later.

Set of soil layers (in the author's practice – about 30...40 layers with total thickness about 120 m) in the conventional soil models is underlain by homogeneous half-space. Usually engineers try to find a hard rock in the depth to use rocky half-space, but it is not always possible. Surely, in every point of the world hard rock exists at a certain depth, but sometimes this depth is so great that one cannot model the whole soft soil column and therefore has to put soft half-space below the layers.

Note that in the US they usually treat rock separately from soil (i.e. rock is not a soil, but some different special material), whereas in the Russian tradition rock is just one of the soil types. Hereinafter, the second approach to the terminology is used.

Of course, horizontally-layered soil is a simplification in many senses. As to the site geometry, it does not account for possible topographic peculiarities or for the internal boundaries like inclined layers. The role of such factors sometimes may be significant, and one should check it. In this book, we will discuss only the sites, which may be reasonably modelled in such a simplified way.

The simplest model of a typical site is a single layer of soft or medium soil resting on a rocky half-space. Even for the rocky sites usually the upper part of the rock is softer (partly weathered) than the lower part. This simple model helps to understand several very important issues.

Seismicity is generally defined as a load originated by waves spreading in the soil. According to the source of waves, seismicity is classified into natural and technological ones. Technological seismicity is caused by sources located either in the soft or in the rocky part of the soil. Subways, surface and underground explosives, or even vibrations from the neighbouring surface sources are considered here. For technological seismicity, the wave path from the source to the considered structure is comparatively short and often goes through the soft soil only. Therefore, the properties of the underlying rock do not control such a wave load; only the soft soil properties matter.

On the contrary, the natural seismicity is never caused by the sources in the soft soil: hypocenters, seismic faults are always in the rock, even if the fault's traces come to the surface through the soft layer. Therefore, seismic waves go from the source located inside or at the surface of the rock to the surface of the soft layer in two variants: (i) directly from the source (located at the boundary between rock and soft soil) through the soft soil up to the surface; (ii) first over the rock surface, then through the soft soil of the site. These two variants are illustrated in *Fig. 1.1*.

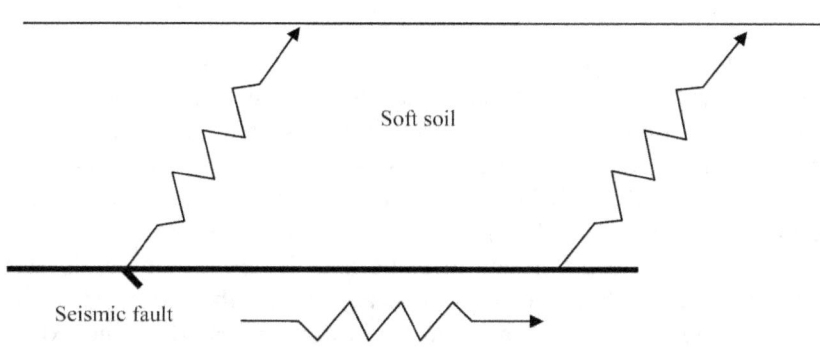

Figure 1.1. Two variants of wave path for natural seismicity

As soft soil has comparatively short wavelengths and greater internal dissipation as compared to the rock, the former variant is typical only for the so-called epicentral zones (epicentre is defined as a projection of deep hypocenter on the surface). The radius of such zone is comparable to the depth of hypocenter plus the length of the fault. In all other regions (sometimes located in hundred kilometres from epicentre) the second variant is observed.

The second variant means that horizontal wave velocity at the bottom of the soft layer is controlled by the rock properties (surface waves in the rock have velocity about 3–4 km/s). What shall we see at the surface of the soft soil?

Let us consider 2D wave field in the soft layers with prescribed wave running over the bottom with high speed C. From each point of the bottom two waves are spreading in the soft soil: (i) primary wave with velocity V_p; (ii) secondary (shear) wave with velocity V_s. The terms "primary" and "secondary" are explained simply by comparative values of these velocities: $V_p > V_s$. Therefore primary waves arrive to the site from the seismic fault first, and secondary waves arrive later. Looking at the seismic motion record, one can distinguish "primary" and "secondary" parts.

Shear (secondary) wave velocity is given by

$$V_s^2 = G/\rho, \qquad (1.1)$$

where G is shear modulus, ρ is mass density. Primary wave velocity is controlled by constrained tension modulus E_c instead of shear modulus G:

$$V_p^2 = E_c / \rho. \qquad (1.2)$$

Mathematical background of this conclusion will be given later. Two short comments should be added here. First, static modules (e.g., controlling settlements) are significantly less than dynamic modules (about ten times). So, if one tries to estimate wave velocities using static modules, the results will be unrealistic. The data about wave velocities are obtained from field dynamic investigations (cross-hole, down-hole, etc.). Physically the difference in static and dynamic modules is partly explained by the behaviour of the porous water. In the static case porous water has enough time to leave the skeleton compressed by the external load, and so does not participate in the effective final stiffness. In the dynamic case the time is too short, and the porous water locked in the compressed volume participates in the effective stiffness of the soil.

Second, constrained modulus E_c is different from the conventional Young modulus E because of the Poisson's effect.

The ratio of two these velocities is controlled by the Poisson's coefficient v:

$$V_p^2 / V_s^2 = 2(1-v)/(1-2v). \qquad (1.3)$$

The relation between shear modulus G and Young modulus E is well-known:

$$G = E / [2(1+v)]. \qquad (1.4)$$

One can easily obtain the relation between constrained modulus E_c and Young modulus E from equations (1.1...1.4).

Let us return to the soft soil layer with a wave source moving at the bottom. Each of the two induced waves mentioned above forms the inclined wavefront, and the inclination angle is controlled by the ratio of velocity V to the source horizontal velocity C. This is illustrated in *Fig. 1.2.*

As source velocity C and wave velocity V for a certain induced wave are constant along horizontal coordinate, the trace of the wave front at the surface of the soft layer will move with the same velocity C, as the source. The same situation we observe when a supersonic jet is flying horizontally. As its velocity is higher than sonic velocity, the so-called "Mach cone" is formed behind a jet. The trace of this cone at the ground surface moves behind the plane with some lag, but the ground velocity of this trace is the same as the super-sonic velocity of the jet. In both cases, it is called "apparent wave velocity".

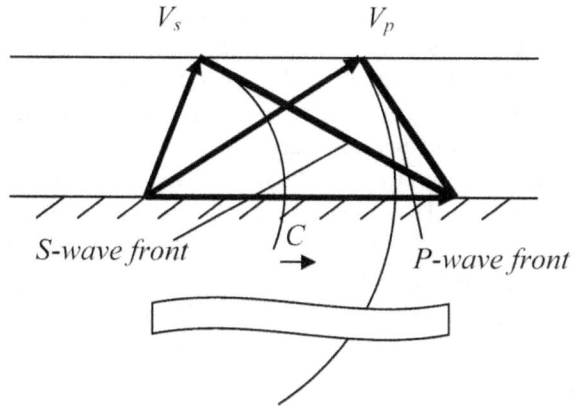

Figure 1.2. Induced wave fronts

One more comment of the same sort. The city of Mexico historically had a lake in the very centre (Montezuma's palace in the time of Cortes stood on the island). Later this lake was filled with soft soil, and buildings were erected, so nowadays one does not see the lake any more. But here we have the situation described above: soft soil resting on the rock. During the earthquake of 1985 number of acceleration time histories were registered, and horizontal apparent wave velocities were calculated based on the correlation lags and distances between the registration points. It turned out that the apparent velocity was very high – several km/s. That was far greater than wave velocities for the soft soil near the surface. Some specialists were surprised, but now the reader should understand the nature of this effect.

If the rock below is very hard, the horizontal velocity at the bottom of the soft layer goes to infinity, and wavefront in *Fig. 1.2* becomes horizontal. In this case, we have the vertically spreading seismic wave.

In reality all wave fronts are surely inclined, but because of the effect described above vertical seismic waves is a reasonable approximation for natural seismicity. This is also an explanation of why wave incoherency is not usually considered (unlike stochastic incoherence). The attempts to link translational motion to the rocking free-field motion usually use apparent horizontal velocity. If it is high, rocking is very small. References to the rocking or torsional structural response here do not work, as the structural response can have rotations because of structural non-symmetry even without free-field rotations. Slow and comparatively short surface waves during natural seismic events may be caused by topographical peculiarities or inclusions (e.g., neighbouring structures). Such waves will be discussed later in this book.

This also explains why the "anti-seismic moats" around buildings proposed by some specialists will not be effective against natural seismicity, though may be effective against technological seismicity induced by neighbouring surface sources.

The conclusion is that vertically propagating seismic wave in horizontally-layered soil conventionally used in site response analysis (SRA) has physical justification. Three translational components of the time history at the surface in three orthogonal directions (two horizontal ones and one vertical one) may be considered as motions in three different vertically spreading waves: two horizontal motions are from two secondary (shear) waves polarized in two orthogonal vertical planes, and vertical motion is from primary wave. Each of these three waves is 1D, so all three waves are described by the same math.

1.2. 1D wave problem. Outcropped motion and motion in depth

Let us consider 1D P-waves in a homogeneous vertical massive rod, modelling soil. The only coordinate is vertical coordinate z. Wave displacements $u(z, t)$ are described by the wave equation

$$V_p^2 \frac{\partial^2 u}{\partial z^2} = \frac{\partial^2 u}{\partial t^2}. \qquad (1.5)$$

Here V_p is wave velocity. In the frequency domain for certain frequency ω there exist two solutions of (1-5):

$$u_1 = U_1 \exp(-i z / \lambda); \quad u_2 = U_2 \exp(i z / \lambda), \quad \text{where} \quad \lambda = V_p / \omega. \qquad (1.6)$$

The first wave u_1 described by (1-6) goes up along Z-axis; the second wave u_2 goes down. Each wave has own amplitude U.

Let U^0 be displacement at the free surface $z = 0$. As we are going to obtain coefficient U_1^0 of the upcoming wave and coefficient U_2^0 of the wave coming down, now we have the first of the two boundary conditions for them:

$$u^0(0) = U_1^0 + U_2^0 = U^0. \qquad (1.7)$$

The second condition comes from the definition of the "free" surface; total stress at the soil surface must be zero:

$$E^0 \frac{\partial u^0}{\partial z}(0) = E^0(i/\lambda)(-U_1^0 + U_2^0) = 0. \qquad (1.8)$$

Two equations (1-7) and (1-8) lead to the well-known "doubling rule": the upcoming wave reaching the free surface is reflected back, and at the free surface displacements of the upcoming wave are doubled:

$$U_1^0 = U^0/2; \quad U_2^0 = U^0/2; \quad u^0(z) = U^0[\exp(-iz/\lambda) + \exp(iz/\lambda)]/2 = U^0\cos(z/\lambda). \quad (1.9)$$

So, (1.9) gives the whole solution of the problem linking wave field in any point to the "control motion" at the surface U^0.

Now let us consider the same rod but consisting of two parts with different properties, with a boundary between them at the depth $z = -H$. Let the upper part have the same properties as in the previous case. Equations (1.7–1.9) remain untouched, but now they are valid for the upper part only. Important note: if "control motion" U^0 stays the same, then the upper part wave field is the same as for the homogeneous soil. It does not depend on the properties of the lower part of the rod.

At the boundary $z = -H$ one has wave displacements given by (1.9) and stress σ given by the analogue of (1.8):

$$\sigma(-H) = E^0 \frac{\partial u}{\partial z}\bigg|_{z=-H}. \qquad (1.10)$$

Both values (displacement and stress) are controlled by surface displacement U^0 and properties of the upper part of the rod. But both displacements and stresses should be continuous at the boundary, so these two values give two conditions for the lower part of the rod. These two conditions enable calculation of two wave amplitudes (upcoming and down-coming ones) for this lower part. Again we have the whole 1D wave field linked to the surface control motion.

If there are more than two parts in a rod, the procedure is the same. Such procedure starting from the surface and going downwards is called "deconvolution". And the same note once again: in the upper part, our wave field is independent of the properties of the lower parts. This is typical for deconvolution.

We see that surface displacement U^0 is linked to the amplitudes of upcoming and down coming waves in each layer of the soil. This link is two-sided: one can start from the wave amplitude in any layer and get all other amplitudes from the same relations. If one starts from the lowest level (i.e. from the surface of the underlying half-space) and then obtains all other amplitudes including the amplitude at the free surface, such procedure is called "convolution".

As we saw above, the motion in a certain point within the soil profile can be described in different ways. First, there is a conventional displacement (like (1.9)). It is called "motion in depth". At the surface, it is surely just U^0. But one can alternatively consider the upcoming wave separately from the down-coming wave. If we imagine that in this very point the artificial free surface is put (i.e. the level of interest is outcropped), then the upcoming wave will be reflected, and displacement in the upcoming wave will be doubled. This doubled displacement in the upcoming wave is called "outcropped motion".

It is not easy to understand the "outcropped motion" concept at once, so let us discuss it more thoroughly. At the free surface of the soil, the upcoming wave is physically doubled, as discussed above. Therefore, the outcropped motion is similar to the motion in depth at the free surface.

For all other points below the surface, there may be two different types of outcrop described in Standard ASCE4-16 (2017). The first type is called "SHAKE outcrop". It means that for the same initial soil profile the amplitude of the upcoming wave in the point of interest is calculated and doubled. SHAKE is the name of popular soft performing calculations of this sort — see Schnabel et al. (1972).

The second type is called "geological outcrop". It means that all layers above the point of interest are fully withdrawn. In fact, one gets some other (i.e. reduced) soil profile as compared to the initial one. How can one be sure that the physical seismic excitation for these two profiles (i.e. the initial one and the reduced one) is the same? The answer is that physically seismic excitation is described by the upcoming wave in the underlying homogeneous half-space (typically the surface of this half-space is considered). This motion is the only motion independent from the properties of the upper layers. Even the down-coming wave in the same point is the result of the reflections from the upper boundaries, making "motion in depth" in this very point dependent on the upper layers. But the upcoming wave in the half-space is a real independent characteristic of the excitation.

Therefore, if one is going to compare two different soil profiles for the same seismic excitation, one has to put the same homogeneous half-space under these layered profiles and to put the same upcoming wave in this half-space. Coming back to the geological outcrop, the resulting motion is calculated at the free surface of the reduced profile (in the point of interest) with the same underlying half-space as in the initial profile and with the same upcoming wave in this half-space.

As mentioned before, at the free surface of the initial soil both types of outcrop give the same result similar to the motion "in depth". Let us consider other levels.

At the surface of the underlying homogeneous half-space, both types of outcrop give similar results, as it is simply the doubled upcoming wave in the half-space independent on the upper layers. This time, however, the resulting outcropped motion is different from the motion "in depth" in the same point.

Let us consider the intermediate point between the free surface of the initial soil and the surface of the underlying half-space and compare two types of the outcrop. In the "geological outcrop", the upper layers (above the point of interest) do not participate at all – they are completely withdrawn. In the "SHAKE outcrop", these upper layers will impact the reflected down-coming wave and change it as compared to the geological outcrop. If below the point of interest there are no boundaries (i.e. the soil is homogeneous) this modified down-coming wave will never impact the upcoming wave. So, the results of both outcrop types will be similar (as mentioned before for the homogeneous half-space). But if there is a physical boundary below the point of interest, the modified down-coming wave will be partly reflected and thus modify the upcoming wave in the point of interest. So the results of two outcrop types will be different. Note that a physical boundary is needed to reflect wave; if this is a "mathematical" boundary (i.e. boundary between layers with similar properties) there is no reflection of the modified down-coming wave.

This is illustrated in *Fig. 1.3*.

Why so much attention is paid to the outcropped motion while most often nobody is going to perform this outcrop physically? The answer is given below. But first let us discuss special technology developed to treat the soil non-linearity.

1.3. The equivalent linear approach to the non-linear soil behavior. Degradation curves

As previously mentioned, the soil is surely a non-linear medium. However, there is an equivalent-linear approach to describe its behaviour, proposed by H.B. Seed and implemented in the SHAKE soft.

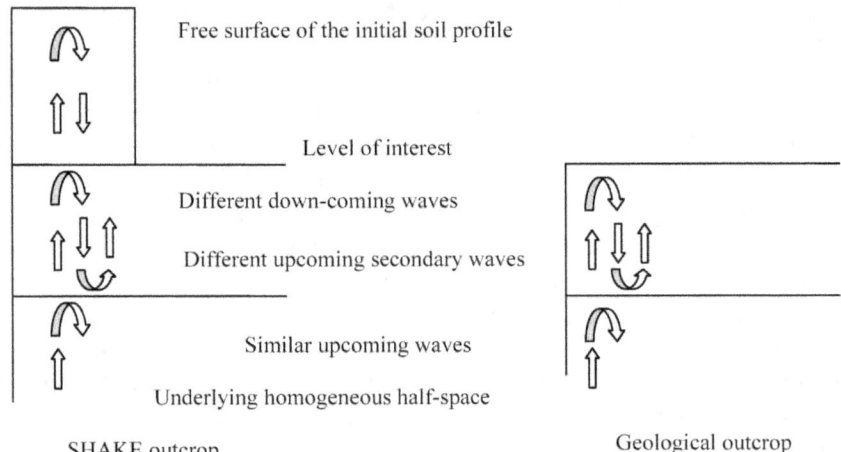

Figure 1.3. Two types of outcrop

Non-linearity means that in every time moment the soil properties in the given point (modules and damping) depend on strains (including strain history). The idea of the equivalent linear approach is to substitute this dependence by the simpler one: let the properties depend on the certain "effective" strain and stay constant over the whole duration of seismic response. This "effective" strain is an integral characteristic of the whole response strain time history (H.B. Seed proposed to take it as 65–70% of the maximal strain value achieved over the duration of seismic response).

If the dependence is known, there should be a sequence of the linear response calculations. Each calculation produces a time history of strains; then effective strains are calculated for each layer (to preserve layering geometry, effective strains are calculated in the middle of each layer and used for the whole layer). Based on these "effective strains" the soil modules and damping are further upgraded layer by layer for the whole soil profile, and then the next linear response calculation is performed. If once the difference in the subsequent properties is small enough, the process is over. The result is not only the wave field but also modified soil properties.

Surely, this is a non-physical simplification, as soil at the beginning of the response cannot "predict" what strains will be achieved later. However, it turned out that the results are quite reasonable in a certain strain range.

The dependence of soil modules and damping on the strains mentioned above is obtained from the lab testing of the soil samples. Therefore, in fact, this approach is just linking seismic response of the soil in the site to the soil sample behaviour in dynamic lab tests (assuming comparable levels of maximal response strains in both cases). Though excitation time histories are not exactly the same (in the lab test excitation is usually almost harmonic unlike true seismic record), general characteristics of the non-linear behaviour should be in the reasonable agreement providing a base for the equivalent-linear approach.

The format of the lab results is the so-called "degradation curves" – two curves for each soil type. The first curve describes relative shear modulus, as shown in *Fig. 1.4*. The second curve describes material (hysteretic) damping, as shown in *Fig. 1.5*.

Let us write down formulae for complex shear modulus accounting for both elastic part and damping. The author met several incorrect expressions in the literature, so it may be useful.

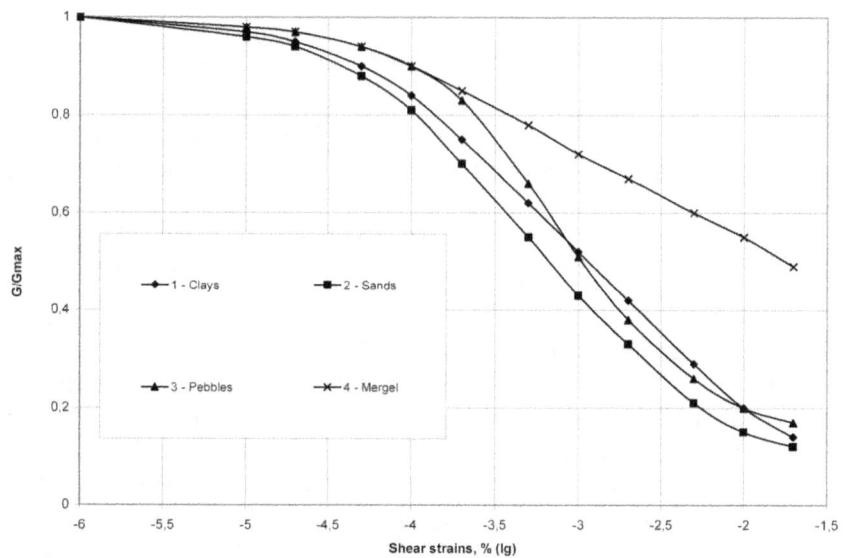

Figure 1.4. Degradation curves for shear modulus

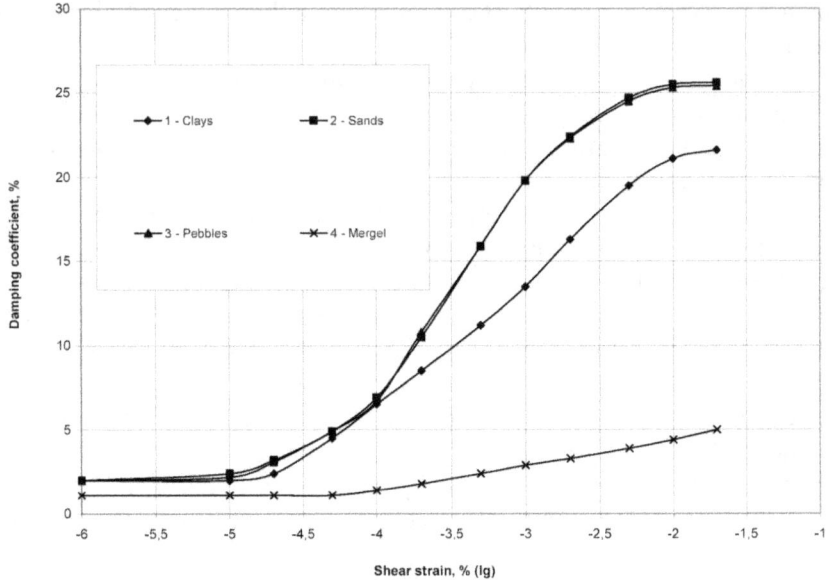

Figure 1.5. Degradation curves for material damping

The internal damping calculation is based on the study of the wave amplitude decay. Therefore complex wave velocity is as follows:

$$V_s = V_s^0 [(1-D^2)^{1/2} + iD]. \qquad (1.11)$$

Here V_s^0 is an absolute value of complex shear wave velocity; D is an internal damping coefficient. Complex shear modulus is then calculated as

$$G = \rho V_s^2 = \rho (V_s^0)^2 [(1-2D^2) + 2i\, D(1-D^2)^{1/2}]. \qquad (1.12)$$

Several comments should be made here.
1) To obtain the effective shear modules from effective strains one should use not only degradation curves, but the low-strain modules (or the low-strain shear wave velocities), as the first degradation curve refers to the relative degradation of G. Therefore one and the same curve may be applied to the soil layers of similar type (e.g., sands) but with different low-strain shear wave velocities. Unlike the first curve in *Fig. 1.4*, the

second degradation curve in *Fig. 1.5* gives damping coefficients in whole, so the low-strain damping is not needed.
2) Modern codes set some upper limits to the values of D – it should not be greater than 0.15. Tests often give greater values, as shown in *Fig. 1.5*. The author understands this limit as a restriction for the implementation of the approximate equivalent-linear method. However, Standards (e.g., ASCE4-16) allow cutting D down to 0.15, in case lab tests give greater values.
3) Degradation curves are applied only to the soil layers, but not to the underlying half-space. The obvious reason is that half-space has no "middle level" to calculate effective strains. Therefore in the sequence of linear iterations, half-space stays the same, unlike layers. Surely the soil in the half-space is physically non-linear, and degradation should be somehow accounted for. This issue is further discussed in the next section.
4) Near the free surface degradation is always very small, as at the free surface stresses and strains are zero. They say that this is "primary" degradation, caused by non-linearity in the free field. Structure will also cause some non-linearity, called "secondary". It can change the effective properties near the soil surface – under the base. This issue is discussed in the next section.
5) All lab tests are performed for shear modules and shear damping only. This is enough for calculating shear wave fields in two orthogonal vertical planes. As time histories in two horizontal directions are different, the resulting effective properties are different also, though usually not very much. Soil properties in each layer are averaged between these two vertical planes. However, there remains a question about degradation of the constrained modules and corresponding damping. There are several approaches. The first one is to keep the Poisson's coefficient, thus leaving the ratio (1.3) untouched. Another variant is to do without degradation for P-waves at all. The author developed his own variant based on the separation of shear and volumetric strains. It turned out, that in P-wave (i.e. in 1D constrained tension strains) one has a mixture of isotropic tension and shear. If isotropic tension goes without degradation at all (and we do not have supporting experimental data about this degradation at the moment), only shear

contributes to the degradation for P-waves. At the end of the day one get the relation for P-wave velocities:

$$V_{p1}^2 / V_{p0}^2 = 1 - \frac{4}{3}\frac{V_{s0}^2}{V_{p0}^2}[1 - \frac{V_{s1}^2}{V_{s0}^2}]. \quad (1.13)$$

As we see, the degradation of S-wave velocities described by the ratio (V_{s1}^2/V_{s0}^2) is translated into the degradation of P-wave velocities with some coefficient controlled by the Poisson's coefficient (1.3). The author suggested the similar equation for damping:

$$D_{p1} = D_{p0} + \frac{4}{3}\frac{V_{s0}^2}{V_{p0}^2}(D_{s1} - D_{s0}). \quad (1.14)$$

Here one needs the low-strain damping coefficients. They can be taken at the level of 0.02.

In practice, the degradation scale is different in different soil layers during one and the same seismic event at the same depth (approximately): in the rock degradation is far less than in the soft soil. There are two reasons for that. First, modules of the rock (both G and E) are far greater, that is why the same stress (and stress profile is continuous unlike strain profile) corresponds to the less strains in the rock as compared to the soft soil. Second, degradation curves for the rock are smoother than for the soft soil.

1.4. Site response analysis with SHAKE. Convolutions and deconvolutions

The standard way to perform site response analysis (SRA) with an equivalent linear approach implemented in SHAKE is a combination of deconvolutions and convolutions as follows.

Suppose control point with given control motion is at the surface of the initial soil profile, hereinafter called "soil profile 1". Soil layering (in terms of soil thickness and mass densities), low-strain profiles (in terms of wave velocities), and degradation curves are provided by seismologists and geotechnical people. These data in the author's practice are based on the boreholes 120 m deep. Further on we will assume the underlying half-space similar to the deepest layer.

The first stage of SRA is to get the effective properties of the whole profile, including underlying half-space, and to get the effective seismic excitation in the half-space.

At this stage, two deconvolutions for horizontal directions are performed. For the first deconvolution, the underlying half-space is taken with properties similar to the deepest layer, though in fact, these properties are of no importance so far. The reason is that during deconvolution the lower layers (as previously shown) do not impact the results in the upper layers – therefore, the displacements, strains and modified properties of the layers after the degradation do not depend on the properties of the half-space. After the first deconvolutions in two vertical planes, one gets averaged (between planes) soil properties after the degradation for the whole profile, except the half-space.

Then one puts the properties of the deepest layer after the degradation manually as the properties of the underlying half-space, puts the averaged properties to all layers and performs the second two deconvolutions in two vertical planes with the same initial time histories at the surface. This time deconvolutions are performed without iterations. After these deconvolutions, the soil properties do not change any more, but the result is the outcropped motion at the surface of the underlying half-space (similar to the deepest layer). Thus we approximately account for the degradation in the underlying half-space. The result is illustrated in Fig. 1.6 for shear wave velocities (note that shear modules G are averaged, and not velocities V_s).

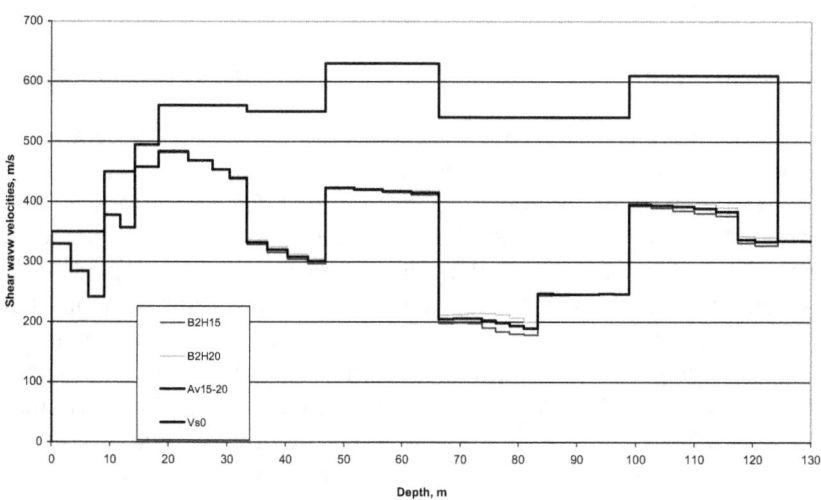

Figure 1.6. The results of deconvolutions in terms of shear wave velocities V_s

Two artificial time histories (marked as B2H15 and B2H20) were applied along two horizontal axes at the free surface. We see considerable degradation (comparing effective velocities after the degradation to initial low-strain velocities V_{s0}) but the difference in two modified profiles in small; so, averaged profile is not far from each of two calculated profiles. The reason is that both artificial time-histories matched the same response spectrum. This is a typical situation. Note also that shear wave velocity V_s in the half-space is set equal to that in the deepest layer.

Averaging of damping coefficients in two vertical planes is illustrated in *Fig. 1.7*.

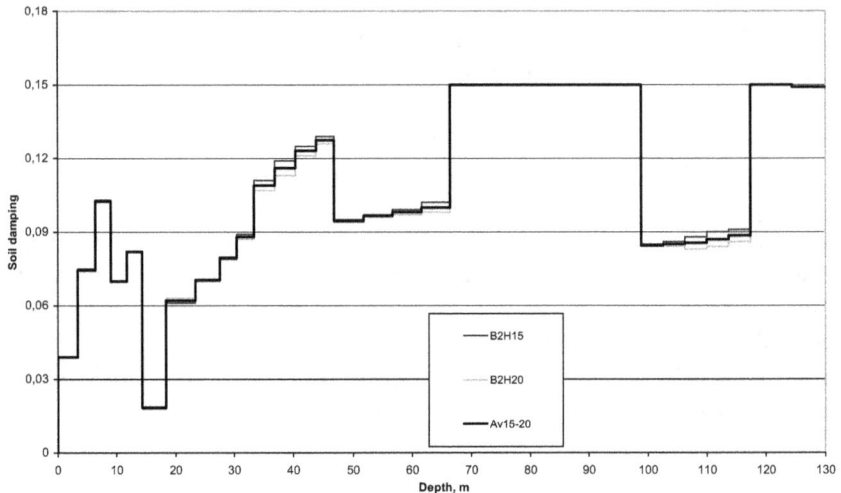

Figure 1.7. The results of deconvolutions in terms of damping coefficients

Note that there is no low-strain damping in *Fig. 1.7*. Note also that D is limited by 0.15 as discussed previously.

An important comment about SHAKE iterations during deconvolution should be added here. In fact, SHAKE iterations do not always converge. Sometimes the soil properties do not stop changing considerably. It means that the motion set up at the surface is inconsistent with the soil properties of the model. In other words, as physically seismic excitation comes from the underlying half-space, this surface motion cannot be achieved whatever motion is set in this half-space. From the author's practice, if 12-14 SHAKE iterations are not enough to reach 2% increment in properties, there are physical problems in the model – iterations will never converge. Convolution procedure (going upwards) does not meet such difficulty.

Another comment is about the thickness of the layers in the soil model. Standards require that thickness of each layer in the model should not exceed $1/5$ of the shortest wavelength of interest. This wavelength is controlled by shear wave velocity after the degradation and highest frequency of interest. It means that if the physical layer is thicker, one must divide it into several sub-layers with similar low-strain properties and with thickness meeting the requirement. This limitation looks like a conventional limitation on finite element method (FEM) in the wave problems, though there $1/10$ of the wavelength is usually used. However, in fact, the meaning of this limitation is completely different. If we take linear calculation by SHAKE (i.e., a single iteration) we find out that inside the layer displacements are represented accurately, so the size (thickness) of the element-layer is of no importance at all. The similar situation is in FEM with a tension of the linear homogeneous rod: a single finite element gives accurate result; it is unnecessary to divide it into several finite elements and care about their size. So, linear SHAKE solution is accurate. The real reason for the limitation refers to the update of the soil properties between two sequential iterations, based on the degradation curves. As previously mentioned, strains in SHAKE are calculated only in the middle of the layer, and then the upgraded soil properties refer to the whole thickness, keeping the layer homogeneous. If one divides the layer into several sub-layers with similar low-strain properties, strains will be calculated in the middle of each sub-layer; they will become different after the first iteration, and the upgraded properties will be different also. The layer will become heterogeneous because of the degradation. Therefore, if the layer is very thick, there will be an error in the final results.

After the second deconvolution is over providing the properties of the underlying half-space and the outcropped motion at the surface of this half-space, the second stage starts. This time up to three convolutions are performed. For the first convolution one develops soil profile called "soil profile 2". This profile has the same underlying half-space as previously "the soil profile 1" during the second deconvolution (i.e. accounting for the degradation). Outcropped time histories for the surface of this half-space obtained from the second deconvolution are now used as outcropped excitation motions. The difference between "soil profile 1" and "soil profile 2" is caused by the construction works. Most often the initial surface of the "soil profile 1" is somehow changed for the construction (e.g., upper layers cut off or replaced, etc.). In principle, "soil profile 2" could be similar to the "soil profile 1", but this never happens in practice.

Two first runs of the first convolution are performed in two vertical planes, and after the iterations, the modified properties of the layers are averaged. Properties of the half-space stay in place.

A second convolution is an option proposed by the author. For the second convolution, the soil profile 2 is modified: extra layer with very high V_s (i.e. very stiff layer) is added at the top. Mass density and thickness are tuned to represent average pressure from the future structure. This is the attempt to approximately account for the secondary non-linearity. Again two runs are performed in two vertical planes, and modified soil properties are averaged. They are different from those obtained after the first convolution for the same soil layers. In particular, there is a certain degradation in the upper soil layer after the second convolution; we remember that after the first convolution the degradation there was insignificant.

After that the resulting soil profile is obtained by the weighted average of the two modified profiles after two convolutions: weight 0.3 is applied to the shear modulus and damping coefficients of the first profile, and weight 0.7 is applied to the second profile (an extra layer of the second profile does not participate). This final soil profile is used for the third convolution without iterations – just to get motions at the free surface.

This procedure is illustrated in *Fig. 1.8* for the shear wave velocities. This is another case from the author's practice: please do not compare to *Fig. 1.5*.

In terms of damping coefficients, the same case is illustrated in *Fig. 1.9*. Damping obtained during deconvolution is added here.

This option with three convolutions is not prescribed by standards. If the structure is embedded, or there is a thick layer of the upgraded soil (say, cemented) under the base, one can be sure that under the base soil properties will account for the degradation even without this option. In this case, the second convolution and weighted averaging of the soil properties are not necessary. In this case after the first convolution the averaged (between two vertical planes) soil properties are put in the soil model, and the third convolution is performed without iterations, as described above.

However, if the base is modeled as a surface one, soil properties right under the base (i.e., near the free surface) after the conventional SHAKE procedure will not get the degradation. If the further SSI analysis will be linear (no secondary degradation), these properties remain untouched. But this is physically wrong because the mass of structure will lead to the non-zero strains under the base.

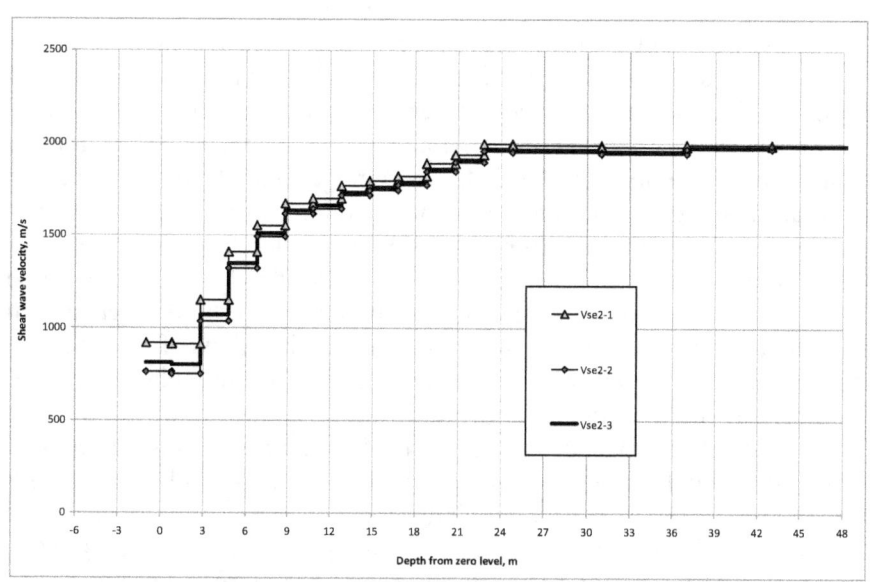

Figure 1.8. Soil profiles after two convolutions (Vse2-1 and Vse2-2) and weighted average (Vse2-3) in terms of the shear wave velocities

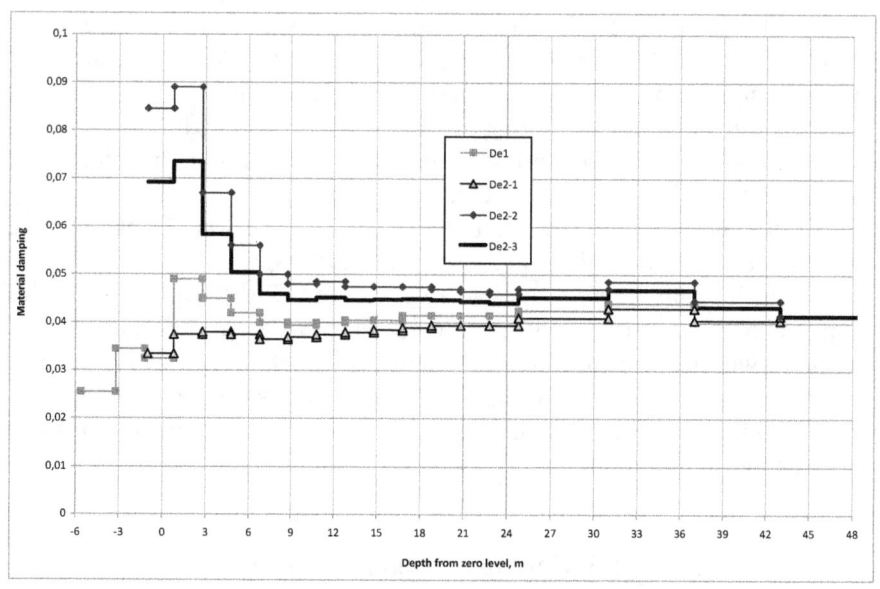

Figure 1.9. Soil profiles after two convolutions (De2-1 and De2-2) and weighted average (De2-3) in terms of the material damping coefficients. De1 is damping obtained during deconvolution

The final comment in this section is not about soil properties, but about the modified seismic motions. From (1.9) we see that motion "in depth" in a homogeneous layer decreases from the surface at least over the first ¼ of the wavelength $L = 2\pi\lambda$ (like a cosine). Is it true for the "outcropped" motion as well? In a homogeneous layer without the internal damping, the amplitude of the upcoming wave is constant over the depth, making the outcropped motion amplitude (doubled upcoming wave, as we remember) also constant over the depth. If there is some internal damping in the soil, the upcoming wave will decrease in amplitude coming upwards. It means that coming down from the free surface and cutting out the upper portion of the soil one obtains greater "outcropped" motions at the new free surface.

Now let us consider layered soil. Most often soil gets stiffer over the depth (though sometimes there appear "abnormal" soil profiles with the opposite trend – e.g., when long ago comparatively soft soil was covered by volcanic lava). In such "normal" profiles the upcoming wave increases in the amplitude at each boundary. Therefore, after cutting out the soft upper layers and outcropping stiffer layers one comes to the fewer amplitudes.

So, if the difference between the initial "soil profile 1" and the upgraded "soil profile 2" is just in cutting out some surface layers, the resulting modified motion at the free surface after deconvolution, and subsequent convolution may be greater than the initial one (in case damping prevail over stiffening with depth) or lesser (in the opposite case). If both profiles are similar, motions are also similar (in spite of the degradation) which is in line with common sense.

One more case, when the upper portion of the soil is not removed but changed instead, will be discussed later, in Chapter 7.

So far, only shear waves were discussed. For the primary waves responsible for vertical displacements the effective properties are obtained without iterations – using degradation of shear wave velocities and damping in different variants, as discussed above. After that only one deconvolution and one convolution are performed without iterations to get the modified motion.

1.5. Half-space tuning method

In the previous sections, the case was discussed when control motion is known at the free surface of the initial soil.

Another case happened some time ago in the author's practice when for a very deep soil site seismologists had to develop seismic excitation based on the attenuation laws (i.e. starting from the seismic fault). The problem was that they were ready to provide response spectra at the surface of homogeneous half-space – but different spectra for different wave velocities in the half-space. But what properties to use for half-space, if degradation is considerable?

The author developed a special approach called "half-space tuning method". Let us present an example. The upper layers of the soil have been investigated preliminarily: low-strain properties and degradation curves for them are known. The goal is to obtain consistent soil profile and excitation avoiding artificial physical boundary at the surface of the underlying half-space.

The basic physical assumption is that there are no signs of sharp physical boundaries (e.g., rock at the visible depth), so there should be no such a boundary in the resulting soil profile (after the degradation). In the initial soil profile, the underlying half-space has low-strain properties similar to the deepest layer known from the boreholes. We set up the upper layer of this half-space with low-strain properties similar to the half-space – therefore no physical boundary appears, but only mathematic boundary separating this new layer from the half-space with the same properties. Then we assume the degradation curves for this layer similar to those of the deepest layer.

Seismic excitation is set up at the surface of the half-space and corresponds to the certain wave velocity V_s which is a prognosis for the wave velocity of half-space after the degradation. One more prognosis is made for damping D. The same V_s together with damping D are manually put as properties of the half-space. Then a standard sequence of SHAKE iterations (convolutions) is performed in two vertical planes, and after averaging, one gets soil properties of all layers after the degradation. Properties of the half-space stay untouched (as always in SHAKE). Effective properties of the deepest layer are of special interest. If they happened to be close to our prognoses for the half-space, no sharp boundary appears between this layer and half-space – this is the desired situation. But if this is not a case, we will have to repeat the calculations with the same outcrop input motion, with the same low-strain properties of all layers, but a new half-space with other prognozed properties (e.g., taken similar to those of the deepest layer in the previous calculation). Properties of the half-space for this new set of the SHAKE iterations are to be changed manually. Unlike deconvolution, the results of convolution depend on the properties of the lower layers and half-space, so the properties of the deepest layer after degradation will change after changing the half-space. Such calculations will go until the properties of the deepest layer and half-space converge within reasonable limits. This is a cycle called "internal tuning cycle". The result is half-space tuned in terms of V_s and D to avoid artificial boundary for the given excitation. This is illustrated in *Fig. 1.10*.

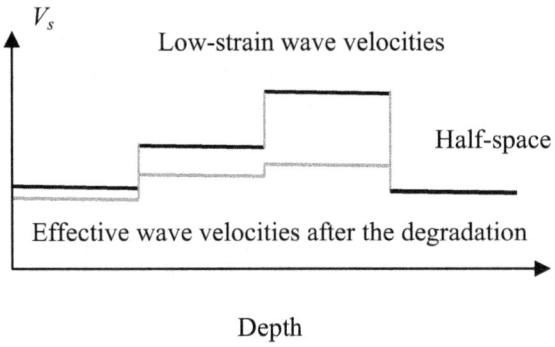

Figure 1.10. Profile of V_s for a single iteration of the internal tuning cycle

But is it the final desired solution? Not yet. We remember that the input motion is given by seismologists for certain V_s (usually it is the velocity in the upper 30 meters, called V_{s30}). At the beginning of the internal tuning cycle, our V_s was compatible with the input motion used. But in the process of the half-space tuning, we have changed V_s to a certain V_H. If the change proved to be considerable, previous input motion is no longer compatible with new V_H, and we have to repeat the internal tuning cycle with the new input motion (e.g., compatible with V_H). This will be an "external tuning cycle": internal tuning cycle is repeated with new input motion until V_H in the internal cycle is close enough to the starting V_s (meaning that input motion compatible with starting V_s is also compatible with final V_H). Damping D must also converge, but damping is usually not used by seismologists to define input motions.

In practice to avoid bothering seismologists many times the author at the beginning ordered a set of ultimate hazard response spectra UHRS (with 5% damping) for different velocities V_{s30} going down with a certain step (50 m/s) from the low-strain V_s for the deepest layer. Changing input motions on the external tuning cycle one can use the interpolation of input response spectra, or just take the ready UHRS compatible with the closest V_{s30}. If the step in V_{s30} is not too much, the results will be reasonable.

The obvious advantage of such an approach is that the resulting motion at the free surface may be used for the standard procedure with deconvolution described in the previous section. The results in terms of the effective properties will be similar to those in the half-space tuning method. Moreover, in standard procedure, we will have guaranteed convergence of iterations during deconvolution.

The author would like to show the real case with the half-space tuning method. Initial soil profile consists of 42 layers total thickness of 120 m resting on the half-space with low-strain V_s = 564 m/s. As described above, a special layer 4 m thick with the properties of the half-space was added at the bottom – therefore the total thickness of the layered package was 124 m.

Three sets of preliminary calculations were performed in the external tuning cycle with different input motions. The author set up three prognosis effective values V_{s30} for half-space as 350, 450 and 500 m/s. For each value UHRS with 5% damping was taken from seismologists as 50% quantile. Two-component horizontal acceleration time-histories were generated for each of these UHRS. Then the internal cycle was performed three times for the three given excitations. Low-strain properties of the layers were the same, including the low-strain V_s = 564 m/s for the bottom layer. Properties of the half-space at the beginning were different corresponding to the assumed V_{s30} – 350, 450 or 500 m/s.

The results for V_{s30} = 350 m/s are shown in *Table 1.1*. At the beginning of each SHAKE standard set of iterations the properties of the half-space were velocity V_H and damping D_H. After the standard iteration set damping D_L was averaged from the effective damping in the bottom layer in two vertical planes. Velocity V_L was calculated using shear modulus G averaged from the effective modules in the bottom layer in two vertical planes.

Table 1.1
Internal tuning cycle for Vs_{30} = 350 m/s

Iteration number	V_H, m/s	D_H,%	V_L, m/s	D_L,%
1	350	5,0	478,6	6,0
2	478,6	6,0	464,5	6,4
3	464,5	6,4	465,6	6,3

As we see from *Table 1.1*, three iterations of the internal tuning cycle were enough to obtain the effective properties of the half-space. However, these properties are considerably different from the initial ones (compatible with input motion).

Similar results for $V_{s30} = 450$ m/s are shown in the *Table 1.2*, and for $V_{s30} = 500$ m/s – in the *Table 1.3*. As we see, two iterations of the internal tuning cycle were enough to obtain the effective properties of the half-space in both cases.

Table 1.2

Internal tuning cycle for $V_{s30} = 450$ m/s

Iteration number	V_H, m/s	D_H, %	V_L, m/s	D_L, %
1	450	5,0	471,0	6,2
2	471,0	6,2	468,5	6,3

Table 1.3

Internal tuning cycle for $V_{s30} = 500$ m/s

Iteration number	V_H, m/s	D_H, %	V_L, m/s	D_L, %
1	500	5,0	466,9	6,3
2	466,9	6,3	470,2	6,2

Note that in spite of different input motions and different starting half-space properties our final results in terms of the effective half-space properties are close to each other. All results show that the effective velocity V_s in the half-space is not far from 450 m/s.

After some additional discussions, it was decided that 84%-quantile UHRS should be taken instead of 50% quantile used for preliminary analysis – to add conservatism. Surely, new UHRS are somewhat greater than the old ones, but it was assumed that $V_s = 450$ m/s will remain the closest value for the half-space properties. New spectra for input motions were obtained by seismologists following the requirements of NUREG 1.208 for $V_s = 450$ m/s. Like before, these spectra were used to generate artificial time-histories – this time 10 one-component time-histories were generated. The comparison of calculated response spectra with a given target response spectrum and 90% of this target spectrum (damping 5%) is shown in *Figure 1.11*. Matching is good.

Correlation coefficients were checked for these time-histories. Maximal coefficient proved to be 0.1383, which is acceptable for statistical independence.

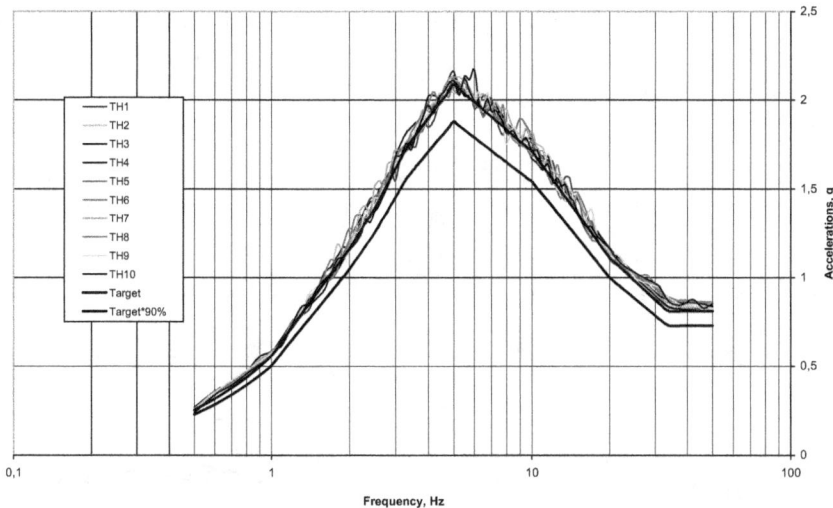

Figure 1.11. Matching of response spectra for 10 artificial time–histories of input motion and target spectrum

Then SHAKE convolutions were performed for these 10 one-component time histories. Half-space parameters were taken as $V_{s30} = 457.2$ m/s and $D = 0.066$ (according to the results of additional preliminary calculations using new input motions). These properties are to be compared to the effective properties of the deepest layer. This comparison will be shown later. The results in the format of response spectra for the free surface are shown in *Fig. 1.12*.

The 85% quantile of these spectra should be used as surface input motion for the further SSI analysis. With 10 results used for statistics the 85% quantile corresponds to the "second greatest" value. As one can see from *Fig. 1.12*, the second greatest spectrum is smooth enough, especially for frequencies above 3 Hz.

Let us perform the promised check for the properties of the half-space. It is shown in *Table 1.4*. N in this Table denotes the random generator input (different for 10 different time-histories) used for phase spectrum during synthesis of the artificial time histories. G in the second line is shear modulus in the deepest layer after the degradation. G_0 and V_0 are correspondingly modulus and shear wave velocity taken for the half-space. G_a and V_a in the last column are averaged shear modulus in the deepest layer and V_s calculated using this shear modulus.

The conclusion is that averaged velocity V_a = 443.1 m/s in the deepest layer is not far from *a*) assumed velocity for the half-space V_s = 457.2 m/s, and *b*) velocity V_{s30} = 450 m/s, used for the selection of the input UHRS.

A similar agreement is for damping D (excluding the choice of UHRS).

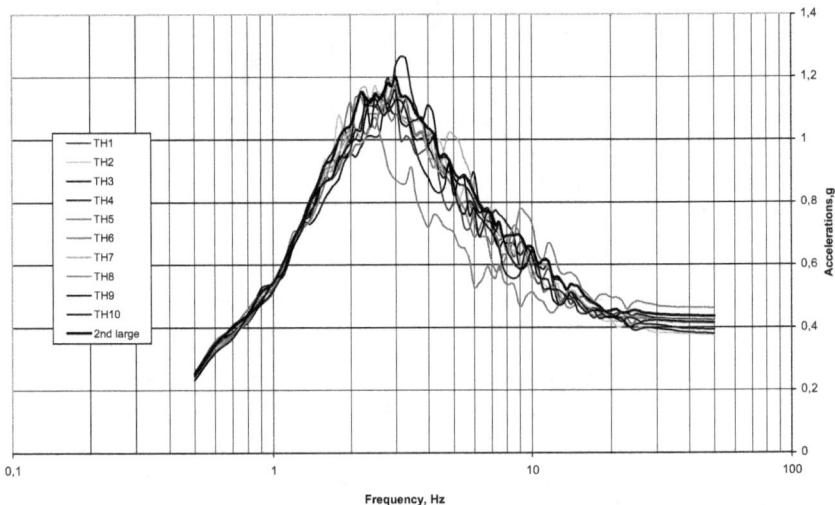

Figure 1.12. Response spectra at the free surface of the soil for 10 artificial time–histories of input motion

Table 1.4.
Check of consistency for the G and V_s in the deepest layer and in the half-space

	$N=7$	$N=13$	$N=19$	$N=24$	$N=27$	$N=33$	$N=36$	$N=40$	$N=43$	$N=48$	G_0, V_0	G_a, V_a
G, MPa	427.2	455.5	450.3	452.5	388.3	453.4	409.4	377.5	376.0	459.5	451.7	425.0
V_s, m/s	444.6	459.1	456.5	457.6	423.9	458.0	435.2	418.0	417.5	461.1	457.2	443.1

Thus the proposed procedure enables obtaining surface response spectrum compatible with effective properties not only of soil layers but also of the underlying half-space. Properties of this half-space after the degradation are obtained as well. No sharp artificial boundary appeared between the deepest layer and the half-space. So, the standard procedure with deconvolution described in the previous section can be used for the further SSI analysis.

Chapter 2. PRIMARY AND SECONDARY SUPERPOSITIONS – COMMON STARTING POINT FOR ALL SSI METHODS

2.1. Primary superposition. Substitution of the initial SSI problem with a new problem

First let us consider the most general case. Let us call the problem with seismic wave, soil and structure as "problem A" and start with completely linear soil-structure model shown in *Figure 2.1*.

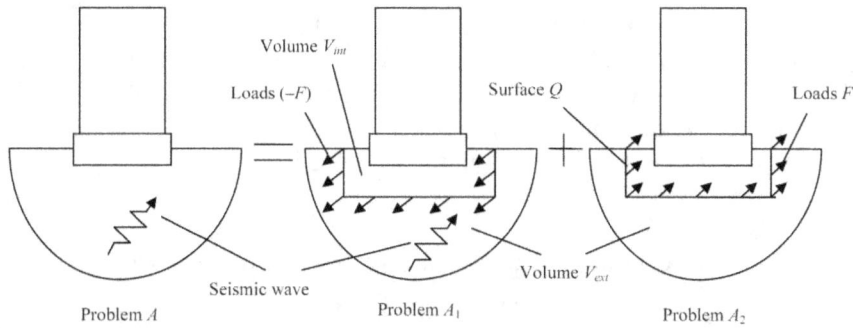

Figure 2.1. Primary superposition: split of the initial "problem A" in the superposition of two problems

Let Q be some surface surrounding the basement in the soil and dividing the soil-structure model into two parts: the "external" volume V_{ext} and "internal" volume V_{int}. Let $(-F)$ be additional external loads distributed over V_{int} and specially tuned so, to provide zero displacements in V_{int} when seismic wave is running in the soil. Then "problem A" can be split in the sum (superposition) of two wave pictures: "problem A_1", including seismic excitation and loads $(-F)$, and "problem A_2" including only loads (F) without seismic wave – see the right-hand part of *Fig. 2.1*. The problem A_1 is called "stopped seismic wave", as the initial seismic wave is stopped at the surface Q by the additional load $(-F)$.

This simple superposition leads to several important conclusions.

1) As in "problem A_1" all displacements in the internal volume V_{int} are zero, the motion of the internal volume V_{int} in "problem A_2" is the same as in "problem A". Hence, if we are interested in the motion of the internal part V_{int} only, we can substitute the initial "problem A" with a

new "problem A_2". As a matter of fact, every time in SSI analysis this substitution is carried out explicitly or implicitly.

2) If seismic wave is stopped at the surface Q by forces $(-F)$ applied at Q only, no displacements will then occur inside V_{int}. So, forces $(-F)$ are not needed inside the volume V_{int}; they are applied only at the surface Q.

3) Surprisingly, primary superposition in *Fig. 2.1* is valid even if some non-linearity appears inside V_{int}. For the internal part V_{int} the non-linear solution from the problem A_2 is combined with zero solution from the problem A_1 – so the superposition works even for non-linear case. For the external part V_{ext} the superposition in *Fig. 2.1* works because of the linearity of this part of the model.

So, the new problem A_2 can substitute the initial problem A, if one (i) knows loads F, and (ii) can somehow model infinite volume V_{ext} (note that this external volume is present in problem A_2, although the initial seismic wave is no longer there!).

Both issues are discussed in the next section.

2.2. Secondary superposition – initial and reflected waves in the free field

In this section, we will further work with problem A_1 from *Fig. 2.1*.

1) As in "problem A_1" all displacements, strains and internal forces inside the internal volume V_{int} are zero, no internal forces are impacting surface Q from the internal part V_{int} (i.e., forces impacting surface Q from the external part V_{ext} due to the seismic wave are balanced in full by loads $(-F)$). Hence, the internal part V_{int} can be fully withdrawn from the model in "problem A_1" or replaced by another medium of the corresponding shape (with zero displacements) without changing the external part V_{ext}, seismic excitation, and loads $(-F)$. The balance at the surface Q will stay in place after such substitution.

2) In particular, V_{int} can be replaced by the initial soil without structure. Let us call this problem with initial soil without structure inside V_{int} and with external loads $(-F)$ as "problem B_1". This problem looks like problem A_1 in *Fig. 2.1*, but without structure and upgraded soil. It may be like "problem A_1" called "problem of the stopped wave" as well, as wave fields in the external volume V_{ext} and loads $(-F)$ are similar in "problem A_1" and in "problem B_1".

3) Let us apply "secondary" superposition to the problem B_1, as shown in *Fig. 2.2*. Problem B_1 can be split in two: (i) "problem B" with initial soil and seismic wave, and (ii) "problem B_2" (reflected wave). However, in "problem A_2" and "problem B_2" (with minus sign) wave fields are different in spite of similar loads F and similar V_{ext} in both problems. Generally, the motions of the surface Q in "problem B_2" and "problem A_2" are different due to the waves, radiating from the structure in "problem A_2". If there is no structure in "problem A_2", and soil in "problem A_2" inside V_{int} is initial, then no difference occurs.

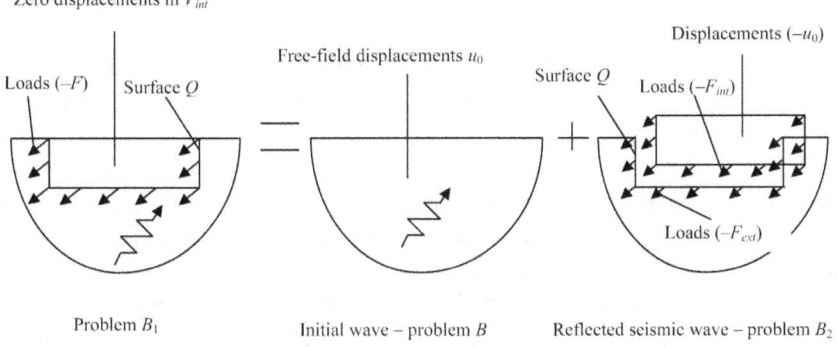

Figure 2.2. Secondary superposition: split of loads F into F_{int} and F_{ext}

4) To provide the desired zero motion in the "problem B_1" the wave field in the internal volume V_{int} in "problem B_2" should be similar to the initial wave field u_0 in "problem B" but with the opposite sign. Very often this initial wave field is known apriori or easily calculated from the control seismic motion at the free surface. This motion is generally given by seismologists.

5) External loads $(-F)$ impacting surface Q in "problem B_1" can be obtained as a sum of the corresponding external loads in the "problem B" (they are zero) and in the "problem B_2". In the "problem B_2", they are obtained from the wave field U_0 (initially set up in the "problem B") inside V_{int} and Green's functions G_0 derived for the initial unbounded soil as follows

$$-F = G_0(-U_0). \qquad (2.1)$$

Formula (2.1) uses operator G_0 in the time domain. This operator is applied to the displacement field in the volume V_{int} and provides the loads, distributed over the volume. For linear initial soil, this operator in the frequency domain will turn into complex frequency-dependent Green's function. This formula can be applied to the whole volume V_{int}, but for the internal nodes the result will be zero. So, the loads (2.1) will be concentrated at the surface Q.

6) Note that for the surface Q loads $(-F)$ in (2.1) can be split in two different parts: (i) loads $(-F_{int})$ acting from the internal volume V_{int}, and (ii) loads $(-F_{ext})$ acting from the external volume V_{ext}. This is shown in the right-hand part of *Fig. 2.2* and may be expressed as

$$-F = G_0(-U_0) = -F_{int} - F_{ext} = G_{int}(-U_0) + G_{ext}(-U_0). \qquad (2.2)$$

With given wave field U_0 in "problem B" one can easily obtain the internal part of the load F_{int} just as surface forces corresponding to the internal stress field in "problem B".

Now let us discuss the external part of the load denoted as F_{ext}, describing the response of the soil in the external volume V_{ext} to the displacements U_0, set up at the surface Q. To get this response one should somehow model the infinite soil volume V_{ext}. But the same modelling is needed for the problem A_2 in *Fig. 2.1*. This creates a powerful tool to verify models suggested for "problem A_2". Each of these models contains some description of the internal part V_{int}, external part V_{ext} and the loads F. It is useful to take the same V_{ext} and F, as proposed for the "problem A_2", and substitute the internal part V_{int} by the initial soil without structure, thus coming from "problem A_2" to "problem B_2" with the opposite sign. The suggested models of V_{ext} and F must provide adequate solution U_0 for "problem B_2" inside V_{int}; otherwise, they cannot be applied to "problem A_2".

As a result of both primary and secondary superposition, the problem A_2 from *Fig. 2.1* may be presented in a way shown in *Figure 2.3*. Bold lines hereinafter mark surfaces with prescribed motion.

Here the external soil volume V_{ext} is substituted by a zero-thickness "soil shell" with stiffness described by operator G_{ext} from (2.2). Kinematical excitation U_0 is applied to the external surface of this shell in the middle part of *Fig. 2.3*. In addition forces F_{int} are loading the internal surface of this shell. The alternative way to describe the same system is to fix the external surface of the "soil shell", but to add the corresponding forces to the loads at the internal surface, making them $F_{int} + G_{ext} U_0$. This variant is shown in the right-hand part of *Fig. 2.3*.

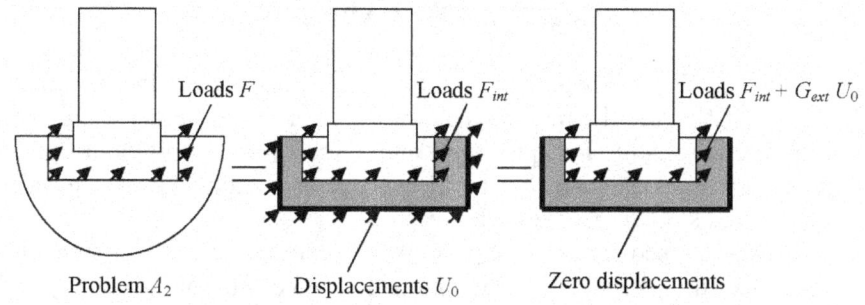

Figure 2.3. Rigorous representation of the problem A_2

Both models (in the middle and in the right in *Fig. 2.3*) can be called "platform models", as there is an external surface of "soil shell" with prescribed motion (U_0 in the middle part and zero in the right-hand part). This surface can be called "platform". Note that if representation G_{ext} of the external volume is accurate, the load in the right model in *Fig. 2.3* is similar to the load F in the left model in *Fig. 2.3*. If this operator G_{ext} is approximate, the structural response in the right model will be approximate too, but the free-field response in the right-hand model in *Fig. 2.3* (i.e. the right-hand model from *Fig. 1.3* for soil but without structure) will be still accurate.

Rigorous representation of the "problem A_2" shown in *Fig. 2.3* enables the systematic classification of the numerous methods for the SSI analysis. The classification is based on the choice of surface Q. Key factor for this classification is the presence of solid soil elements in the internal part V_{int} of the model. The so-called "direct approach" as a particular case of the general approach deals with solid soil part inside the internal volume V_{int}. On the contrary, simplified sub-structuring approach deals with "problem A_2" without solid soil inside V_{int}. Each of these two basic approaches can be understood as a particular case of the common general rigorous approach presented in *Fig. 2.3*.

Two mentioned basic approaches will be discussed in the next two chapters.

Chapter 3. DIRECT APPROACH

In the "direct" method they put surface Q apart from the basement. It means that inside the internal volume V_{int} there is some portion of soil around the basement. This portion is modelled by solid soil elements. In addition the external part V_{ext} of the soil is also modelled, but usually without solid soil elements (see below).

As a consequence, two principal directions of development are opened for this approach (leaving aside modelling of structure): (i) sophistication of finite element modelling soil in the internal volume V_{int}, and (ii) sophistication of modelling soil in the external volume V_{ext}.

The first direction is focused on modelling the multi-phase structure of soils (skeleton, water and air) and non-linear behaviour (we remember from Chapter 2, that soil and structure inside V_{int} can be non-linear). It is worth mentioning that for a long time soil in dynamic problems (unlike static problems) was modelled as isotropic linear-elastic material with certain internal damping. Effective equivalent linear properties of such material were obtained from experimental data (field tests for small strains and lab tests for medium strains), as described in Chapter 1. Up to now, this approach is considered reasonable, provided strains in the soil are not too high. Equivalent linear modelling of soil usually is performed together with equivalent linear modelling of the structure. If there is no non-linearity on the soil-structure contact surface, the whole system becomes linear. It helps a lot with building models for the V_{ext} and with dynamic analysis. In particular, calculation may be performed in the frequency domain using the Fourier Transform.

If "true" non-linearity is present either in the soil, or in the structure, or at the soil-structure contact (e.g., uplift or sliding), one has to perform calculations in the time domain. One can find some details in Appendix B to ASCE4-16.

The second direction is focused on the modelling of the response of external soil volume V_{ext} to the motion of surface Q. In other words, they try to find some boundary conditions to be set at the surface Q instead of infinite volume V_{ext} to provide the same response inside V_{int} with the model of the finite volume. From Chapter 2 we remember that soil in V_{ext} must be linear – otherwise, the basic superposition will not work.

Most often they try to put the bottom of the surface Q on the underlying rock assuming that this rock is so stiff that it moves similarly with or without structure. In this case they can avoid soil support at the bottom of Q (see *Fig. 2.3*) and directly put the free-field motion of the rock U_0 as kinematical excitation on the bottom of V_{int}. Then only lateral boundaries with corresponding loads and dynamic stiffness need to be developed in the model (see *Fig. 2.3*). If these boundaries are set far away from the basement (3...4 basement dimensions), then even their very approximate modelling should not spoil the basement motion obtained in the analysis. This is illustrated in *Fig. 3.1* (the left-hand part is similar to the right-hand part of *Fig. 2.1*).

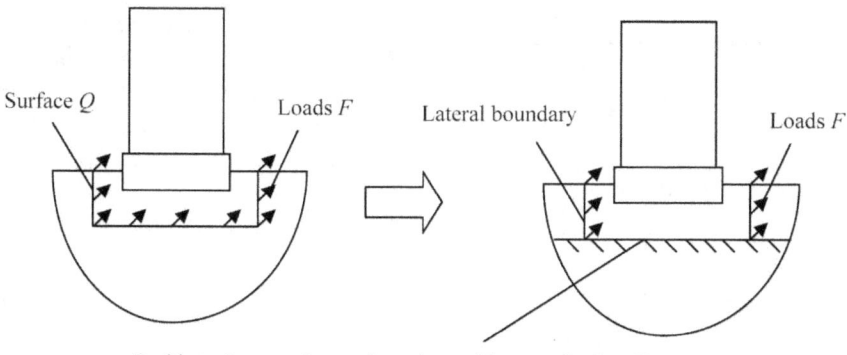

Figure 3.1. The typical representation of the problem A_2 in direct approach in case of underlying rock

These lateral boundaries in direct method have their own history and classification. We will describe main groups of them.

3.1. Elementary Boundaries

The first group is called "elementary boundaries". The simplest variant is free boundaries, shown in *Fig. 3.2*.

Let us assume vertical seismic waves in the horizontally-layered soil profile. Rigid rock at the bottom of the model is moving according to the free-field rock motion. Flexible soil and structure will also move somehow (their motion will be calculated from the SSI analysis). But let us imagine the same model with initial soil, i.e. without structure. One can see that in this auxiliary problem without structure the model in *Fig. 3.2* will not reproduce the free-field motion in the flexible soil. The reason is that in the real infinite free-field there are certain internal stresses loading the lateral boundaries from the external part of the soil. For vertical S-waves there will be shear stresses; for vertical P-waves there will be pressures due to the Poisson's effect. In the model shown in *Fig. 3.2* these stresses are missing. One should put such boundaries very far from the structure not to spoil structural response.

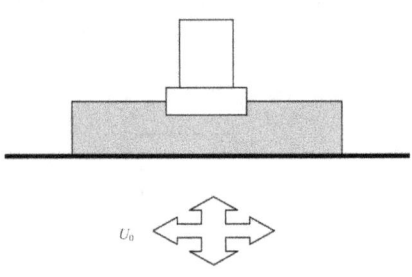

To resolve this "free-field" issue they proposed another variant of elementary boundaries – "fixed boundaries" shown in *Fig. 3.3*. Instead of free lateral boundaries in *Fig. 3.2* here we prescribe the motion of these boundaries using the free-field motion $U_0(z)$. This motion varies along the depth.

Figure 3.2. Free lateral boundaries

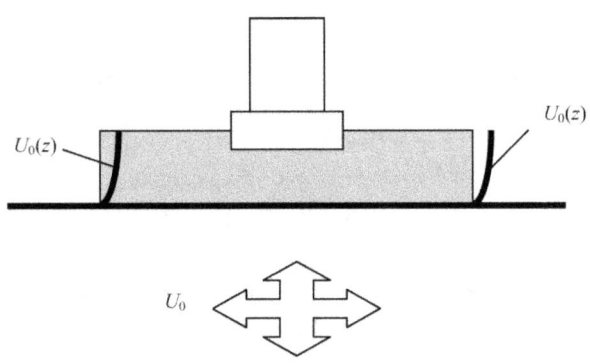

Figure 3.3. Fixed lateral boundaries

Free-field motion $U_0(z)$ may be calculated separately in advance. The alternative way is to put somewhere on the same moving bottom rock some special "soil column" with artificially very high elasticity modules and high mass densities reproducing wave velocities of the initial soil. This soil column has symmetrical lateral boundaries, so it will reproduce the free-field soil motion created by vertical seismic waves in horizontally-layered soil. Then lateral boundaries of the flexible soil in *Fig. 3.3* are linked to the lateral boundaries of this soil column (in the format of similar displacements) as shown in *Fig. 3.4*. Here soil column is shown as a hollow ring surrounding V_{int}. Due to the very high stiffness of the soil column, its motion will not be changed by these links and will remain similar to the free-field. This trick helps to avoid two analyses and to perform a one-step calculation instead.

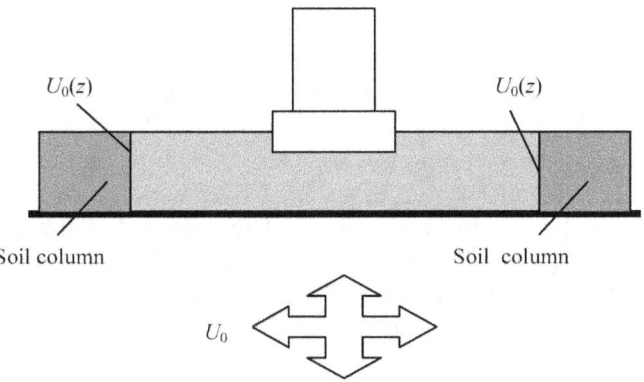

Figure 3.4. Fixed lateral boundaries – variant with soil column

As we see, in the auxiliary free-field problem (i.e. a problem without structure) the model shown in *Fig. 3.3* will give accurate results, as all the motions at the boundaries (lateral ones and the bottom) are accurate for the free-field case. However, this is not enough for the accurate solution of the main problem shown in *Fig. 3.3* (i.e. a problem with structure). The moving structure will produce additional (to the free-field motion) waves radiating from the basement. These additional waves reaching the boundaries will meet fixed (with zero displacements) boundary conditions (as prescribed displacements U_0 correspond only to the free-field wave field). As a consequence, these additional waves will be reflected from fixed boundaries back into the soil volume V_{int}. This is true both for the bottom and for the lateral boundaries.

If there is a real stiff rock at the bottom, this reflection will correspond to the physical effect existing in the real world. But at the lateral boundaries it has no physical justification, so the resulting wave field in V_{int} will be spoiled by these reflected additional waves. The error in the structural response will depend on the distance from these lateral boundaries to the basement, and on the degree of the internal damping in the soil. Radiated waves are decreased by the internal damping in the soil on their wave to the lateral boundaries and back to the structure (after the reflection from the fixed boundaries). These are the same factors as for free lateral boundaries, and the early studies in 1970-s showed that the necessary distances from the basement to the lateral boundaries to obtain reasonable results are almost the same for free and fixed boundaries.

The next generation of the non-reflecting lateral boundaries was "acoustic boundaries" proposed by J. Lysmer and R.L. Kuhlemeyer (1969).

3.2. Acoustic boundaries

Three viscous dampers were placed in each point of the lateral boundary (i.e. dampers were distributed over the area of the boundary) along each of three translational axes. The viscosity of these distributed dampers was equal to the so-called "seismic stiffness" – the product of the wave velocity and mass density. For the direction normal to the boundary, the "acoustic" viscosity is

$$c_p = \rho V_p. \tag{3.1}$$

For each of the two tangential directions the "acoustic" viscosity is

$$c_s = \rho V_s. \tag{3.2}$$

Here ρ is a mass density of the soil in the given point of the boundary, V_p and V_s are velocities of the primary and secondary waves in the soil. Note that material damping in the soil is not present here.

It may be shown that such dampers can rigorously substitute half-infinite rod of constant cross-section area with shear of primary waves in it. It is schematically shown for P-waves in *Fig. 3.5*.

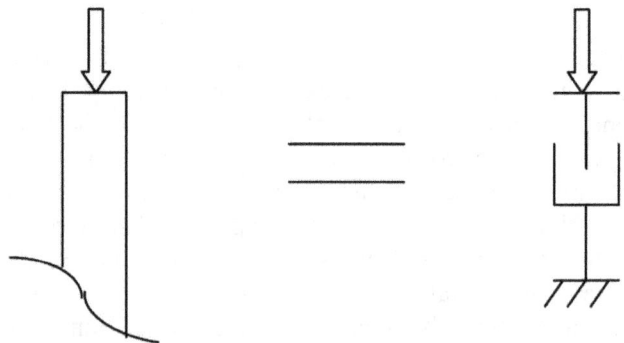

Figure 3.5. Analogue between half-infinite rod of unit cross-section area and viscous dashpot with viscosity parameter $b = \rho V$

So, if primary or secondary body wave is crossing the lateral boundary at the angle 90 degrees (e.g., running horizontally through vertical boundary) it will pass the boundary without the non-physical reflection. This is a desirable solution. However, the problem is that not everywhere body waves cross the boundary at this angle. Surface waves and body waves in depth are not transmitted "properly" – as a consequence, they are still partly reflected by these "acoustic boundaries". So, the success was only partial: "acoustic boundaries" can be placed closer to the structure, as compared to elementary boundaries, but still need certain considerable distance.

Nevertheless, it was a great step forward. With acoustic boundaries the model from *Fig. 3.3* can be modified to the model schematically shown in *Fig. 3.6*. This model corresponds to the middle model from *Fig. 2.3*. In the auxiliary free-field problem the lateral boundaries of the internal volume V_{int} will move according to the free-field motion $U_0(z)$, and viscous dampers composing the acoustic boundaries will not produce any forces, as the relative displacements in all these dampers will be zero. However, the loads F_{int} applied at the lateral boundaries will force flexible soil move similarly to the free field (surely, this motion is also caused by kinematical excitation at the bottom).

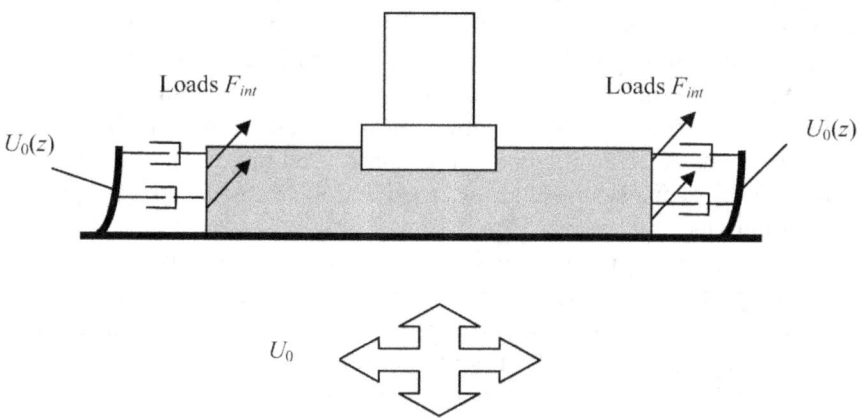

Figure 3.6. Model with acoustic lateral boundaries

When structure appears in the model and radiates additional waves, these additional waves change the motion of the lateral boundaries and thus cause relative displacements in the dampers composing the acoustic boundaries. These dampers provide certain response forces approximately modelling the response of the infinite external part of the soil. The accuracy depends on the angle and internal damping, as stated before.

Unfortunately, often the model from *Fig. 3.6* is used in practice without loads F_{int} applied at the lateral boundaries. This is an error! This error will spoil the results starting from the auxiliary free field problem. Indeed, if in *Fig. 3.6* flexible soil without structure and without loads F_{int} moves like free field (which is a desirable solution), then dampers composing the acoustic boundaries do not work because of zero relative displacements. But then the lateral boundary is simply not balanced: from the internal part V_{int} there are certain free-field loads, and from the external part there are no loads at all, as F_{int} is missing.

Loads F_{int} for the free field motion should be calculated together with wave field $U_0(z)$ – for example, from the separate analysis of the soil columns with symmetrical lateral boundaries. After $U_0(z)$ are calculated, one should multiply them by dynamic stiffness matrices for the soil elements and get nodal forces. These forces (after assembling) should be used as nodal loads for the model shown in *Fig. 3.6*.

It is important to note that finite elements for the soil column should be similar in type and geometry to those further used in SSI analysis with structure. It is important, because simple analytical solutions of 1D wave problems are available, and one can try to use them instead of performing FEM analysis for the soil column. Analytical practice shows that this is the wrong way. Soil profile underlain by a rock has specific resonant frequencies. At these frequencies, even comparatively small difference between mesh solution obtained from FEM and the analytical solution may cause the considerable difference in response. And this small difference will surely occur, as displacement shapes used in finite elements do not reproduce wave solutions.

If the underlying rock is in place, one can put acoustic boundaries far enough from the basement and get reasonable results in terms of structural response. However, from time to time we have to deal with so-called "deep soil profiles" without rock at visible depth (e.g., even for nuclear facilities boreholes during a field survey in the site are usually made down to 120 m only). In such cases, one has to assume the homogeneous flexible half-space below the investigated layered profile. The properties of this half-space correspond to the properties of the deepest layer investigated, as it was discussed in Chapter 1.

In such a situation the whole approach of *Fig. 3.1* becomes doubtful and we have to return to the general approach of *Fig. 2.3*. Fortunately, 1D seismic analysis of the soil column with given surface motion is still possible even without rigid boundary below. It can be shown that the solution in the upper part of the column does not depend on the lower part (both boundary conditions – prescribed displacements and zero stresses – are set up at the surface). This type of soil column analysis is called "deconvolution". It may be performed either analytically, of by FEM. The details were discussed in Chapter 1.

The results of this analysis give us boundary displacements U_0 and loads F_{int} for the middle model in *Fig. 2.3*. Now the loads refer not only to the lateral boundaries but to the bottom as well. The missing part is now only a model of the external soil described by operator G_0. As shown in Chapter 2, the free-field part of the final solution does not depend on G_0, but the additional part – the wave field radiated by the structure – is controlled by G_0.

If the volume V_{int} is stretched in the horizontal direction, the lateral part of G_0 may be described by acoustic boundaries as previously discussed for the rock case. Technically speaking, acoustic boundaries can be used for the bottom as well, but there appear several concerns about the accuracy of such an approach.

As stated before, acoustic boundaries physically are equivalent to the set of half-infinite rods. So, for the additional wave field the system will look like one shown in *Fig. 3.7*.

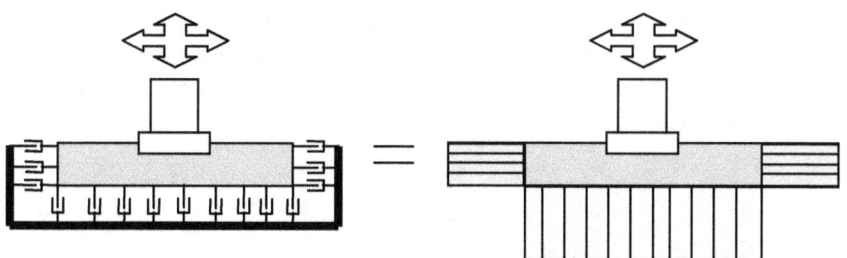

Figure 3.7. Model with acoustic lateral and bottom boundaries

Side parts of the bottom receive the waves radiated by the structure at the angles far from 90°. Besides, considerable parts of the infinite external volume adjacent to the corners of Q are not represented in the model at all. So, the accuracy cannot be justified in such cases.

For some period acoustic boundaries were very popular (e.g., LUSH soft used them see Lysmer et al. (1974)), but later on they were changed for the next generation of "non-reflecting" or "transmitting" boundaries, developed by G. Waas (see Lysmer and Waas (1972)) and intensively used in the code SASSI (see Lysmer et al. (1981)).

But before we get to these boundaries, let us have a deeper insight into the wave processes in layered soil.

3.3. Surface wave in layered soil. Analytical transmitting boundaries in the frequency domain

If we look at the right-hand part of *Fig. 3.7* and imagine two half-infinite neighboring horizontal rods, modeling neighbouring layers with different properties, we see that the displacements at the horizontal boundary between these layers are not continuous even in case of horizontally propagating waves: in two neighboring rods they are different. The reason is that wavelengths are different because of the different properties of rods. Therefore the displacements in two layers that were continuous at the vertical lateral boundary become non-continuous apart from this vertical boundary.

So, the first goal at the new stage of development was to develop some analytical solution for the horizontally layered soil resting on the rigid half-space. As this solution was intended to be used for the waves propagating from the structure, the surface of the rigid half-space should be fixed. Surely, this solution should be continuous at all the horizontal boundaries between layers, unlike the acoustic solution shown in *Fig. 3.7*. So, it was, in fact, the problem of the surface waves spreading in the horizontally-layered medium underlain by rigid half-space. Scheme of this problem is shown in *Fig. 3.8*.

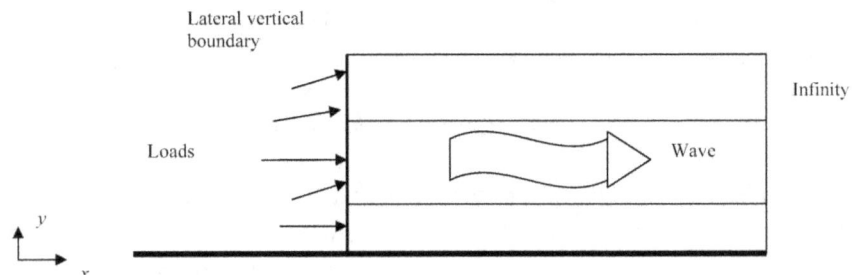

Figure 3.8. Scheme of the surface waves problem for horizontally layered medium

Let us start with a two-dimensional problem for a single layer resting on the fixed rigid half-space. Let us put the internal damping zero. Equations of motion can be written as follows:

$$(\lambda+\mu)\frac{\partial^2 u_k}{\partial x_j \partial x_k}+\mu \Delta u_j - \rho \frac{\partial^2 u_j}{\partial t^2} = 0. \quad (3.3)$$

Here ρ is a mass density; λ and μ are Lame parameters. Using the conventional technical Young modulus E, Poisson's coefficient v and shear modulus G, one has:

$$\lambda = \frac{vE}{(1+v)(1-2v)}; \quad \mu = \frac{E}{2(1+v)} = G. \quad (3.4)$$

In (3.3) index k is used for summation (k = 1, 2, 3), and index j = 1, 2, 3 is a number of equation in the system. Besides, the conventional operator is used:

$$\Delta = \frac{\partial^2}{\partial x_1^2} + \frac{\partial^2}{\partial x_2^2} + \frac{\partial^2}{\partial x_3^2}. \quad (3.5)$$

Let x_1 be horizontal axis, x_2 be vertical axis, x_3 be the second horizontal axis normal to the considered plane. As a problem is two-dimensional, all derivatives over x_3 are zero. Then (3.3) can be rewritten as

$$(\lambda+2\mu)\frac{\partial^2 u_1}{\partial x_1^2} + \mu\frac{\partial^2 u_1}{\partial x_2^2} + (\lambda+\mu)\frac{\partial^2 u_2}{\partial x_1 \partial x_2} = \rho\frac{\partial^2 u_1}{\partial t^2}, \quad (3.6)$$

$$(\lambda+2\mu)\frac{\partial^2 u_2}{\partial x_2^2} + \mu\frac{\partial^2 u_2}{\partial x_1^2} + (\lambda+\mu)\frac{\partial^2 u_1}{\partial x_1 \partial x_2} = \rho\frac{\partial^2 u_2}{\partial t^2}, \quad (3.7)$$

$$\mu\frac{\partial^2 u_3}{\partial x_1^2} + \mu\frac{\partial^2 u_3}{\partial x_2^2} = \rho\frac{\partial^2 u_3}{\partial t^2}. \quad (3.8)$$

One can see that (3.8) is uncoupled with (3.6) and (3.7). They say that (3.6) and (3.7) describe SV-waves, and (3.8) describes SH-waves. We will start with the SV-waves.

We will look for the SV-solution in the form

$$\begin{pmatrix} u_1 \\ u_2 \end{pmatrix} = \begin{pmatrix} U \\ V \end{pmatrix} \exp[i(\omega t - k_x x_1 - k_y x_2)]. \quad (3.9)$$

Here k_x and k_y are complex wave numbers.

Substituting (3.9) into (3.6) and (3.7) one gets homogeneous algebraic system of two equations for the unknown U and V:

$$(\lambda + 2\mu)k_x^2 U + \mu k_y^2 U + (\lambda + \mu)k_x k_y V = \rho \omega^2 U, \quad (3.10)$$

$$(\lambda + 2\mu)k_y^2 V + \mu k_x^2 V + (\lambda + \mu)k_x k_y U = \rho \omega^2 V. \quad (3.11)$$

This system has a non-zero solution only if the determinant is zero. So, we get the equation linking wave numbers k_x and k_y to ($\rho \omega^2$):

$$\begin{vmatrix} (\lambda + 2\mu)k_x^2 + \mu k_y^2 - \rho\omega^2 & (\lambda + \mu)k_x k_y \\ (\lambda + \mu)k_x k_y & (\lambda + 2\mu)k_y^2 + \mu k_x^2 - \rho\omega^2 \end{vmatrix} = 0. \quad (3.12)$$

One can solve (3.12) easily as quadratic equation over ($\rho \omega^2$) and get two roots:

$$\rho\omega^2 = \mu(k_x^2 + k_y^2), \quad (3.13)$$

$$\rho\omega^2 = (\lambda + 2\mu)(k_x^2 + k_y^2). \quad (3.14)$$

Now let us remember (1.1) and (1.2). Note that

$$E_c = \lambda + 2\mu. \quad (3.15)$$

From (3.14) one gets

$$k_x^2 + (k_y^s)^2 = \omega^2 \rho / \mu = \omega^2 / V_s^2. \quad (3.16)$$

This equation describes shear SV-wave. If $k_x = 0$, we get vertically propagating shear wave from Chapter 1. For non-zero k_x shear wave is inclined.

From (3.15) one gets

$$k_x^2 + (k_y^p)^2 = \omega^2 \rho / (\lambda + 2\mu) = \omega^2 / V_p^2. \quad (3.17)$$

This equation describes primary (i.e. compression) SV-wave. If $k_x = 0$, we get vertically propagating primary wave from Chapter 1. For non-zero k_x primary wave is inclined.

For the given k_x equations (3.16) and (3.17) give four (two pairs with opposite signs) different k_y. Opposite signs of k_y mean two different wavefronts, symmetrical about horizontal axis OX.

For each given pair of k_x and k_y the system (3.5) provides certain U/V. For shear waves the substitution of (3.13) into (3.10) gives

$$V^s/U^s = -k_x/k_y. \qquad (3.18)$$

For primary waves the substitution of (3.14) into (3.10) gives

$$V^p/U^p = k_y/k_x. \qquad (3.19)$$

So, for a given k_x one has four waves in a layer, controlled by four different values of k_y and corresponding different values of (U/V).

These waves are scaled by four amplitudes U_j ($j = 1, ..., 4$). Values of U_j must satisfy four boundary conditions. Two of them are zero stresses at the free surface:

$$\sigma_y = (\lambda + 2\mu)\frac{\partial u_2}{\partial x_2} + \lambda \frac{\partial u_1}{\partial x_1} = 0, \qquad (3.20)$$

$$\tau = \mu(\frac{\partial u_1}{\partial x_2} + \frac{\partial u_2}{\partial x_1}) = 0. \qquad (3.21)$$

Other two conditions are set at the fixed bottom:

$$u_1 = 0; \quad u_2 = 0. \qquad (3.22)$$

Let us put the origin of the coordinate system to the free surface. Then with four waves corresponding to a single k_x, equations (3.20) and (3.21) may be rewritten as:

$$\sum_{j=1}^{4}[(\lambda + 2\mu)ik_{yj}V_j + \lambda ik_x U_j] = 0, \qquad (3.23)$$

$$-\mu \sum_{j=1}^{4}[ik_x V_j + ik_{yj} U_j] = 0. \qquad (3.24)$$

At the bottom $x_2 = -H$ (H is a layer thickness), the equations (3.22) can be rewritten as:

$$\sum_{j=1}^{4}[U_j \exp(ik_{yj}H)] = 0, \quad (3.25)$$

$$\sum_{j=1}^{4}[V_j \exp(ik_{yj}H)] = 0. \quad (3.26)$$

Equations (3.23–3.26) are in fact a linear system with unknown U_j, because V_j are expressed via U_j. Let us denote four values of k_y as k_y^s, $-k_y^s$, k_y^p and $-k_y^p$. First two of them are expressed via k_x using equation (3.16), other two – using (3.17). Corresponding V_j will be V_1^s, V_2^s, V_1^p, V_2^p (similar for U_j). First two of them are expressed via U_j using equation (3.18), other two – using (3.19).

We arrive to the following system of linear algebraic equations

$$\begin{bmatrix} (\lambda+2\mu)k_y^s(-k_x/k_y^s)+\lambda k_x & (\lambda+2\mu)(-k_y^s)(k_x/k_y^s)+\lambda k_x & (\lambda+2\mu)k_y^p(k_y^p/k_x)+\lambda k_x & (\lambda+2\mu)(-k_y^p)(-k_y^p/k_x)+\lambda k_x \\ \mu[k_x(-k_x/k_y^s)+k_y^s] & \mu[k_x(k_x/k_y^s)-k_y^s] & \mu[k_x(k_x/k_y^p)+k_y^p] & \mu[k_x(-k_y^p/k_x)-k_y^p] \\ \exp(ik_y^s H) & \exp(-ik_y^s H) & \exp(ik_y^p H) & \exp(-ik_y^p H) \\ -(k_x/k_y^s)\exp(ik_y^s H) & (k_x/k_y^s)\exp(-ik_y^s H) & (k_y^p/k_x)\exp(ik_y^p H) & -(k_y^p/k_x)\exp(-ik_y^p H) \end{bmatrix} \begin{pmatrix} U_1^s \\ U_2^s \\ U_1^p \\ U_2^p \end{pmatrix} = \begin{pmatrix} 0 \\ 0 \\ 0 \\ 0 \end{pmatrix}$$

This system can be rewritten as

$$\begin{bmatrix} -2k_x & -(k_x)^2/k_y^s + k_y^s & -2k_x & (\lambda/\mu+2)(k_y^p)^2/k_x + (\lambda/\mu)k_x \\ -(k_x)^2/k_y^s + k_y^s & (k_x)^2/k_y^s - k_y^s & (\lambda/\mu+2)(k_y^p)^2/k_x + (\lambda/\mu)k_x & (\lambda/\mu+2)(k_y^p)^2/k_x + (\lambda/\mu)k_x \\ \exp(ik_y^s H) & \exp(-ik_y^s H) & \exp(ik_y^p H) & \exp(-ik_y^p H) \\ -(k_x/k_y^s)\exp(ik_y^s H) & (k_x/k_y^s)\exp(-ik_y^s H) & (k_y^p/k_x)\exp(ik_y^p H) & -(k_y^p/k_x)\exp(-ik_y^p H) \end{bmatrix}$$

$$\begin{pmatrix} U_1^s \\ U_2^s \\ U_1^p \\ U_2^p \end{pmatrix} = \begin{pmatrix} 0 \\ 0 \\ 0 \\ 0 \end{pmatrix}$$

And one more step forward, using (3.17) and (3.18) in the first two lines:

$$\begin{bmatrix} -2k_x & -2k_x & \frac{\lambda+2\mu}{\mu}[\frac{\rho\omega^2}{\lambda+2\mu} - k_x^2]/k_x + \frac{\lambda}{\mu}k_x & \frac{\lambda+2\mu}{\mu}[\frac{\rho\omega^2}{\lambda+2\mu} - k_x^2]/k_x + \frac{\lambda}{\mu}k_x \\ -[\frac{\rho\omega^2}{\mu} - (k_y^s)^2]/k_y^s - k_y^s & [\frac{\rho\omega^2}{\mu} - (k_y^s)^2]/k_y^s - k_y^s & 2k_y^p & -2k_y^p \\ \exp(ik_y^s H) & \exp(-ik_y^s H) & \exp(ik_y^p H) & \exp(-ik_y^p H) \\ -(k_x/k_y^s)\exp(ik_y^s H) & (k_x/k_y^s)\exp(-ik_y^s H) & (k_y^p/k_x)\exp(ik_y^p H) & -(k_y^p/k_x)\exp(-ik_y^p H) \end{bmatrix}$$

$$\begin{pmatrix} U_1^s \\ U_2^s \\ U_1^p \\ U_2^p \end{pmatrix} = \begin{pmatrix} 0 \\ 0 \\ 0 \\ 0 \end{pmatrix}$$

(3.27)

This system can be rewritten as

$$\begin{bmatrix} -2k_x & -2k_x & \dfrac{\rho\omega^2}{\mu k_x} - 2k_x & \dfrac{\rho\omega^2}{\mu k_x} - 2k_x \\ -\dfrac{\rho\omega^2}{\mu k_y^s} + 2k_y^s & \dfrac{\rho\omega^2}{\mu k_y^s} - 2k_y^s & 2k_y^p & -2k_y^p \\ \exp(ik_y^s H) & \exp(-ik_y^s H) & \exp(ik_y^p H) & \exp(-ik_y^p H) \\ -\dfrac{k_x}{k_y^s}\exp(ik_y^s H) & \dfrac{k_x}{k_y^s}\exp(-ik_y^s H) & \dfrac{k_y^p}{k_x}\exp(ik_y^p H) & -\dfrac{k_y^p}{k_x}\exp(-ik_y^p H) \end{bmatrix} \begin{pmatrix} U_1^s \\ U_2^s \\ U_1^p \\ U_2^p \end{pmatrix} = \begin{pmatrix} 0 \\ 0 \\ 0 \\ 0 \end{pmatrix} \quad (3.27)$$

If the excitation wave is running across the bottom of the layer (like we discussed in Chapter 1), the right-hand part of (3.27) is non-zero in two last lines. Besides, k_x is fixed by the excitation wave apparent velocity. Then (3.27) becomes the non-homogeneous system for the determination of U_j. This is the case of the induced waves in the layer, discussed in Chapter 1 of this book. Note once more, that in this case k_x given by the apparent excitation wave at the bottom of the layer is common for all four induced waves and control the apparent wave velocity at the free surface of the layer.

Now we are going to study the alternative variant when the right-hand parts of (3.27) are zeroes, i.e. the underlying half-space is fixed. Then the system (3.27) is homogeneous. Once more we have the situation when the determinant of this system must be zero to enable non-zero solution:

$$\det \begin{bmatrix} -2k_x & -2k_x & \dfrac{\rho\omega^2}{\mu k_x} - 2k_x & \dfrac{\rho\omega^2}{\mu k_x} - 2k_x \\ -\dfrac{\rho\omega^2}{\mu k_y^s} + 2k_y^s & \dfrac{\rho\omega^2}{\mu k_y^s} - 2k_y^s & 2k_y^p & -2k_y^p \\ \exp(ik_y^s H) & \exp(-ik_y^s H) & \exp(ik_y^p H) & \exp(-ik_y^p H) \\ -\dfrac{k_x}{k_y^s}\exp(ik_y^s H) & \dfrac{k_x}{k_y^s}\exp(-ik_y^s H) & \dfrac{k_y^p}{k_x}\exp(ik_y^p H) & -\dfrac{k_y^p}{k_x}\exp(-ik_y^p H) \end{bmatrix} = 0 \quad (3.28)$$

This time (3.28) is an equation with the only unknown, and this is k_x. This equation is called the "wave equation". The roots of this equation are frequency-dependent wave numbers, controlling surface waves in a layer. Each root corresponds to four U_j; actual U_j are controlled by the displacements at the lateral vertical boundary (see *Fig. 3.8*). We will not discuss methods of the solution of wave equation; instead, we will discuss the results of the solution, i.e. the behaviour of the roots.

The number of these roots is infinite but countable; the whole spectrum is discrete. This spectrum in the complex plane is anti-symmetric (i.e. if k_x is a root, then $(-k_x)$ is also a root). Usually, instead of k_x they use dimensionless $(k_x H)$. The complex lower half-plane of k_x according to (3.9) describes waves with exponent reduction towards positive X-direction; therefore these roots will describe waves in the right half-layer with excitation applied at the vertical boundary as shown in *Fig. 3.8*. The upper complex half-plane corresponds to the waves with exponent reduction towards negative X-direction, therefore describing the left half-layer.

Let us study the lower complex half-plane. For small frequency, all roots have non-zero imaginary parts. Physical meaning is that all waves will have exponential decay along X-direction even without any internal damping in the soil. They will not take energy in the horizontal direction from the vertical boundary.

When frequency ω increases, roots k_x continuously move from their static position. There are different variants of this motion for different roots.

1) The first root moves along an imaginary axis towards the real axis and reaches it when frequency ω reaches the characteristic value

$$\omega_1 = \frac{2\pi V_s}{4H}. \quad (3.29)$$

When it happens, the first root is zero. It means that the corresponding wave field does not depend on coordinate x. This frequency value is very important; it is called "critical frequency of the layer". Note that due to the anti-symmetry mentioned before, at the same time, when our first root k_x is approaching zero from the lower complex half-plane, "twin" root $(-k_x)$ is approaching the same zero point from the upper half-plane. If internal damping in soil is zero (i.e. λ and μ are real values), two these roots will "meet" in zero point at a frequency given in (3.29). But if we introduce some internal damping making λ and μ slightly complex values, then two roots will not "meet", though they will approach each other. When the frequency increases further above the critical value (3.29), the roots k_x in the complex plane turn 90°. The root coming from the lower complex half-plane turns to the right and starts moving along the real axis. Physically it means that wave amplitude does not decrease along positive X-axis any more. "Dying" wave turned into "running wave". Such a wave takes the energy away from the vertical boundary of excitation. That is why critical frequency (3.29) is often called "opening frequency" of the layer: above this frequency the layer is opened as a wave-conductor. The whole phenomenon of mechanical "running" waves taking energy away from the excitation vertical boundary is called "wave damping", or "radiation damping". This phenomenon is physically different from the conventional internal damping: the energy is not transferred to heat but remains mechanical. However, the consequences for the excitation source are the same as with the internal damping: energy is taken from the source. In reality, there exists the internal material damping in the soil; so, the trajectory of the root in the complex plane is somewhat different, as shown in *Fig. 3.9*. There is certain decay of the "running ways" due to the internal damping, but it is rather small.

2) Other roots in the lower complex half-plane are grouped in pairs. Initially (for zero frequency) each pair is symmetrical over the imaginary axis. The behaviour of the second and third roots depends on the Poisson's ratio. For the high ratio (typical for saturated soils) both roots approach the real axis in the complex plane, keeping symmetry and meeting their "twins" coming from the upper complex half-plane. After the "meeting" they turn 90° to the right and move along the real axis as shown in *Fig. 3.9*. One of them (Root # 2 in *Fig. 3.9*) just follows the way of the first root, creating one more "running" way taking the energy away. Another root (Root # 3 in *Fig. 3.9*) moves in the same direction. After it reaches zero, it turns 90° to the right once more and goes down

the imaginary axis, as shown in *Fig. 3.9*. Such behaviour (shift along the real axis towards zero point) is called "abnormal dispersion". The term "abnormal" is used because the apparent velocity of the corresponding wave is directed to the source of excitation, and energy is taken in the opposite direction.

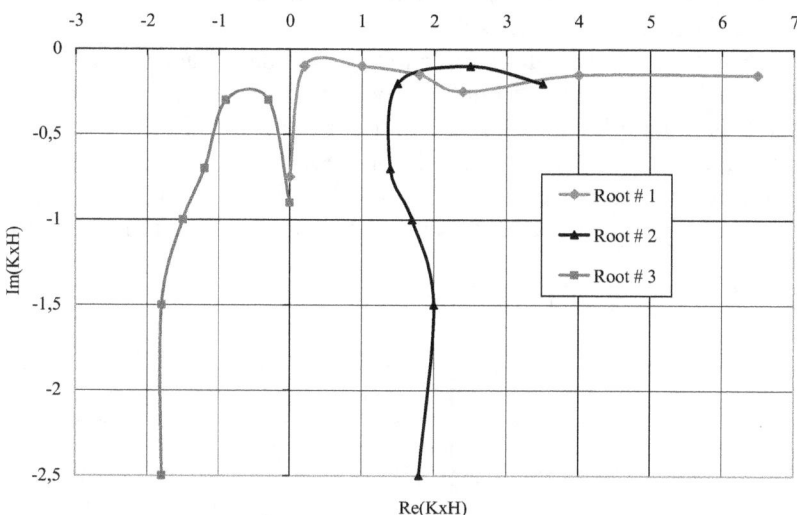

Figure 3.9. Trajectories of the first three roots k_x in the complex plane with 2.5% internal damping and Poisson's coefficient 0.48

3) Other pairs of roots are first coming to the imaginary axis. After "meeting with each other" they go in the opposite directions along this axis.

We will not go into further details. The main conclusions are as follows.

1) For the low frequencies (below critical frequency of the layer) no wave damping exists in the layer.

2) For the frequencies above critical frequency of the layer there appear "running waves" taking the energy away from the excitation source. For each given frequency the number of "running waves" is finite.

Note that this effect (sudden appearance of running ways) cannot be described by acoustic boundaries (i.e. infinite rods), as viscous dashpots there start to work from very low frequency. It was investigated in detail (and probably discovered) by John Wolf from Switzerland (e.g., see Wolf (1985)).

Now, what is the reason for the study of the surface waves? Suppose we know the displacements at the vertical lateral boundary in *Fig. 3.8* being kinematical excitation for the half-layer. Then these boundary displacements can be presented as a linear combination of these waves (taken at $x_1 = 0$) with certain coefficients. Wave field in the whole half-layer shown in *Fig. 3.8* will be the sum of the infinite number of such waves with the same coefficients. But then we are able to obtain stresses acting from the infinite half-layer to the lateral boundary as a response to the kinematical excitation.

Suppose finite volume down to the rigid half space to the left of the half-layer is modelled by finite elements. It means that the displacement field at the lateral boundary is a linear combination of elementary "unit" displacements (unit displacement in one node and zero displacements in all other nodes at the boundary) controlled between the nodes by the shape functions in finite elements as schematically shown in *Fig. 3.10*.

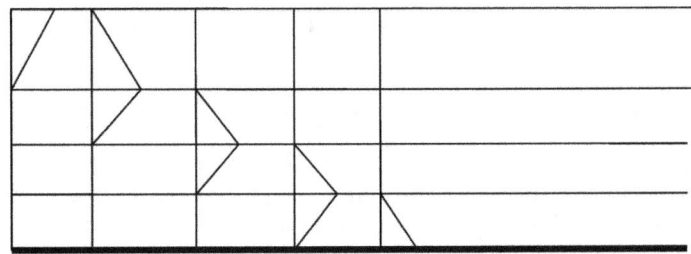

Figure 3.10. Elementary FEM displacements at the lateral boundary

Each of these triangle "unit" FEM displacements may be represented as a sum of surface waves, causing response stresses from half-layer. These stresses can be lumped into nodal response forces. And nodal forces in response to unit nodal displacements by definition form stiffness matrix of the half-layer. This is a matrix of the desired "transmitting boundary". The accuracy of this boundary is controlled by the accuracy of the approximation of the unit FEM displacements by surface waves. As the number of roots and waves is infinite, the accuracy can be improved to any given extent (surely, it cannot exceed the accuracy of the FEM representation of the adjacent finite volume).

Several important comments should be added here.

1) Such transmitting boundary is frequency-dependent as surface waves are frequency-dependent (starting from wave numbers, as we saw above). Unlike acoustic boundaries, this boundary will reflect the

appearance of "running waves" above the "opening frequency". Even without the internal damping (i.e. with real λ and μ) we get complex stiffness for running waves out of complex wave numbers.

2) Such transmitting boundary, unlike acoustic boundary, is not local, i.e. the response forces to the unit FEM displacements act not only on the node with unit displacement but on all other nodes as well (not only the neighbouring ones). In other words, stiffness matrix will be not diagonal (as for acoustic boundary) but fully populated. It makes calculations more complicated but reflects physics (the so-called "distributive ability" of the soil).

Now let us consider waves, described by (3.8), i.e. with out-of-plane displacements u_3. If the waves considered before can be called "generalized Rayleigh waves", now we are going to study "generalized Love waves". The sequence is the same. We are looking for the solution in the form

$$u_3 = W \exp[i(\omega t - k_x x_1 - k_y x_2)]. \qquad (3.30)$$

Substituting (3.30) into (3.8), one gets the same equation for the shear waves as we had before (the old number is used here):

$$\rho \omega^2 = \mu(k_x^2 + k_y^2). \qquad (3.13)$$

The given value of k_x corresponds this time only to two values of k_y, and not to four ones, as before; however, these two values participated in the previous four ones. Let W_1 be amplitude for k_y, and W_2 be the amplitude for $(-k_y)$. Upper indices should be s, but we will omit them as there are no other variants this time.

The boundary condition at the free surface is

$$\tau = \mu \frac{\partial u_3}{\partial x_2} = 0. \qquad (3.31)$$

At the fixed bottom of the layer ($x_2 = -H$) the fixed boundary condition is

$$u_3 = 0. \qquad (3.32)$$

Analogue of the system (3.28) has only two equations and unknowns:

$$\begin{bmatrix} k_y & -k_y \\ \exp(ik_yH) & \exp(-ik_yH) \end{bmatrix} \begin{pmatrix} W_1 \\ W_2 \end{pmatrix} = \begin{pmatrix} 0 \\ 0 \end{pmatrix}. \qquad (3.33)$$

The determinant of the matrix in (3.33) is simply $2k_y\cos(k_yH)$ and it should be zero to get non-zero displacements. Thus, the wave equation is simply

$$\cos(k_yH) = 0. \qquad (3.34)$$

From this we get

$$k_yH = \frac{\pi}{2} + \pi k, \quad k = 0, \pm 1, \ldots . \qquad (3.35)$$

But we are looking for k_x, which we get from (3.13):

$$k_x^2 = \frac{\rho\omega^2}{\mu} - \frac{\pi^2}{H^2}(\frac{1}{2} + k)^2. \qquad (3.36)$$

For small frequency ω the right-hand part of (3.36) is negative, so k_x is imaginary value. Along with increasing frequency, each root goes to zero (without internal damping), as we saw it before for the first root of the previous wave equation. The first root will reach zero at the frequency

$$\omega = \frac{\pi}{2H}\sqrt{\frac{\mu}{\rho}}. \qquad (3.37)$$

This is exactly the opening frequency of the layer from (3.29). When frequency ω further increases, the right-hand part of (3.36) becomes positive, and we obtain increasing real root k_x. So, the conclusion is that each root of (3.36) behaves like the first root of (3.28): it comes to zero, then turns 90° to the real axis and goes away. We see that the 90° "turns" in the trajectory of k_x correspond to the crossing of zero by the second degree of k_x.

One more comment should be added here. When $k_x = 0$, the whole free surface (and any other horizontal surface in the soil) moves as a rigid body. But then there is no physical difference between Love wave and

Rayleigh shear wave with zero vertical displacements. It means that set of frequencies

$$\omega_k = \frac{\pi}{H}\sqrt{\frac{\mu}{\rho}}(\frac{1}{2}+k). \qquad (3.38)$$

corresponds to zero k_x for the Rayleigh wave equation also. In the corresponding Rayleigh wave field, the coefficients U_1^s and U_2^s will be non-zero; V_1^s and V_2^s will be zero because of (3.18); all amplitudes of primary waves will be zero. It means that (3.36) is a simple tool to find not only the first "critical" frequency but the whole set of "critical" frequencies corresponding to the appearance of the additional "running" waves.

Now let us extend the scope. How to be if not a single layer, but several flexible horizontal layers with different properties are resting on rigid half-space? It turns out that physically we have the same picture as before: there exists certain "opening" frequency of his package, corresponding to zero k_x common both for Rayleigh and for Love waves. Below this frequency, there is no "wave damping"; above this frequency there appear "running waves". Mathematically each root k_x in the generalized Rayleigh wave corresponds now not to 4, but to $4n$ values of k_y (n is a number of layers). On the other hand, each new layer brings four additional consistency terms: two ones describing continuity of displacements between two layers, and two other terms describing continuity of stresses σ_y and τ_{xy}. So the number of unknowns and the number of terms are balanced. The similar situation is for Love waves: there each new layer brings two additional unknowns and two additional terms (one for the continuity of displacements; another one for the continuity of stresses τ between the layers).

And one more step forward. Suppose we have finite volume in the form of cylinder coming down to the rigid half-space. Instead of two infinite half-layers from the left and from the right of the finite volume we have now infinite 3D layer with the cylinder cut out. Suppose displacements at cylindrical lateral vertical boundary are set as a Fourier sum along angular cylindrical coordinates. In turns out that instead of (3.9) and (3.30) one can use almost similar equations substituting exponents along x_1 by Hankel's functions along x_1. The general idea is as follows. When we considered plane wavefront, the transfer of energy without losses due to the internal damping meant constant amplitudes without decay. This is expressed in complex exponents (3.9), when wave number k_x is real. Now we consider cylindrical wave spreading from some source. The area of wavefront increases with radius. It means that to keep energy at the front constant the amplitude should decrease with radius. This "geometric" decay in displacements amplitudes without physical decay in energy content is described by Hankel's functions. The non-zero internal damping causes additional decay both for the plane and cylindrical waves.

The most impressive result is that the wave equations for generalized Rayleigh and for Love waves remain completely the same as for the two-dimensional case considered above. It was rigorously proven. And physical consequences (i.e. the appearance of the running waves above certain frequency) remain the same.

In the middle of 1980-s, the author developed effective computer tools to solve wave equations and implemented the analytical transmitting boundary described above. However, later this approach was not further developed, because the home-made soft was replaced by SASSI. Nevertheless, the author described this approach, because it gives the insight in the SASSI ideology.

It may seem that too much attention was paid to the surface waves here. However, the author considers their behaviour to be a key issue to the understanding of several SSI effects. We will return to these results later in Chapter 5.

3.4. Semi-analytical transmitting boundaries in the frequency domain

At the beginning of 1970-s Guenter Waas (see Lysmer and Waas (1972)) developed a new semi-analytical approach to the description of the wave field in the horizontally-layered package resting on rigid half-space. He used instead of (3.9) the equation

$$\begin{pmatrix} u_1 \\ u_2 \end{pmatrix} = \begin{pmatrix} U(x_2) \\ V(x_2) \end{pmatrix} \exp[i(\omega t - k_x x_1)]. \qquad (3.39)$$

One can see that if functions of $U(x_2)$ and $V(x_2)$ are taken as exponents, we come to (3.9). But G. Waas instead took these functions according to the FEM ideology: having a set of nodes at the lateral boundary, he took unit displacements (see *Fig. 3.10*) and multiplied by nodal displacements. Therefore along vertical axis displacements between nodes were linear.

In FEM ideology (3.39) can be rewritten as

$$\{u(x_1,x_2)\} = \exp[i(\omega t - k_x x_1)][S(x_2)]\{V\}. \qquad (3\text{-}40)$$

Here $\{u\}$ in the left-hand part is a vector (2×1), $[S(x_2)]$ in the right-hand part is a matrix of unit displacement shape forms ($2 \times 2n$), where n is number of nodes at the lateral boundary (without the fixed one at the bottom); $\{V\}$ is the column of nodal displacements ($2n \times 1$). Functions $S(x_2)$ consist of n functions $S_{jx}(x_2)$ and n functions $S_{jy}(x_2)$ similar in shape forming sub-matrices (lines) $[S_x(x_2)]$ and $[S_y(x_2)]$. Usually, they are placed in turn:

$$[S(x_2)] = \begin{bmatrix} [S_x(x_2)] \\ [S_y(x_2)] \end{bmatrix} = \begin{bmatrix} S_{1x}(x_2) & 0 & S_{2x}(x_2) & 0 & ... \\ 0 & S_{1y}(x_2) & 0 & S_{2y}(x_2) & ... \end{bmatrix}, \qquad (3.41)$$

$$\{V\} = \{U_1 \ V_1 \ U_2 \ V_2 \ ...\}^T. \qquad (3.42)$$

Then G. Waas substituted (3.40) into (3.6) and (3.7), taking derivatives along t and x_1 analytically and leaving derivatives along x_2 for a while. After eliminating exponents he got from (3.6) and (3.7) two equations in the frequency domain with functions of x_2:

$$\{-(\lambda+2\mu)k_x^2[S_x(x_2)] + \mu[\frac{\partial^2 S_x(x_2)}{\partial x_2^2}] -$$
$$-(\lambda+\mu)ik_x[\frac{\partial S_y(x_2)}{\partial x_2}] + \omega^2\rho[S_x(x_2)]\}\{V\} = 0, \qquad (3.43)$$

$$\{(\lambda+2\mu)[\frac{\partial^2 S_y(x_2)}{\partial x_2^2}] - \mu k_x^2[S_y(x_2)] -$$
$$-(\lambda+\mu)ik_x[\frac{\partial S_x(x_2)}{\partial x_2}] + \omega^2\rho[S_y(x_2)]\}\{V\} = 0. \qquad (3.44)$$

After that G. Waas performed standard Galerkin procedure: multiplied equation (3.43) by $[S_{kx}]^T$ ($k = 1,2,..., n$) from the left and integrated along x_2 over vertical lateral boundary $x_1 = 0$. Thus he received n equations. Another set of n equations he got multiplying (3.44) by $[S_y]^T$.

But what was actually integrated during this procedure?

First, all integrals along the lateral boundary are sums of integrals along each of *n* vertical parts of this boundary located between neighbouring nodes. So let us consider one of these parts – part number *j* between node *j* – 1 and node *j*. Only two shape functions are non-zero for this single part – let them be $S_j(x_2)$ and $S_{j-1}(x_2)$. Let *L* be the length of this part.

The first and the last terms in (3.43); the second and the last terms in (3.44) in this procedure will contain integrals:

$$I^0_{11} = \int_L S_j(x_2) S_j(x_2) dx_2 = \frac{1}{3}L; \quad I^0_{12} = \int_L S_j(x_2) S_{j-1}(x_2) dx_2 = \frac{1}{6}L. \quad (3.45)$$

The second term in (3.43) and the first term in (3.44) in this procedure will contain integrals:

$$I^2_{11} = \int_L S_j(x_2) \frac{\partial^2 S_j(x_2)}{\partial x_2^2} dx_2 = -\int_L \frac{\partial S_j(x_2)}{\partial x_2} \frac{\partial S_j(x_2)}{\partial x_2} dx_2 = -\frac{1}{L}$$

$$I^2_{12} = \int_L S_j(x_2) \frac{\partial^2 S_{j-1}(x_2)}{\partial x_2^2} dx_2 = -\int_L \frac{\partial S_j(x_2)}{\partial x_2} \frac{\partial S_{j-1}(x_2)}{\partial x_2} dx_2 = \frac{1}{L}. \quad (3.46)$$

The third terms in (3.43) and in (3.44) in this procedure will contain integrals:

$$I^1_{11} = \int_L S_j(x_2) \frac{\partial S_j(x_2)}{\partial x_2} dx_2 = \frac{1}{2},$$

$$I^2_{12} = \int_L S_j(x_2) \frac{\partial S_{j-1}(x_2)}{\partial x_2} dx_2 = -\frac{1}{2}. \quad (3.47)$$

After the described procedure which started from (3.43) and (3.44) and after changing the signs we get the equation

$$\{k_x^2[A] + i k_x[B] + [G] - \omega^2[M]\}\{V\} = 0. \quad (3.48)$$

Here all matrices are $(2n \times 2n)$; they are assembled from the matrices (4×4) obtained for each part of the boundary according to the conventional FEM rule, illustrated in *Fig. 3.11*.

Matrix $[A_j]$ for part j between nodes $j - 1$ and j will be composed of integrals (3.45) and will look as follows (indices j in the right-hand part omitted):

$$[A_j] = \frac{L}{6} \begin{bmatrix} 2(\lambda+2\mu) & 0 & (\lambda+2\mu) & 0 \\ 0 & 2\mu & 0 & \mu \\ (\lambda+2\mu) & 0 & 2(\lambda+2\mu) & 0 \\ 0 & \mu & 0 & 2\mu \end{bmatrix} \quad (3.49)$$

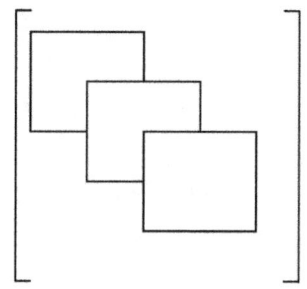

Figure 3.11. Conventional assembling rule for matrices

Formally speaking, matrix $[M_j]$ should be composed of the same integrals (3.45) and look as follows

$$[M_j] = \frac{\rho L}{6} \begin{bmatrix} 2 & 0 & 1 & 0 \\ 0 & 2 & 0 & 1 \\ 1 & 0 & 2 & 0 \\ 0 & 1 & 0 & 2 \end{bmatrix}. \quad (3.50)$$

This is "consistent" inertia matrix of the rod. But G. Waas introduced an additional tuning, averaging this matrix with the conventional lumped matrix for the same rod. So, he got

$$[M_j] = \frac{\rho L}{12} \begin{bmatrix} 2 & 0 & 1 & 0 \\ 0 & 2 & 0 & 1 \\ 1 & 0 & 2 & 0 \\ 0 & 1 & 0 & 2 \end{bmatrix} + \frac{\rho L}{4} \begin{bmatrix} 1 & 0 & 0 & 0 \\ 0 & 1 & 0 & 0 \\ 0 & 0 & 1 & 0 \\ 0 & 0 & 0 & 1 \end{bmatrix} = \frac{\rho L}{12} \begin{bmatrix} 5 & 0 & 1 & 0 \\ 0 & 5 & 0 & 1 \\ 1 & 0 & 5 & 0 \\ 0 & 1 & 0 & 5 \end{bmatrix}. \quad (3.51)$$

The reason for this additional tuning was that the computational experience for wave problems has shown that lumped mass matrix and consistent mass matrix lead to the numerical errors in opposite directions. Averaging make the numerical results more accurate. This approach was generally used in SASSI.

Let us return to matrices from (3.48). Matrix $[G_j]$ is composed of integrals (3.46) and looks as follows:

$$[G_j] = \frac{1}{L}\begin{bmatrix} \mu & 0 & -\mu & 0 \\ 0 & (\lambda+2\mu) & 0 & -(\lambda+2\mu) \\ -\mu & 0 & \mu & 0 \\ 0 & -(\lambda+2\mu) & 0 & (\lambda+2\mu) \end{bmatrix}. \qquad (3.52)$$

Matrix $[B_j]$ is composed of integrals (3.47) and looks as follows:

$$[B_j] = \frac{\lambda+\mu}{2}\begin{bmatrix} 0 & 1 & 0 & -1 \\ 1 & 0 & -1 & 0 \\ 0 & 1 & 0 & -1 \\ 1 & 0 & -1 & 0 \end{bmatrix}. \qquad (3.53)$$

Now all matrices in (3-48) are defined. The determinant of this system should be zero to provide non-zero solutions. Therefore we get the equation

$$\det\{k_x^2[A] + i k_x[B] + [G] - \omega^2[M]\} = 0. \qquad (3.54)$$

Usually, equations of this type are used to find natural frequencies. But this time frequency ω is a given parameter, and equation (3.54) is used to find wave numbers k_x. In fact, this is the approximate analogue of the wave equation (3.28). The error of the approximation depends on the relations between surface wave shapes and unit FEM displacements. For the first roots of the wave equation, if FEM mesh at the lateral boundary is fine, the error is acceptable. As wave damping is always controlled by the finite number of running waves, the phenomenon of wave damping is reflected reasonably. Higher roots will be modelled less accurate, but they correspond to the "dying waves". Surely, equation (3.54) has only $2n$ roots, and exact wave equation (3.28) has an infinite number of roots; so, part of higher roots is just lost in (3.54).

For some time the author was proud that his approach with wave equation (3.28) is more accurate than the approach (3.54). But later the author realized that this fact does not improve the accuracy of the final solution, as even for the precise modelling of the infinite part of the soil the final accuracy of the SSI solution is limited by the accuracy of FEM in the finite part of the soil.

Like in the previous section of the book, Love waves are treated separately from the Rayleigh waves. Displacements are obtained in the form

$$\{w(x_1,x_2)\} = \exp[i(\omega t - k_x x_1)][S(x_2)]\{W\}. \qquad (3.55)$$

This time $\{W\}$ is a column ($n \times 1$) of the nodal displacements; $[S(x_2)]$ is just a line of n unit shape functions similar to those used before. Equation (3.8) after analytical calculation of derivatives along t and x_1 gives

$$\{-\mu k_x^2[S(x_2)] + \mu[\frac{\partial^2 S(x_2)}{\partial x_2^2}] + \omega^2 \rho[S(x_2)]\}\{W\} = 0. \qquad (3.56)$$

After the Galerkin procedure similar to that described above we come to the system

$$\{k_x^2[A^w] + [G^w] - \omega^2[M^w]\}\{W\} = 0. \qquad (3.57)$$

All matrices here may be extracted from the corresponding matrices for Rayleigh waves. This time for each part of the boundary they are (2×2):

$$[M_j^w] = \frac{\rho L}{12}\begin{bmatrix} 5 & 1 \\ 1 & 5 \end{bmatrix}, \qquad (3.58)$$

$$[G_j^w] = \frac{\mu}{L}\begin{bmatrix} 1 & -1 \\ -1 & 1 \end{bmatrix}, \qquad (3.59)$$

$$[A_j^w] = \frac{\mu L}{6}\begin{bmatrix} 2 & 1 \\ 1 & 2 \end{bmatrix}. \qquad (3.60)$$

Wave equation this time is

$$\det\{k_x^2[A^w] + [G^w] - \omega^2[M^w]\} = 0. \qquad (3.61)$$

After the eigenvalue problems in wave equations (3.54) and (3.61) are solved (all $2n$ roots k_x for Rayleigh waves and n roots k_x for Love waves are obtained), matrices $[V]$ of the eigenvectors are obtained. Matrix $[V]$ consists of $2n$ eigenvectors $\{V_j\}, j = 1, 2, \ldots, 2n$. Matrix $[W]$ consists of n eigenvectors $\{W_j\}, j = 1, 2, \ldots, n$. The further procedure looks very much like the previous one, but even simpler.

For Rayleigh waves each eigenmode $\{V_m\}$ corresponds to horizontal and vertical stresses at the vertical lateral boundary, which may be obtained in the same manner:

$$\sigma_x(x_2) = \left\{-(\lambda + 2\mu)\, ik_x [S_x(x_2)] + \lambda \left[\frac{\partial S_y(x_2)}{\partial x_2}\right]\right\} \{V_m\}, \quad (3.62)$$

$$\tau(x_2) = \left\{-\mu i k_x [S_y(x_2)] + \mu \left[\frac{\partial S_x(x_2)}{\partial x_2}\right]\right\} \{V_m\}. \quad (3.63)$$

Corresponding nodal forces in the node k are obtained by multiplication of these stresses by shape functions $S_{kx}(x_2)$ in the horizontal direction and by $S_{ky}(x_2)$ in vertical direction with further integration along x_2. Integration will take part in the first brackets in the right-hand parts of (3.62) and (3.63), as $\{V_j\}$ does not depend on x_2. The whole matrix $[D]$ will be assembled from matrices corresponding to separate parts like shown in *Fig. 3.11*. Separate matrix $[D_j]$ will have the form

$$[D_j] = ik_x[P_j] + [Q_j], \quad (3.64)$$

$$[Q_j] = \frac{1}{2}\begin{bmatrix} 0 & \lambda & 0 & -\lambda \\ \mu & 0 & -\mu & 0 \\ 0 & \lambda & 0 & -\lambda \\ \mu & 0 & -\mu & 0 \end{bmatrix}, \quad (3.65)$$

$$[P_j] = \frac{L}{6}\begin{bmatrix} -2(\lambda+2\mu) & 0 & -(\lambda+2\mu) & 0 \\ 0 & -2\mu & 0 & -\mu \\ -(\lambda+2\mu) & 0 & -2(\lambda+2\mu) & 0 \\ 0 & -\mu & 0 & -2\mu \end{bmatrix}. \quad (3.66)$$

One can see from (3.49) and (3.66) that $[P_j] = -[A_j]$. Another note is that (3.64) depends on k_x in the first term; and k_x, as we remember from (3.63), is the m-th root of the wave equation. So, the resulting matrix $[D]$ after assembling, in fact, depends on m in the first part. The resulting nodal forces corresponding to $\{V_m\}$ are as follows:

$$\{F^m\} = [D^m]\{V_m\} = \{-ik_x^m[A] + [Q]\}\{V_m\}. \qquad (3.67)$$

Full matrix $[F]$ of these resulting forces (column after column) corresponding to the full set $[V]$ of eigenmodes (column after column) is

$$[F] = -i[A][V]\,diag[k_x^m] + [Q][V]. \qquad (3.68)$$

To get stiffness matrix (i.e. corresponding to the unit displacements, and not to $[V]$) one should multiply (3.68) by $[V]^{-1}$ from the right:

$$[R] = -i[A][V]\,diag[k_x^m][V]^{-1} + [Q]. \qquad (3.69)$$

Matrices $[Q]$ and $[A]$ here are frequency-independent and "almost local" (only neighbouring nodes participate in the response). However, the product $\{[V]\,diag\,[k_x^m]\,[V]^{-1}\}$ in the first term is frequency dependent in every part and besides makes the whole matrix fully populated.

This was transmitting boundary for Rayleigh waves in plane problem. To complete this section, let us derive the equation for Love waves for the plane case. The only stress at the vertical lateral boundary is

$$\tau(x_2) = -\mu i k_x[S(x_2)]\{V_m\}. \qquad (3.70)$$

Nodal forces corresponding to the eigenform number m are

$$[F^w] = -i[A^w][V^w]\,diag[k_x^{wm}]. \qquad (3.71)$$

The resulting stiffness matrix of the transmitting boundary is

$$[R^w] = -i[A^w][V^w]\,diag[k_x^{wm}][V^w]^{-1}. \qquad (3.72)$$

One should carefully choose the complex half-plane for the roots k_x to provide physical decay in the right direction as discussed in the previous section.

These were transmitting boundaries for the plane case. We will not explain the details of obtaining transmitting boundaries for axisymmetrical 3D case – principal approach is the same. Wave numbers, as mentioned before, are exactly the same as for the plane case.

These boundaries are so accurate that they can be placed near the structure, decreasing the internal volume V_{int}. So, it was a great step forward in the development of the SSI software in 1970-s – from LUSH (see Lysmer et al. (1974)) to FLUSH (Fast LUSH; see Lysmer et al. (1975)) and ALUSH (Axisymmetrical LUSH; see Lysmer (1982)).

The important limitation still was rigid half-space at the bottom of the layered soil. What if the half-space is flexible? We will discuss it in the next section.

3.5. Flexible half-space

Now let us return to section 3.3 and change the layer for the flexible half-space with similar soil properties. Equations (3.3–3.19) stay valid for flexible half-space. The only difference is that now we must leave only one of two values for each of k_y^s and k_y^p. This value should correspond to the SV-ways, decreasing downwards (i.e. coming from the surface source). That means that the imaginary part of k_y should be positive. These two conditions substitute conditions (3.25) and (3.26); so instead of (3.28) we get

$$\det \begin{bmatrix} -2k_x & \dfrac{\rho\omega^2}{\mu k_x} - 2k_x \\ -\dfrac{\rho\omega^2}{\mu k_y^s} + 2k_y^s & 2k_y^p \end{bmatrix} = 0. \qquad (3.72)$$

This wave equation for the homogeneous half-space will lead to the conventional Rayleigh waves. Let us use the unknown

$$\alpha = \frac{\rho\omega^2}{\mu k_x^2}. \qquad (3.73)$$

Then from (3.13)

$$\frac{(k_y^s)^2}{k_x^2} = \alpha^2 - 1. \qquad (3.74)$$

Similarly from (3.14)

$$\frac{(k_y^p)^2}{k_x^2} = \beta^2 \alpha^2 - 1. \qquad (3.75)$$

Here

$$\beta^2 = \frac{\mu}{\lambda + 2\mu} = \frac{1-2\nu}{2(1-\nu)} = \frac{V_s^2}{V_p^2}. \qquad (3.76)$$

Using these parameters one gets from (3.72) the equation of the fourth order, but luckily one root is zero. So, finally we come to the well-known cubic equation for the Rayleigh waves:

$$\alpha^3 - 8\alpha^2 + 8(3 - 2\beta^2)\alpha - 16(1 - \beta^2) = 0. \qquad (3.77)$$

This equation has a single root providing the desired Rayleigh wave. Displacements are decaying downwards. The author should like to note, that Rayleigh wave, in fact, is not a special wave, different from S- and P-waves; it is rather a special combination of S- and P-waves, as shown above.

But there is a certain physical paradox here. From a physical point of view, half-space is the limit case of a very thick layer. But what about an infinite discrete spectrum of wave numbers in (3.28)? Only one Rayleigh wave exists in the half-space!

To understand these phenomena let us rewrite wave equations using dimensionless wave numbers (k_x H) and corresponding (k_y^s H) and (k_y^p H). We must also use the dimensionless frequency θ, which we define using (3.13):

$$\theta^2 = (\rho \omega^2 H^2)/\mu = (k_x H)^2 + (k_y^s H)^2. \qquad (3.78)$$

Then (3.14) transfers to

$$\beta^2\theta^2 = (\rho\omega^2 H^2)/(\lambda+2\mu) = (k_x H)^2 + (k_y^p H)^2;$$

$$\beta^2 = \frac{\mu}{\lambda+2\mu} = \frac{1-2\nu}{2(1-\nu)} = \frac{V_s^2}{V_p^2}. \tag{3.79}$$

Wave equation (3.28) in the first two lines transfers to

$$\det \begin{bmatrix} -2(k_x H) & -2(k_x H) & \frac{\theta^2}{k_x H}-2(k_x H) & \frac{\theta^2}{k_x H}-2(k_x H) \\ -\frac{\theta^2}{k_y^s H}+2(k_y^s H) & \frac{\theta^2}{k_y^s H}-2(k_y^s H) & 2(k_y^p H) & -2(k_y^p H) \\ \exp(ik_y^s H) & \exp(-ik_y^s H) & \exp(ik_y^p H) & \exp(-ik_y^p H) \\ -\frac{k_x}{k_y^s}\exp(ik_y^s H) & \frac{k_x}{k_y^s}\exp(-ik_y^s H) & \frac{k_y^p}{k_x}\exp(ik_y^p H) & -\frac{k_y^p}{k_x}\exp(-ik_y^p H) \end{bmatrix} = 0. \tag{3.80}$$

As a result, dimensionless wave number ($k_x H$) depends on dimensionless frequency θ with some additional parameter β depending on the Poisson's coefficient (β does not participate in (3.75) explicitly; however, it implicitly participates in k_y^p). Thickness H does not participate in this dependence. Here we have an infinite spectrum described above and continuous trajectories of the roots.

Let us fix certain dimensionless frequency θ with the corresponding spectrum of dimensionless wave numbers and start increasing thickness H of the layer. With fixed dimensionless parameters ($k_x H$) and θ the corresponding physical parameters k_x and ω will go to zero.

What is going on at the lateral vertical boundary? Each single surface wave corresponding to certain root remains the same in shape along the vertical boundary and is just stretched along with the increase in thickness. If the wave source is localized (and not stretched), higher and higher waves dominate in the linear combination. But one should remember that corresponding physical frequency goes to zero.

Alternatively, if one increases thickness H fixing physical frequency ω, dimensionless frequency θ will increase following (3.78).

The conclusion is that the infinite wave numbers spectrum at finite physical frequency should not be compared to wave numbers in infinite half-space, as the physical frequency with the increase of the layer thickness goes to zero. Infinite number of surface waves is transferred into body waves spreading downwards from the source at an infinite number of inclination angles.

Let us return to the question about transmitting boundaries at the bottom in case the underlying half-space is flexible. Fixed value of α for the Rayleigh wave obtained from (3.77) means according to (3.73) that k_x is proportional to the frequency ω. Fixed ratios (3.74) and (3.75) mean that k_y^s and k_y^p are proportional to k_x, i.e. also proportional to the frequency. But it means that characteristic wavelength is proportional to the inverse frequency.

The idea about the bottom boundary (implemented in SASSI) is that if we put the fixed boundary (i.e. "rock-like") at the depth where displacements in the Rayleigh wave are almost zero, the effect of such substitution of the flexible half-space by rigid half-space will be not disastrous. In this case, we may use only lateral transmitting boundaries for layered package underlain by rigid underlying half-space described above. Thus we add one more layer (in practice it is divided into several sub-layers) at the bottom of the physical layered package in order to model half-space. The problem, however, is that this depth (i.e. the thickness of this additional layer) physically depends on the frequency ω as mentioned in the previous paragraph. Mathematically, if we are solving SSI problem frequency by frequency, it makes no problem: we just vary the thickness of the additional layer with frequency (when frequency increases, the thickness decreases). But physically it creates the situation when the geometry of the model changes with frequency. This is unacceptable for the time-domain analysis. Note also that this idea is used only for the development of the vertical transmitting boundaries; as to the bottom of the FEM model of the finite volume, conventional acoustic boundaries are used, because body waves there are more important than surface waves. The resulting scheme is shown in *Fig. 3.12*.

So, the general conclusions about transmitting boundaries in the frequency domain (both analytical and semi-analytical) are as follows.

1. Transmitting boundary matrices are complex and frequency-dependent. This fact enables treating wave damping phenomena for the layered soils, impossible for the acoustic boundaries. Thanks to that, these transmitting boundaries are so accurate that they can be placed in the vicinity of the structure. On the other hand, such frequency dependence creates problems in the representation of such boundaries in the time domain (e.g. if there is non-linearity somewhere in the internal part of the SSI model).

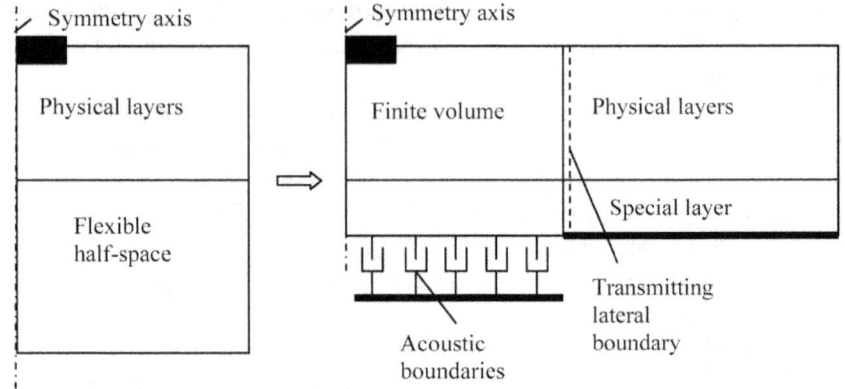

Figure 3.12. The SSI model for flexible underlying half-space

2. These boundaries are not local. This fact enables accounting for the "distribution ability" of the soil and additionally contributes to the accuracy of these boundaries.

3. If the underlying half-space is flexible, one can approximately substitute it with the additional layer, but then physically the depth of the model depends on frequency. This fact creates additional problems for the calculations in the time domain, though in the frequency domain no additional problems appear.

For several decades the limitations listed above were considered acceptable. First such transmitting boundaries were used in FLUSH and ALUSH. These codes implemented classical direct approach: finite volume in *Fig. 3.12* was an actual great volume around the structure. However, in 3D case, the geometry of structure usually is not axisymmetrical, so ALUSH cannot be used directly. Then SASSI appeared, where the axisymmetrical scheme of *Fig. 3.12* was used not for the physical soil volume around the structure, but in a certain auxiliary problem with a lumped point load at the symmetry vertical axis, as shown in *Fig. 3.13*.

In this auxiliary problem, finite volume was just a vertical cylinder with radius R modelled in each soil layer by a single cylindrical axisymmetrical element in the horizontal direction. In vertical direction, this finite volume was a column including both physical layers and special layer at the bottom. Unit loads for the given frequency were applied in turn node by the node at vertical axis in vertical and horizontal directions. The result of the solution of this auxiliary problem for each loaded node and for each of two load directions was: (i) transfer functions from the load to the displacements of all nodes at the vertical axis; (ii) transfer functions from the load to the displacements of all nodes at the vertical lateral boundary, leading to the participation factors of all generalized Rayleigh and Love waves in the infinite volume beyond this lateral boundary. These participation factors were used together with semi-analytical expressions for the displacements in the infinite module (like (3.40) and (3.55) but with Hankel's functions along radius instead of exponents for 3D case, as previously mentioned). As a result, they provided transfer function from the loads applied at the vertical axis in vertical and horizontal directions to the displacements of any point in the infinite volume. In fact, it is analogue of Green's function for any point of the infinite volume. So, for a set of nodes located either on the vertical axis or inside the infinite volume in *Fig. 3.13*, this auxiliary problem provides transfer functions from the load to the displacements. Furthermore, if all these nodes are located at the boundaries between horizontal layers or at the horizontal surface, one needs the solution just for one column applying loads at the surface and at the boundaries between layers (but only the boundaries carrying nodes). This procedure (in SASSI is performed separately in the POINT module) gives Green's functions for all the nodes of the system. Surely, radius R of the column should be less than the minimal horizontal distance between neighbouring nodes (if FEM mesh is regular, they recommend taking column radius R as 90% of the minimum horizontal distance).

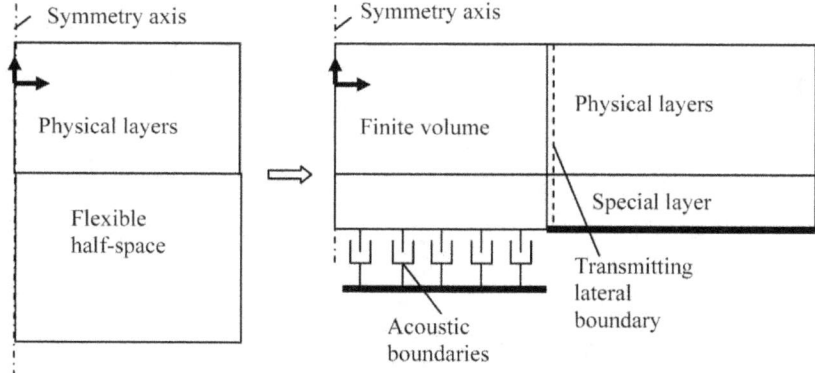

Figure 3.13. Auxiliary problem with nodal lumped load at the vertical axis of symmetry

But here one leaves a direct approach and comes to some different approach, which will be discussed in the next Chapters.

Thanks to these ideas (and using several great ideas more, see below) SASSI became the leading soft in SSI. This position was proved especially after the large-scale experiments and observations in Lotung, Taiwan, when SASSI was able to predict the observed results.

But in the last decade there grows an interest to the non-linear problems, so they have to return to the acoustic boundaries, as they work in the time domain.

The problem of "transmitting boundaries" remains one of the key problems for the direct approach. The attempts to create better non-reflecting boundaries in the time domain are in progress now.

Chapter 4. SUB-STRUCTURING APPROACH

4.1. Winkler models

Now we return back to Chapter 2 to take another way from that point.

The alternative approach (contrary to the direct approach described in Chapter 3) is to put surface Q in *Fig. 2.1* right on the soil-structure contact surface, avoiding the soil in the internal volume V_{int}. Surely the external part V_{ext} of the soil is still present in the model (again modelled not by solid elements – usually by some combination of soil springs and soil dashpots). As mentioned in Chapter 2, this external part should be linear in properties. The typical approach of this sort for a structure with flexible basement is a "quasi-Winkler" one: soil springs and viscous dashpots are somehow distributed (uniformly or not) over the bottom and embedded walls of the basement.

Two problems are important here. First, due to the soil inertia, the values of soil stiffness and viscosity are frequency-dependent. The degree of the volatility depends on soil profile: for layered profiles the volatility is greater than for almost homogeneous ones.

Second, the soil medium has a so-called "distributive capacity". It means that the response to the applied local force is not local in terms of displacements. Winkler's models are principally local (whatever shape is chosen for the distribution), so they cannot reproduce the interaction effect in full. One of the consequences is that any set of distributed vertical soil springs or dashpots cannot reproduce simultaneously integral vertical and rocking stiffness for the rigid stamp (known from contact problems) even in static case.

Let us discuss the simplest versions of Winkler's models for the surface basements. According to the central picture in *Fig. 2.3*, for the surface base mat we have $F_{int} = 0$, so they put free-field motion U_0 of the soil surface as a kinematical excitation to the rigid half-space under the base, and then try to model the soil by springs and dashpots as shown in *Fig. 4.1*.

Usually, they start from integral stiffness and damping for rigid stamp resting on the surface of homogeneous half-space. There exist approximate formulae for simple (circular and rectangular) base mats – e.g., in Standard ASCE4-98. For circular base mats they are given below in *Table 4.1*. One more table of the same sort in the same standard is given for rectangular base mats.

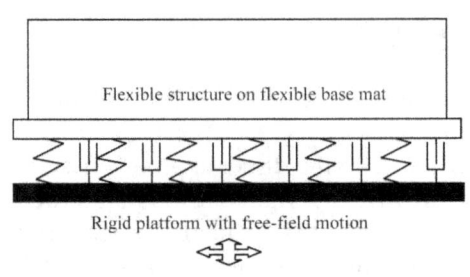

Figure 4.1. Schematic view of the simplest Winkler model for the surface base mat

Then they distribute vertical translational springs and dashpots over the bottom. Usually, the distribution shape is uniform, but sometimes they use more sophisticated shapes (e.g., static shape for springs). After that, they calculate rocking integral stiffness and damping arising from the distributed vertical springs and compare them to the values from Standards. It turns out that rocking stiffness from Standard is underestimated by Winkler's model, and rocking damping is overestimated.

Table 4.1

Extract from ASCE4-98

Table 3.3-1
Lumped Representation of Structure-Foundation Interaction at Surface for Circular Base

Motion	Equivalent Spring Constant	Equivalent Damping Coefficient
Horizontal	$k_x = \dfrac{32(1-\nu)GR}{7-8\nu}$	$c_x = 0.576 k_x R\sqrt{\rho/G}$
Rocking	$k_\psi = \dfrac{8GR^3}{3(1-\nu)}$	$c_\psi = \dfrac{0.30}{1+B_\psi} k_\psi R\sqrt{\rho/G}$
Vertical	$k_z = \dfrac{4GR}{(1-\nu)}$	$c_z = 0.85 k_z R\sqrt{\rho/G}$
Torsion	$k_t = 16GR^3/3$	$c_t = \dfrac{\sqrt{k_t I_t}}{1+2I_t/\rho R^3}$

Notes: ν = Poisson's ratio of foundation medium; G = shear modulus of foundation medium; R = radius of circular base mat; ρ = mass density of foundation medium; $B_\psi = 3(1-\nu)I_0/(8\rho R^5)$; I_0 = total mass moment of inertia of structure and base mat about the rocking axis at the base; I_t = polar mass moment of inertia of structure and base mat.

Two alternative ways are usually used to overcome this difficulty. The first way (in Russia it was proposed by A. Roleder and described in Birbraer (1998)) is to add rotational springs (distributed over the bottom) with integral stiffness compensating the gap. But in this case, they will get distributed soil-structure interaction moments at the bottom, which is not physically the case. As the initial goal of leaving flexible (and not rigid) base mat in the model was to obtain internal forces in the base mat, the spoiled interaction forces will surely spoil the internal forces. Besides, for damping, they will have to use negative viscosity.

The alternative way is to use two sets of vertical springs and dashpots instead of one set in order to separate vertical response and rocking response of the soil supports. Two pairs of vertical springs and dashpots linked to two rigid weightless plates: one with only rocking motion allowed; another one with only vertical motion allowed, as shown in *Fig. 4.2*. The first set of vertical springs and dashpots (denoted as K_1 and C_1) is responsible for rocking response. If the base mat is moving vertically, the corresponding rigid plate just moves similarly, and these springs and dashpots do not provide any forces. The second set of vertical springs and dashpots (denoted as K_2 and C_2) is responsible for the vertical translational response. If the base mat is rocking without vertical translation, the corresponding rigid plate is just rocking similarly, and these springs and dashpots do not provide any forces.

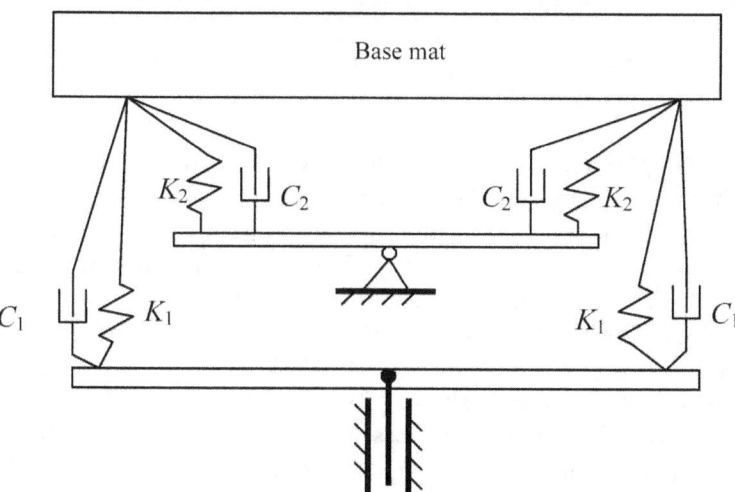

Figure 4.2. Scheme of the two pairs of vertical springs and dashpots providing the separate response to vertical translational and to rocking displacements of rigid base

One should note, however, that all these ways are approximate, as they do not account for two effects (frequency dependence and distribution capacity) mentioned above.

Some time ago the author studied the accuracy limits of the Winkler type models. Having accurate solution from SASSI, he obtained the best fit shapes of distribution of springs and dashpots in Winkler models and compared the results in the format of interaction forces and internal forces in the base mat with the exact ones (see Tyapin (2011)).

All that referred to the surface base mats. Sometimes Winkler models are used for the embedded basements also – in this case springs and dashpots should be distributed not only over the bottom but over the embedded lateral walls as well.

A typical mistake in the SSI analysis for embedded structures is that they use the model shown in the middle of *Fig. 2.3* with excitation U_0 only, i.e. forgetting about the load F_{int}. This load F_{int} is zero only for surface basements, but for the embedded basement it is more or less proportional to the mass of the outcropped soil. Another mistake is to take kinematical excitation U_0 constant over the lateral boundaries for the embedded basement. Even if they take it from the surface and not from the depth, the conservatism of such an approach is very doubtful.

4.2. Impedance approach as a particular case of simplified approach

*4.2.1. The simplest case: surface basement,
horizontally-layered soil, vertical seismic wave*

The approach described in the previous section may be called the simplified approach, but there exists further simplification. Often they additionally assume the rigidity of the soil-structure contact surface. Physical justification is that very often a base mat is reinforced from above by shear walls making a box-like stiff substructure.

Rigid Base Assumption (RBA), if justified, helps a lot in SSI analysis. Distributed soil springs and dashpots can be substituted by lumped soil springs and dashpots. As rigid base has only six degrees of freedom (DOFs), dynamic stiffness of the linear soil is described in full by 6×6 matrix. This is an operator matrix in the time domain, but in the frequency domain it turns into a symmetrical complex frequency-dependent matrix called "impedance matrix". The whole approach is often called "impedance approach". The problem with the distribution of springs and dashpots under the bottom, discussed in the previous section, now goes: rocking impedances and translational impedances are set independently.

Several comments should be made here about the further simplifications often used in practice. First, they often neglect the off-diagonal terms of the impedance 6 × 6 matrix, leaving just six diagonal terms. Is it accurate enough? For symmetrical basements, the part of the off-diagonal terms is zero indeed. But there always exists a link between horizontal translation and rocking in the same vertical plane (i.e. at least two off-diagonal terms are non-zero – one for each of two vertical planes). The error caused by neglecting of these links depends on the embedment depth and on frequency. In static (i.e. for low frequency) for surface basements the error is small indeed, but for embedded basements and for some frequencies in layered soil profiles it can become significant.

Second, after leaving six complex diagonal impedances they often simplify the frequency dependence of these impedances: they assume real parts constant over the frequency and imaginary parts proportional to the frequency. If so, impedances can be represented in the model by conventional springs and conventional linear viscous dashpots. Values of stiffness and viscosity for homogeneous soil profile, surface foundations and simple base shape (circle or rectangular) are given in the tables, e.g., in ASCE4-98 or ASCE4-16. There are some other proposals for soil half-space with modules, linearly increasing with depth.

The error resulting from such a simplification is different in different directions even for homogeneous soil profile, surface foundations and simple base shape. Horizontal diagonal translational impedances for homogeneous half-space indeed follow the simplified rule. However, vertical translational stiffness is considerably frequency-dependent even for surface rigid basement resting on homogeneous half-space. The situation with rotational impedances is even worse (especially with rocking damping). It resulted in the recommendation to set rocking dashpot dependent on the upper structure, which is physically absurd but helps to reproduce frequency-dependent viscosity at least at one certain selected frequency. So, any proposed formulae for constant values are approximate.

Seismic load for the rigid basement (see the right-hand part of *Fig. 2.1*) can be also lumped to six components. Let us consider several particular cases.

For every surface basement, the load F_{int} introduced in section 2.2 is zero, as there is no solid soil part inside V_{int} in impedance approach, and there is no outcropped soil in case of the surface basement. If seismic wave (primary or secondary) is running vertically through the horizontally layered (or horizontally smooth) soil profile, each horizontal plane in the free field moves as a rigid surface. For a surface basement, it means that the spot under the base in the free field also moves rigidly (though it is not physically rigid), so this spot motion is fully described by the motion U_0 of any single point at the free surface. Thus, the middle model from *Fig. 2.1* is transformed to the model shown in *Fig. 4.3*.

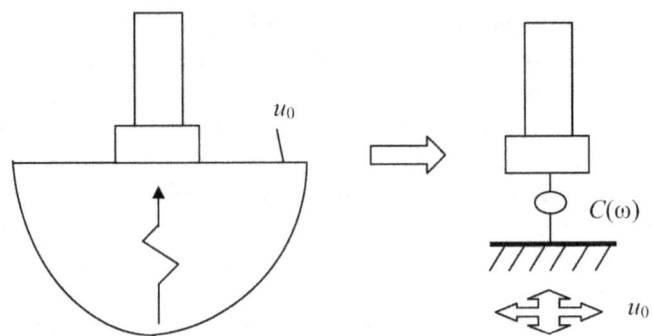

Figure 4.3. The typical representation of the problem A_2 for the simplest case in "impedance" approach

Impedances for layered half-space may be obtained by CLASSI or SASSI programmes. For homogeneous soil profile, one can further simplify the model substituting impedance matrix $C(\omega)$ by six pairs of springs and dashpots, as discussed before.

From *Fig. 4.3* there is one step to the conventional scheme for analysis without SSI: if impedances $C(\omega)$ become great, the motion of the base mat becomes similar to the motion of the platform. So, this conventional scheme is a limit case for SSI model from *Fig. 4.3*.

Often they prefer to change the coordinate system placing it at the moving platform in *Fig. 4.3*. Then the platform for the relative displacements is fixed, but there appear inertial loads in the structure.

4.2.2. Embedded rigid basement.
Vertical wave in horizontally-layered soil

If the rigid basement is embedded, several changes need to be introduced into the simple model discussed above. First, the load F_{int} (see

Fig. 2.2) is not zero any more. As a consequence, the right-hand model from *Fig. 4.3* should be changed for the model with fixed platform and excitation force instead of the excitation platform motion. Thus we return to the right-hand model from *Fig. 2.1*. This excitation force F is composed of two parts: F_{int} and F_{ext} (see *Fig. 2.2*). The second part F_{ext} refers to the reflected wave; it is linked to the surface free-field motion U_0 by special transfer function (and not by impedance $C(\omega)$ as in *Fig. 4.3*), but the first part F_{int} is linked to U_0 in a different way, so the total excitation force F should be calculated accurately and separately from impedances.

Second, the impedance matrix must be taken non-diagonal. Moreover, there is a physical separation of the upper parts of the embedded lateral walls from the soil. ASCE4-98 Standard (1999) allows modelling it as a full loose of contact over the upper half, but not more than upper 6 m in depth. This effect must be accounted for during the calculation of impedances. Impedances for embedded basement can be obtained by SASSI code.

If the seismic wave is not vertical, the model with excitation forces will not change in format. Moreover, the impedances will be the same as for vertical wave, but excitation force (six component one) will change accounting for actual wave type.

If one wants to keep kinematical excitation at the platform for the embedded case, then this excitation is different from the free-field motion. It can be calculated as a result of "kinematical SSI" – i.e., as a motion of the weightless embedded rigid basement, as shown in *Fig. 4.4*.

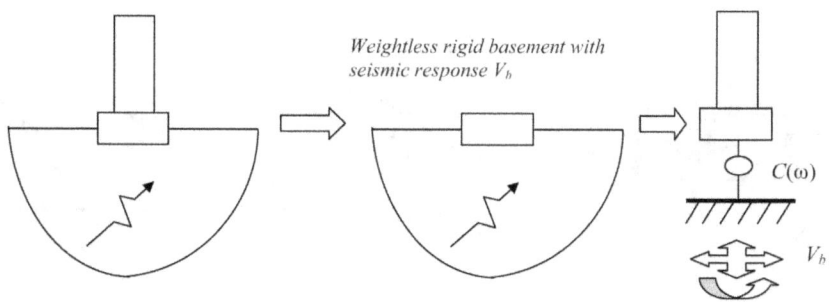

Figure 4.4. Impedance model with kinematical excitation for the embedded basement

Some additional comments about impedances are given in the next Chapter.

4.2.3. Complicated soil environment for rigid base

"Complicated soil environment" means that near rigid base there is a certain finite volume of the soil with modified properties breaking the horizontal soil layering of the initial profile assumed previously. It may be an improved soil, or soil with piles, etc. It looks somehow like the previous case with embedded rigid basement, but now the embedded "basement" is partly flexible.

The final impedance platform model is similar to the previous one (with excitation forces), but both impedances and excitation forces should be calculated differently. The author proposed a SASSI-based approach for this purpose in Tyapin (2015).

It turns out that soil improvement can significantly impact the results of the kinematical SSI, reducing the effective seismic load on the upper structure. The effect is governed by the thickness of the improved volume and by the ratio of seismic stiffness of initial and improved soils, as shown in Tyapin (2017). The details of this case are discussed in this book in Chapter 7.

4.2.4. Multiple rigid basements

Impedance approach is easily extended for the case of structure-soil-structure interaction (SSSI). The model is shown in *Fig. 4.5* for the complicated soil environment.

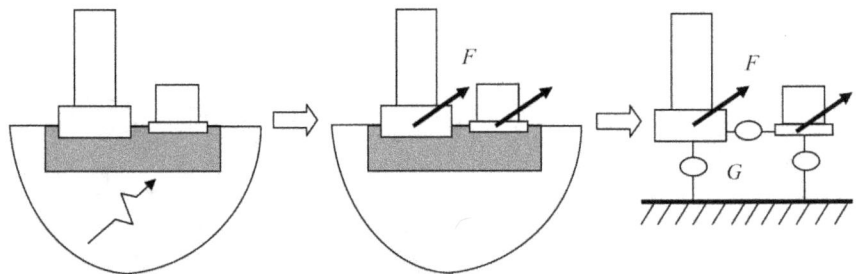

Figure 4.5. Impedance model with kinematical excitation for multiple embedded basements in the complicated soil environment

If N structures having rigid bases are considered, the impedance matrix will be $6N \times 6N$, and loading forces will have $6N$ components (6 for each of N basements).

4.3. Problems with damping in modal and linear-spectral approach to SSI analysis

4.3.1. Conventional modal and spectral analysis

There is one more issue in SSI analysis deserving special discussion. In fact, it refers both to direct and to impedance approaches, but it is manifested more for the impedance approach, as the soil is considered fully linear here.

One of the popular approaches to the linear analysis is the modal approach. It is a base for conventional linear-spectral approach common for the civil codes. Let us remember basic relations. The equation of motion describing the system from *Fig. 4.1*, is as follows (see ASCE4-98):

$$[M]\{\ddot{X}\}+[C]\{\dot{X}\}+[K]\{X\} = -[M][U]\{A^0\}. \qquad (4.1)$$

Here $[M]$, $[C]$, $[K]$ are matrices of inertia, damping and stiffness of size $n \times n$ (n – number of DOFs in the system); $[U]$ is a matrix of size $n \times 3$, describing nodal displacements caused by unit static displacements of the platform along three coordinate axes; $\{X\}$ is a column of size $n \times 1$ describing relative nodal displacements; $\{A_0\}$ is a column of size 3×1 describing platform accelerations along three coordinate axes.

Then they apply modal decomposition of the relative motion conventionally using natural modes of the fixed-base system without damping:

$$\{X\} = [\Phi]\{Y\}. \qquad (4.2)$$

Here $[\Phi]$ is a full matrix of natural modes of size $n \times n$; $\{Y\}$ is a column of modal displacements of size $n \times 1$.

Substituting (4.2) into (4.1) and multiplying (4.1) by $[\Phi]^T$ from the left one comes to the equation of motion in the so-called "main coordinates of the system without damping":

$$([\Phi]^T[M][\Phi])\{\ddot{Y}\}+([\Phi]^T[C][\Phi])\{\dot{Y}\}+([\Phi]^T[K][\Phi])\{Y\} = \\ = -([\Phi]^T[M][U])\{A^0\}. \qquad (4.3)$$

When natural modes are normalized by mass, three matrices in the left-hand part of (4.3) are as follows:

$$[\Phi]^T[M][\Phi] = [E]; \qquad (4.4)$$

$$[\Phi]^T[K][\Phi] = diag[\Omega_j^2]; \qquad (4.5)$$

$$[\Phi]^T[C][\Phi] \approx diag[2\lambda_j \Omega_j]. \qquad (4.6)$$

Here E is a unit matrix; Ω_j is natural frequency of mode number j calculated for the system without damping; λ_j is modal damping coefficient of mode number j.

In the right-hand part of (4.3) one can see the "participation coefficients" matrix

$$[Q] = [\Phi]^T[M][U]. \qquad (4.7)$$

As matrices in the left-hand part of (4.3) are all diagonal (see 4.4—4.6), the whole matrix equation (4.3) may be decomposed into n modal equations for SDOF (single degree of freedom) oscillators:

$$\ddot{y}_j + 2\lambda_j \Omega_j \dot{y}_j + \Omega_j^2 y_j = -\{q_j\}\{A^0\}. \qquad (4.8)$$

Here $\{q_j\}$ is a line number j of the matrix $[Q]$, consisting of three participation coefficients for mode number j along three coordinate axes.

Let us introduce "elementary" SDOF responses $z_{jk}(t)$:

$$\ddot{z}_{jk} + 2\lambda_j \Omega_j \dot{z}_{jk} + \Omega_j^2 z_{jk} = -a_k. \qquad (4.9)$$

Then from the linearity of (4.8)

$$y_j = \{q_j\}\{Z_j\}. \qquad (4.10)$$

Here $\{Z_j\}$ is a column 3×1 composed of three z_{jk} ($k = 1, 2, 3$).

Equation (4.10) describes modal components of relative displacements. Absolute displacements can be also decomposed in modal components if we remember the "participation" of modes in "rigid" displacements:

$$[U] = [\Phi][Q]. \qquad (4.11)$$

Then absolute nodal accelerations are

$$\{\ddot{W}\} = [U]\{A^0\} + [\Phi]\{\ddot{Y}\} = [\Phi]([Q]\{A^0\} + \{\ddot{Y}\}). \qquad (4.12)$$

The modal coefficient for the mode number j stands in the right-hand part of (4.12) in the line j of the column in the round brackets:

$$w_j = \{q_j\}(\{A^0\} + \{\ddot{Z}_j\}). \qquad (4.13)$$

This equation describes absolute modal acceleration in the time domain. As $[Q]$ is constant over time, maximal absolute modal acceleration for excitation along axis k is given by

$$\max_t |w_{jk}| = |q_{jk}| \max_t |a_k(t) + \ddot{z}_{jk}(t)|. \qquad (4.14)$$

Maximum in the right-hand part of (4.14) is called "response spectral accelerations":

$$S_A^k(\Omega_j, \lambda_j) = \max_t |a_k(t) + \ddot{z}_{jk}(t)|. \qquad (4.15)$$

These accelerations are the absolute accelerations of SDOF oscillator with parameters Ω_j and λ_j on the platform with excitation $a_k(t)$.

Static inertial nodal load is obtained by moving the first term from the left-hand part of (4.1) to the right-hand part. Maximal value of the relative displacement corresponds to the zero relative velocity. So, in the left-hand part of (4.1) only the third term remains non-zero. In the right-hand part of (4.1) we use (4.2) together with (4.11) and obtain the modal composition for static inertial loads. A single term of this modal composition with maximal value

$$\{\varphi_j\} \max_t |w_{jk}| = \{\varphi_j\} |q_{jk}| S_A^k(\Omega_j, \lambda_j) \qquad (4.16)$$

corresponds to the mode number j and excitation along axis k. It leads to the static internal forces corresponding to this mode and excitation component (both loads and response forces are maximal in time). Here $\{\varphi_j\}$ describes nodal displacements in mode number j.

Then a certain double combination of these maximal modal internal forces (accounting for their different times of occurrence) would provide the resulting estimates of the maximal internal forces.

The combination is double because one must first combine different modal responses for each single excitation component and after that combine responses to different excitation components.

This approach is called "linear spectral method". It was developed in the middle of the twentieth century. The main advantage was that structural engineers were not to solve the equations of motion: they got spectral accelerations S_A^k as ready curves from the seismologists or from the codes and then performed static calculations using seismic loads (4.16) as one more type of conventional static loads (together with dead weight, snow, etc.).

This approach is plain enough but it is rigorous only for SDOF systems; for the real-life multi-degrees-of-freedom systems it is approximate. The main uncertainty is about the rules for the combination of different maximal modal responses. This issue in detail is described in ASCE4-98.

4.3.2. Inhomogeneous damping

Both modal approach and spectral approach in the conventional form described above are based on the assumption (4.6) which is not rigorous (unlike equations (4.4) and (4.5)). In fact, this assumption means the following. One can calculate damping matrix in the main coordinates of the system (i.e. main coordinates calculated for the system without damping):

$$[D] = [\Phi]^T [C][\Phi]. \quad (4.17)$$

Equation (4.6) means that the off-diagonal diagonal terms of this matrix, which are neglected in (4.6), must be small in order not to spoil the solution. The criterion for this is as follows:

$$d_{ij}^2 << |d_{ii}\, d_{jj}|, \quad i \neq j. \quad (4.18)$$

Let us discuss when this criterion is met.

First, there exist systems with homogeneous damping (e.g., linear systems made of one and the same material). Damping in the construction materials is in reality not viscous, but hysteretic (i.e. controlled by strains and not by strain velocities). So, the best model to describe it is frequency-independent material damping. In the frequency domain calculations real elasticity modules are just changed for the complex modules:

$$E = E^0 [(1 - 2\gamma^2) + 2i\gamma\sqrt{1-\gamma^2}]. \qquad (4.19)$$

Here γ is a material damping coefficient set up for certain material and for a certain general stress level in this material.

It means that the equation of motion (4.1) in the frequency domain in the left-hand part instead of viscosity matrix $[C]$ multiplied by velocity column $-i\omega\{X\}$ and stiffness matrix $[K]$ multiplied by displacement column $\{X\}$ will have the same stiffness matrix $[K]$ multiplied by displacement column $\{X\}$ and additionally by complex value from the right-hand part of (4.19). As this complex value is common for the whole system, in the main coordinates the analogue of (4.6) will be just proportional to (4.5) – i.e. fully diagonal.

The shortcoming of this approach with "material" damping is that it is not converted to the time domain. Usually, they try to replace material damping by viscous damping, convenient for the time-domain calculations. To keep modal equations of motion one has the following options.

1. If the system is homogeneous and made of construction material (e.g., steel or concrete), modal damping values can be set directly equal to those prescribed for the given material – instead of starting from matrix $[C]$ and using (4.6) for this purpose.
2. If the system is inhomogeneous, but still made of several construction materials (e.g., steel and concrete), one can also put the modal damping coefficients directly, though they should be somehow averaged between different values prescribed for different materials. Weighted averaging of damping is made element by element with assembling of the whole system. Two options are commonly used for the averaging procedure – with different weights. The first one is called "stiffness-weighted"

damping. Damping coefficient λ_j for the mode $\{\varphi_j\}$ is obtained using the stiffness matrix $[K]$ as follows:

$$\lambda_j = \frac{\{\varphi_j\}^T (\sum_{i=1}^{N} \lambda_i [K_i]) \{\varphi_j\}}{\{\varphi_j\}^T (\sum_{i=1}^{N} [K_i]) \{\varphi_j\}} = \frac{\{\varphi_j\}^T (\sum_{i=1}^{N} \lambda_i [K_i]) \{\varphi_j\}}{\Omega_j^2}. \quad (4.20)$$

Here the summation in brackets is performed following FEM assembling rules; N is the number of finite elements (each of them is homogeneous in terms of material); $[K_i]$ is stiffness matrix for element number i; λ_i is damping value prescribed for element i.

The alternative is "mass-weighted damping" where instead of (4.20) they use

$$\lambda_j = \{\varphi_j\}^T (\sum_{i=1}^{N} \lambda_i [M_i]) \{\varphi_j\}. \quad (4.21)$$

Here $[M_i]$ is the mass matrix for element number i.
3. If one knows somehow the full damping matrix $[C]$, he may obtain the modal damping coefficient directly using (4.6) as

$$\lambda_j = \frac{\{\varphi_j\}^T [C] \{\varphi_j\}}{2\Omega_j}. \quad (4.22)$$

Note that for inhomogeneous system modal damping coefficients are different for different modes. Such damping is called "composite" modal damping.

It may seem that equations (4.20 – 4.22) solve all problems for the Winkler model of the soil-structure system shown in *Fig. 4-1*. Some specialists believe it is really the case. Their logic is as follows.

• Damping is additive, i.e. if damping matrix $[C]$ in (4.1) is a sum of matrices $[C_1]$ and $[C_2]$, then modal damping λ_j should be a sum of λ_{j1} and λ_{j2}.

• The soil-structure system consists of two parts: soil and structure. For the soil modelled by Winkler springs and dashpots, we know damping matrix $[C_{soil}]$ composed of viscosity coefficients. So, we can apply (4.22) and get the soil contribution to all modal damping coefficients. The structure is made of construction materials, so we use (4.20) or (4.21) to obtain the contribution of structural damping to the total modal damping. Then we just add "soil" modal damping to the "structural" modal damping for each mode and get the resulting modal damping to be used in the modal or spectral analysis.

What is the trouble with this logic? The problem arises in the equation (4.6). After the transfer of the linear equations of motion into the "main" coordinates, using natural modes of the system without damping, mass matrix (4.4) and stiffness matrix (4.5) become diagonal. This is accurate and precise. But this is not the case for the damping matrix (4.6). To keep uncoupling between different equations of motion they simply neglect the off-diagonal terms of the matrix (4.6). The question is whether the error arising from this operation is significant for the results. It turns out that sometimes the error can spoil the results. So, the problem is that the whole modal approach with modes and frequencies calculated without damping and with the further solution of the uncoupled equations is not always acceptable.

Let us investigate this problem, assuming structure to be homogeneous (i.e. non-homogeneity of damping in the system is only between soil and structure). To obtain non-diagonal terms of $[D]$ (4.17) needed to check criterion (4.18) one has to obtain full damping matrix $[C]$ for the Winkler model of the soil-structure system in the initial coordinates. In fact, they are to obtain a structural part of this matrix, as the soil part is obvious. The most popular way to do it is the so-called "Rayleigh damping model", sometimes called also "proportional damping". Viscosity matrix $[C]$ is set as a linear combination of the mass matrix $[M]$ and stiffness matrix $[K]$:

$$[C] = \alpha [M] + \beta [K]. \qquad (4.23)$$

According to (4.4) and (4.5), equation (4.6) after substitution of (4.23) will give fully diagonal matrix in the main coordinates. For diagonal terms one gets

$$[D] = \alpha [E] + \beta \, diag\left[\Omega_j^2\right]. \qquad (4.24)$$

According to (4.6) modal damping coefficients λ_j will be

$$\lambda_j = (\alpha / \Omega_j + \beta \Omega_j) / 2. \qquad (4.25)$$

This relation (4.25) is not frequency-independent, but two coefficients (α and β) enable to get target values of λ (known from the structural material input data) at two certain frequencies Ω chosen by the analyst. In the range between these two frequencies (they are called "Rayleigh frequencies") damping coefficient (4.25) will be less than a target one; out of the frequency interval between these frequencies, it will be greater than a target one. So, they believe that if all important frequencies will be inside the interval between two Rayleigh frequencies, then modal damping will be generally underestimated, and that will lead to conservative results. Is it really so?

Let us use for the illustrative purposes a very simple sample 1D model with 3 DOFs shown (without damping) in *Fig. 4.6*. Parameters of the model are given in *Table 4.2* together with natural frequencies and natural modes of the fixed-base system without damping.

Natural frequencies in *Table 4.2* are typical for SSI models of the NPP reactor buildings in the vertical direction. Let the lower spring in *Fig. 4.6* represent "soil stiffness" and let other two springs together with three masses represent structure. Then we can use formulae from ASCE4-98 (see *Table 4.1* above) linking coefficient of viscosity c_{soil} for soil dashpot to the stiffness coefficient k_{soil} of the soil spring

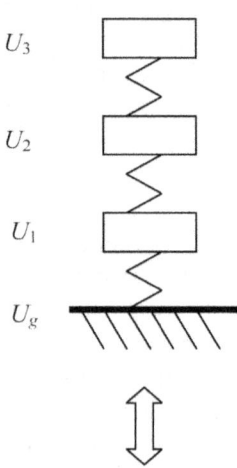

Figure 4.6. Sample 1D model has shown without damping

$$c_{soil} / k_{soil} = 0{,}85r / V_s. \qquad (4.26)$$

Table 4.2
Parameters of the sample model and natural frequencies/modes of the fixed-base SSI system

Number from below	Mass, tones	Stiffness of springs, kN/m	Natural frequencies, Hz	Modal displacement of the lower mass, $t^{-1/2}$	Modal displacement of the middle mass, $t^{-1/2}$	Modal displacement of the upper mass, $t^{-1/2}$
1	1	1.3E3	3.0025	0.4703	0.6069	0.6407
2	1	3.25E3	11.297	0.8535	-0.1281	-0.5051
3	1	6.75E3	20.073	-0.2245	0.7844	-0.5782

Here r is the equivalent radius of the base mat, V_s is shear wave velocity in the soil. For further calculations $r = 40$ m, $V_s = 400$ m/s; so soil viscosity coefficient in $kN/(m/s)$ is

$$c_{soil} = k_{soil} \times (0.85r / V_s) = 1.3 \times 10^3 \times 0.85 \times 40 / 400 = 110.5. \quad (4.27)$$

Viscosity coefficient c_z should be directly added to the term (1,1) of the damping matrix $[C]$ in the initial coordinates.

Let us consider the equation of motion in the frequency domain. It is written in the absolute displacements U:

$$-\omega^2 [M]\{U\} + \{[K_{str}] + [K_{soil}]\}\{U\} = [K_{soil}]\{U_g\}. \quad (4.28)$$

Here ω is a circular frequency; $[M]$ is a mass matrix (real matrix $n \times n$; in our sample case $n = 3$); $[K_{str}]$ is a stiffness matrix for structure (complex matrix $n \times n$); $[K_{soil}]$ is a stiffness matrix for soil spring and dashpot (complex matrix $n \times n$ with a single non-zero element (1,1) in our sample case); $\{U_g\}$ is a platform displacement in the frequency domain (complex column matrix $n \times 1$ with a single non-zero element (1,1) in our sample case); $\{U\}$ is a structural response displacement (complex column matrix $n \times 1$). Imaginary part of the only non-zero element of complex matrix $[K_{soil}]$ is "viscous", i.e. proportional to ω with coefficient c_{soil}.

The frequency domain is convenient for research, as both viscous and material models of damping are easily implemented (unlike calculations in the time domain).

As previously mentioned, the best damping model for structure (though not appropriate in the time domain) is material damping. Let us consider it in the form

$$[\operatorname{Im} K_{str}] = 2\lambda [\operatorname{Re} K_{str}]. \quad (4.29)$$

It is slightly different from (4.19), but the approximation is good for small λ. Let us use $\lambda = 0.05$ in our sample case. Equation (4.28) leads to

$$\{U\} = [TF]\{U_g\}; \quad [TF] = \{-\omega^2[M] + [K_{str}] + [K_{soil}]\}^{-1}[K_{soil}]. \quad (4.30)$$

Now we have all the information necessary to obtain [*TF*] – the transfer functions from platform to all three masses (from displacements to displacements; the same from accelerations to accelerations). The results will be shown below. This is the end of the "accurate" solution, which will be later used for the comparison. We will call it "material structure with viscous soil" (referring to the damping models).

Now let us apply to the structural part the Rayleigh damping model (4.23) which we rewrite as

$$[C_{str}] = \alpha [M] + \beta [K_{str}]. \qquad (4.31)$$

Let us set up two boundary frequencies (i.e. Rayleigh frequencies) for our sample structure $f_b = 3$ Hz and $f_e = 20$ Hz. Let us take the "target" value of damping $\lambda = 0.05$ mentioned above. Then the Rayleigh coefficients α and β are calculated as

$$\alpha = 4\pi \lambda \frac{f_b f_e}{f_b + f_e} = 1{,}639\ s^{-1},\ \beta = \lambda \frac{1}{\pi(f_b + f_e)} = 6{,}91978 \times 10^{-4}\ s. \qquad (4.32)$$

Structural part [C_{str}] of damping matrix [*C*] in $t\ s^{-1}$ ($kN/(m/s)$) is given by Equation (4.31):

$$[C_{str}] = 1.639 \times \begin{bmatrix} 1 & 0 & 0 \\ 0 & 1 & 0 \\ 0 & 0 & 1 \end{bmatrix} + 6.91978 \times 10^{-4} \times \begin{bmatrix} 3.25 \times 10^3 & -3.25 \times 10^3 & 0 \\ -3.25 \times 10^3 & 10.0 \times 10^3 & -6.75 \times 10^3 \\ 0 & -6.75 \times 10^3 & 6.75 \times 10^3 \end{bmatrix} =$$

$$= \begin{bmatrix} 3.8879 & -2.2489 & 0 \\ -2.2489 & 8.5588 & -4.6709 \\ 0 & -4.6709 & 6.3099 \end{bmatrix}. \qquad (4.33)$$

After the addition of the soil dashpot viscosity coefficient c_{soil} given by Equation (4.27) we get full damping matrix

$$[C] = \begin{bmatrix} 114.3879 & -2.2489 & 0 \\ -2.2489 & 8.5588 & -4.6709 \\ 0 & -4.6709 & 6.3099 \end{bmatrix}. \qquad (4.34)$$

Let us transfer our sample damping matrix given by Equation (4.34) to the generalized coordinates using the matrix of modes taken from *Table 4.2*:

$$[\Phi] = \begin{bmatrix} 0.4703 & 0.8535 & -0.2245 \\ 0.6069 & -0.1281 & 0.7844 \\ 0.6407 & -0.5051 & -0.5782 \end{bmatrix}. \quad (4.35)$$

In generalized coordinates we get

$$[D] = [\Phi]^T [C][\Phi] = \begin{bmatrix} 26.127 & 43.994 & -11.572 \\ 43.994 & 84.965 & -21.001 \\ -11.572 & -21.001 & 18.170 \end{bmatrix}. \quad (4.36)$$

This is the end of the second variant for the further comparison – we will call it "Rayleigh structure with viscous soil". Transfer functions will be obtained from the equation (4.3) transferred to the frequency domain.

Now let us come to the modal approach. The conventional modal approach requires neglecting the off-diagonal terms of this damping matrix (4.36).

Using conventional "modal full" damping one comes to the following formulae for the transfer functions from platform to masses:

$$\{TF\} = [1 \ 1 \ 1]^T + [\Phi]\{Y\}, \quad Y_j = \Gamma_j \omega^2 [-\omega^2 + i\omega c_j + \Omega_j^2]^{-1}. \quad (4.37)$$

Here modal damping parameters c_j for our sample system are taken from the diagonal of the matrix given by (4.36). They correspond to the following dimensionless parameters $\lambda_j = c_j/(2\Omega_j)$: $\lambda_1 = 0.6925$; $\lambda_2 = 0.5985$; $\lambda_3 = 0.0720$. We see that the first two coefficients are far greater than conventional "material" values of λ, usually making 4...7%. This is typical for soil-structure interaction, where "wave" damping dominates over "material" one. We will call this variant of the transfer functions (4.37) "full modal damping".

One more option is called "cut-down modal damping". It is similar to the previous option, but in (4.37) two first values of c_j ($j = 1, 2$) are artificially cut down to $0.4\Omega_j$ (corresponding to $\lambda_1 = \lambda_2 = 0.2$); c_3 and λ_3 stay the same as before, as $\lambda_3 < 0.2$. Some specialists still believe that such cutting down of λ below 0.2 can provide necessary conservatism. Threshold value 0.2 for λ is written in ASCE4-98. We will comment on it later.

Now let us look at the results in terms of absolute values of the transfer functions from platform to structural masses. "Material structure plus viscous soil" results are compared to "Rayleigh structure plus viscous soil" results, to the "full modal damping" results and to the "cut-down modal damping" results. The results for the lower mass are shown in *Fig. 4.7*, the results for the middle mass – in *Fig. 4.8*, the results for the upper mass – in *Fig. 4.9*.

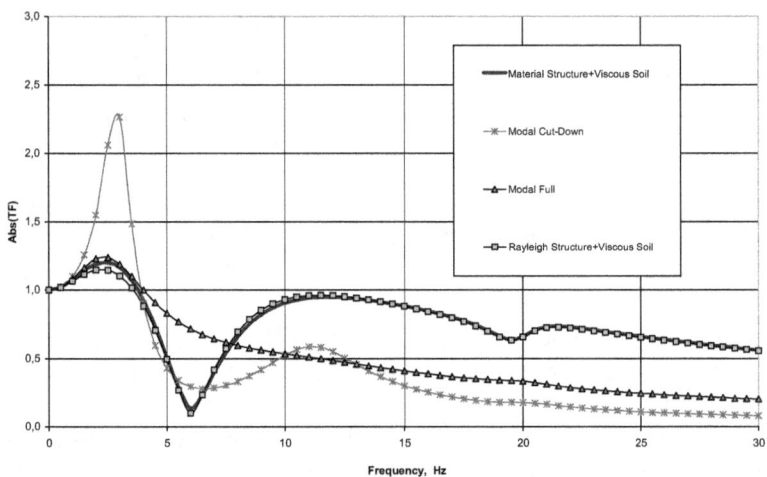

Figure 4.7. Absolute values of the transfer functions from the platform to the lower mass

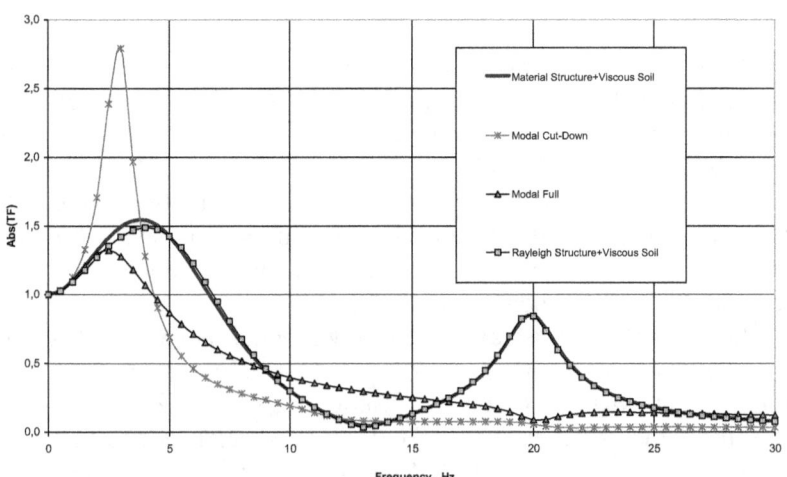

Figure 4.8. Absolute values of the transfer functions from the platform to the middle mass

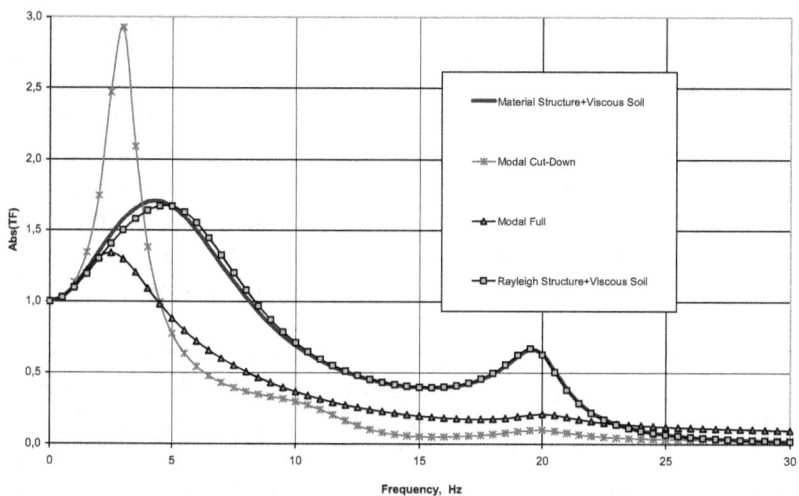

Figure 4.9. Absolute values of the transfer functions from the platform to the upper mass

The "Rayleigh structure" results are close to the "material structure" ones. Some difference can be seen, but it is small. The reason is that soil damping is represented in full in all variants ("material" and "Rayleigh" ones), and it is more important in our case than structural damping.

The "full modal damping" results are satisfactory only for very low frequencies. For upper frequencies, they are considerably non-conservative. It means that the attempt to use conventional modal approach (simply neglecting the off-diagonal terms in (4.36)) failed. If we look at (4.36) we see that the off-diagonal matrix term (1,2) breaks the criterion (4.18). One should not neglect it. There exist various technologies to overcome this difficulty. One can account for damping in the modal analysis, getting complex modes and complex frequencies. Alternatively, one can leave conventional real modes and frequencies, but then solve the system of modal equations coupled through the damping matrix. Finally, one can do without modal superposition at all, performing direct integration of equation (4.1) in the time domain.

Let us return to our sample case results. The "cut-down modal damping" option is often understood as a tool to save conventional modal approach after it meets the above-mentioned problem. We see in *Fig. 4.7—4.9* that the results are excessively conservative around the first peak, but non-conservative for the upper frequencies. Note that the "modal cut-down" results in the higher frequency range are less than the "full modal" results. The conclusion is that this attempt also failed. If the off-diagonal terms are great, they should be properly accounted for, and not neglected "at a price of" decreasing the remaining diagonal terms of the damping matrix $[D]$.

In our sample problem, we had an opportunity to estimate the off-diagonal terms directly. But what if one uses equations (4.20—4.22) to get modal damping values and does not see the off-diagonal terms? How can he or she discover the presence of the excessive terms off the diagonal?

The answer is, in fact, empirical and physical. Either soil works in the soil-structure system, or it does not work (because the soil is too stiff). If it does not work, the effective damping is not far from the fixed-base structural damping. Calculated modal damping values are close to the material values (about 4…7%). But if soil really works, great wave damping in soil dashpots impacts not only the off-diagonal terms but also the diagonal ones. One will see modal damping values after (4.20—4.22) far above the material ones, as we saw them in our example. Therefore, high modal damping values got from (4.20 –4.22) are the alert signal about the significant role of the soil damping in the inhomogeneous soil-structure system – the empirical threshold, as mentioned above, is 0.2. The attempt to artificially cut the calculated modal damping values down to 0.2 looks like turning off the alert signal instead of the proper response to the problem – it is unreasonable and dangerous.

Chapter 5. COMBINED ASYMPTOTIC METHOD (CAM)

5.1. General remarks

Combined Asymptotic Method (CAM) is a special computational technology (in fact, just a variant of the sub-structuring method) adjusted for the soil-structure interaction (SSI) problems. As for every sub-structuring method, the goal is to substitute a single direct analysis of the large-size system by a series of analyses of partial subsystems composing the initial system. Of course, these partial analyses will be of smaller size, thus enabling either more refined models or savings in computational resources.

If everything is done accurately, the results of the sub-structuring method are similar to those of direct method performed for the same models of all subsystems composing the initial system and assembled together (if such direct analysis is possible). So, sub-structuring is not about physical assumptions – it is about mathematics and computational efficiency. As a consequence, sub-structuring standing alone needs only verification (mathematical check), but not validation (physical check). Validation of the physical assumptions is an important, but different issue – it refers not only to sub-structuring, but to the direct analysis as well.

In our particular case the initial soil-structure system is clearly split into two subsystems: structure and soil, divided by a certain boundary, called "contact surface". If the response motion of this surface during a seismic event is somehow obtained, then the subsequent analyses can be performed for structure and for soil separately – using the obtained contact surface motion as a boundary condition for each subsystem standing alone.

Traditionally everybody is interested mostly in the subsequent analysis of structure. Thus, sub-structuring method CAM consists of two stages: (i) obtaining the contact surface response motion, (ii) analysis of structure without soil with prescribed contact surface motion. In the seismic analysis (ii) this motion is an effective seismic excitation for the structure. Step (ii) of seismic analysis is conventional – it is performed using general software (like ABAQUS for spectra or SCAD for internal forces – both used in the author's practice). The only difference with the conventional fixed-base analysis is that the kinematical excitation of the base is six-component and not three-component (it includes three rotational components in addition to three translational ones). These general computer codes have verification reports and special certificates. So, the real need for verification is only in step (i) – the obtaining of the contact surface motion.

5.2. The basic scheme of the first step of CAM

CAM is based on two physical assumptions clearly stated in the Standards (e.g., ASCE4-16): (i) soil and structure are linear with full contact between them – so, the whole soil-structure system is linear; (ii) contact surface moves as a rigid body. Both assumptions are simplifications of the real world, and they have certain limits in the application. But this is the issue of the basic assumptions' validation – not about the verification of CAM standing alone. Until 2010 both simplifications were used without alternatives; nowadays there are some alternative approaches.

The linearity of the system enables the separation of seismic analysis from all other analyses (deadweight, etc.). Besides, linearity has the following important consequences.

• The forces acting from the soil to the contact surface during the seismic event may be calculated as a sum of (i) loads acting from the soil to the fixed contact surface – they will appear due to the seismic wave in the soil reflected from the fixed contact surface; (ii) forces acting from the soil to the moving contact surface without seismic wave. Moreover, the forces (ii) are linearly dependent on the contact surface motion (general format is Green's functions in the frequency domain). This was discussed in Chapter 2.

• The forces acting from the structure to the same contact surface are originated only by the contact surface motion, so they are somewhat like forces (ii) mentioned above. Let us call them the forces (iii). Like forces (ii), the forces (iii) are also linearly dependent on the contact surface motion (once again general format is Green's functions in the frequency domain – of course, different from the Green's functions for forces (ii)).

Forces (i), (ii) and (iii) are balanced at the contact surface – we can write the equilibrium equation for every point of the contact surface in terms of the distributed forces (i), (ii) and (iii).

Now let us consider the second basic assumption (i.e. about the rigidity of the contact surface) – the so-called Rigid Base Assumption

(RBA). It means, that one can imagine contact surface as a very thin weightless rigid shell between soil and structure. The contact surface motion is fully described by the six-component displacement vector $U_b(t)$ consisting of three translational and three rotational displacements. Instead of writing equilibrium equations for each point of the contact surface one can write equilibrium equations just for three integral (resultant) forces and three integral moments. Forces (ii) and (iii) caused by the contact surface motion are now integral ones having six components each. The linear links of these forces to the contact surface displacements may be fully described by 6 × 6 dynamic stiffness matrices in the frequency domain (instead of Green's functions). These are two complex symmetrical frequency-dependent matrices of this sort: one for the soil, another one for the structure.

The resulting scheme for the first step of CAM looks as shown in Fig. 5.1.

Here rigid contact surface is in the centre of the picture. $F(\omega)$ represents seismic loads (i) condensed to the contact surface (6 × 1 matrix); $G(\omega)$ represents the link to forces (ii) acting to the contact surface from the soil when the contact surface moves (this is 6 × 6 matrix called "soil impedance matrix"); $D_{str}(\omega)$ represents the link to forces (iii) acting to the contact surface from the structure when the contact surface moves (this is another 6 × 6 matrix called "structural dynamic stiffness matrix"). Both links are depicted not by springs, but by circles instead, because: *a)* they have damping parts; *b)* they are frequency-dependent.

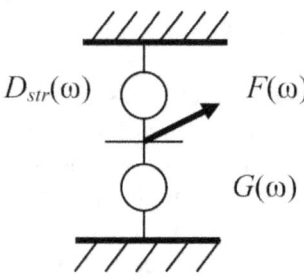

Figure 5.1. The general scheme for the first step of CAM

The equilibrium equation for the contact surface in the frequency domain looks as follows

$$[G(\omega) + D_{str}(\omega)]U_b(\omega) = F(\omega). \qquad (5.1)$$

Here $U_b(\omega)$ is the six-component displacement vector of the contact surface displacements mentioned above.

In fact, (5.1) is just a 6 × 6 linear algebraic system with complex frequency-dependent coefficients. It is solved frequency by frequency to get the transfer functions from F to U_b. In practice, F is linearly (in the frequency domain) linked to the seismic wave displacements U_0 in the control point in the soil without structures. As a result, one gets the transfer function from U_0 to U_b. The same transfer function links response accelerations to the accelerations in the control point. So, having time-history of accelerations in the control point and transfer functions to the response accelerations of the rigid contact surface one can obtain time-histories of the rigid base motions. Fast Fourier Transform (FFT) is used for this purpose. That will be the end of step 1 in CAM.

What might be a subject for verification at this stage (apart from the verification of F, G and D_{str} discussed further on)? It might be: *a*) the solution of 6 × 6 algebraic equations, and *b*) the FFT implementation. The subroutine for the inversion of fully populated matrices of moderate size based on Gauss method was written long ago and tested many times by means of multiplication of initial and inverse matrices – the result is the unit matrix. Usually, the possible problems with the inversion occur due to special block storage of matrices. In our case, the whole matrix 6 × 6 is stored plainly in one block, so there are no problems of this sort. Another kind of problems with the inversion occurs due to the possible zero matrix determinants (causing infinite resonance). However, in our practice the damping is high enough, and we never met difficulties in that.

As to the FFT, the corresponding subroutines were taken directly from the source text of SASSI.

5.3. Illustration of the CAM methodology

Let us consider the simplest illustration of CAM methodology with 1D motion. The goal is to let the reader follow the logic of CAM without the computer. The soil-structure model is shown in *Fig. 5.2*.

Here the structure is represented by two masses: M_{top} and M_{bas} connected by spring K_{str}. The soil is represented by mass M_{soil} attached to the basement and by soil spring K_{soil}. The seismic load is represented by platform motion with platform displacement U_0 (in the frequency domain).

First, let us obtain the direct solution without CAM. The system has two DOFs. In the time domain the equations of motion are as follows:

$$M_{top}\ddot{U}_{top} + K_{str}(U_{top} - U_b) = 0;$$
$$(M_{bas} + M_{soil})\ddot{U}_b + K_{str}(U_b - U_{top}) + K_{soil}(U_b - U_0) = 0. \quad (5.2)$$

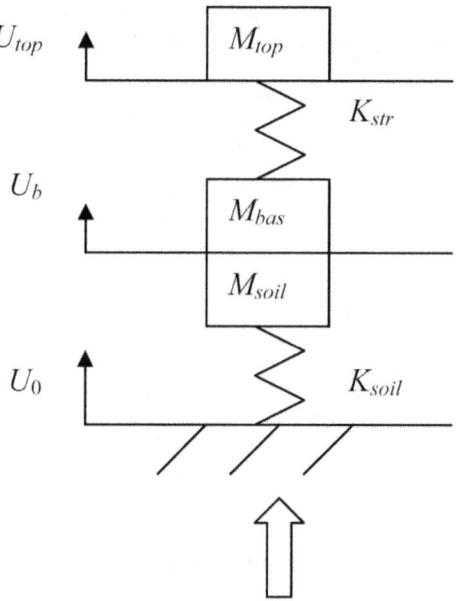

Figure 5.2. The simplest soil-structure model

In the frequency domain these equations are

$$-\omega^2 M_{top} U_{top} + K_{str}(U_{top} - U_b) = 0;$$
$$-\omega^2 (M_{bas} + M_{soil}) U_b + K_{str}(U_b - U_{top}) + K_{soil}(U_b - U_0) = 0. \quad (5.3)$$

This system is easy to solve. As a result, one gets

$$U_b = U_0 K_{soil} / \{K_{soil} - \omega^2 (M_{bas} + M_{soil}) - \omega^2 M_{top} \frac{K_{str}}{K_{str} - \omega^2 M_{top}}\}. \quad (5.4)$$

That was the direct solution without CAM – we will use it as a benchmark later on.

Now let us apply the CAM approach. We are to obtain three values participating in (5.1): F, G and D_{str}. From *Fig. 5.2* one directly gets the load $F(\omega)$ impacting the fixed base:

$$F(\omega) = K_{soil} U_0. \quad (5.5)$$

Now let us consider the fixed-base model of the structure with the prescribed base displacement V_b shown in *Fig. 5.3*.

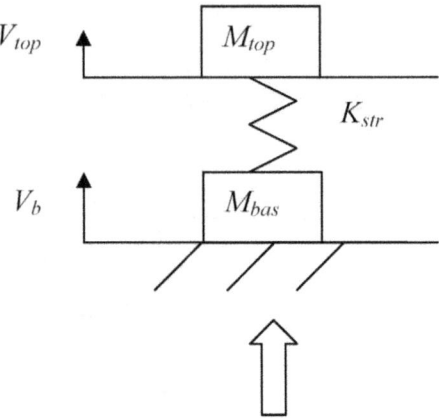

Figure 5.3. Fixed-base model of the structure without soil

The motion of the upper mass can be obtained from the equation similar to the first equation in (5.3):

$$-\omega^2 M_{top} V_{top} + K_{str}(V_{top} - V_b) = 0. \qquad (5.6)$$

One can easily get

$$V_{top} = V_b \frac{K_{str}}{K_{str} - \omega^2 M_{top}}. \qquad (5.7)$$

The force acting from the structure to the base is a resultant of inertial forces in all nodes. Using (5.7) one gets

$$D_{str}V_b = -\omega^2 M_{bas}V_b - \omega^2 M_{top}V_{top} = -\omega^2 V_b [M_{bas} + M_{top}\frac{K_{str}}{K_{str} - \omega^2 M_{top}}]. \qquad (5.8)$$

From this one gets

$$D_{str} = -\omega^2 [M_{bas} + M_{top}\frac{K_{str}}{K_{str} - \omega^2 M_{top}}]. \qquad (5.9)$$

Finally, let us consider soil and rigid basement without structure, as shown in *Fig. 5.4*.

The equation of motion for the soil mass with displacement W loaded by external force Q is as follows:

$$-\omega^2 M_{soil} W + K_{soil} W = Q. \quad (5.10)$$

From this one gets the dynamic stiffness of the soil (i.e. the soil impedance)

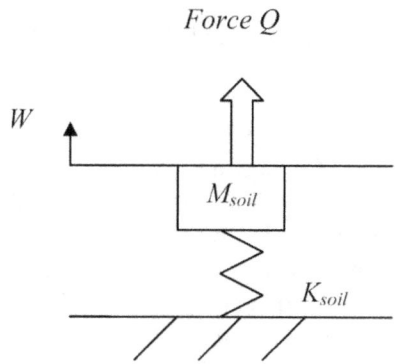

Figure 5.4. Soil without structure

$$G(\omega) = Q/W = K_{soil} - \omega^2 M_{soil}. \quad (5.11)$$

Note that this soil impedance is frequency-dependent like we usually see in practice for layered soil profiles.

So, now we have (5.5), (5.9) and (5.11) for F, D_{str} and G accordingly. From (5.1)

$$U_b = F(\omega)/[G(\omega) + D_{str}(\omega)]. \quad (5.12)$$

One can easily check, that (5.12) after the substitution of (5.5), (5.9) and (5.11) is exactly the same as the direct solution (5.4). This is a verification of the general CAM methodology for the considered simple case.

5.4. Dynamic inertia condensation procedure

The author in addition to the general CAM logic described above offers also an effective method to obtain $D_{str}(\omega)$ from the results of the modal analysis of the fixed-base structural model. Let us return to (5.9) and rewrite it as follows:

$$D_{str} = -\omega^2[(M_{bas} + M_{top}) + (M_{top}\frac{K_{str}}{K_{str} - \omega^2 M_{top}} - M_{top})] =$$

$$= -\omega^2[(M_{bas} + M_{top}) + \omega^2 M_{top}\frac{M_{top}}{K_{str} - \omega^2 M_{top}}] =$$

$$= -\omega^2 [(M_{bas} + M_{top}) + M_{top} \frac{\omega^2}{(K_{str}/M_{top}) - \omega^2}]. \quad (5.13)$$

First of all, $(M_{bas} + M_{top})$ is a full conventional "rigid" structural mass M_{str}. Second, (K_{str}/M_{top}) is a second degree of the natural frequency of the fixed-base model Ω^2. Third, in the only fixed-base natural mode of our sample structure normalized by mass, the modal displacement of the top mass is $\varphi = (M_{top})^{-0.5}$. This means that the participation factor S of this mode is equal to $M_{top}\varphi = (M_{top})^{0.5}$. So, $M_{top} = S^2$. Now one may re-write (5.13) once more:

$$D_{str} = -\omega^2 M(\omega); \quad M(\omega) = M_{str} + S^2(\frac{\omega^2}{\Omega^2 - \omega^2}). \quad (5.14)$$

If the structure is rigid, natural frequency Ω goes to infinity. This means that only "rigid" mass M_{str} plays a role in total $M(\omega)$. That is why the author calls $M(\omega)$ "dynamic inertia". For low frequencies ω dynamic inertia $M(\omega)$ goes to "rigid" inertia M_{str}. With the increase of frequency ω the dynamic inertia goes up, having peak at the natural frequency $\omega = \Omega$ (here the peak is infinite; in practice structural damping makes it finite). When the current frequency ω is far greater than the natural frequency Ω, the coefficient in brackets goes to minus one. This means that corresponding modal mass S^2 is subtracted from the total mass.

It may be rigorously shown that in the general case the dynamic inertia is described by 6 × 6 complex matrix $M(\omega)$. It looks very much like (5.14), but instead of scalar equation (5.14) there is a matrix equation of size 6 × 6. Besides, as there are many natural modes, their contribution is combined. Finally, modal damping also plays a certain role. The final formula looks as follows:

$$D_{str} = -\omega^2 M(\omega); M(\omega) = M_{str} + \sum_{j=1}^{N}(S_j^T S_j)(\frac{\omega^2}{\Omega_j^2 - \omega^2 + 2i\omega\lambda_j\Omega_j}). \quad (5.15)$$

Here S_j is a line of six participation factors for the fixed-base natural mode number j (so $S_j^T S_j$ is a 6 × 6 matrix); Ω_j and λ_j are accordingly natural frequency and modal damping for this mode; i is an imaginary unit, making dynamic inertia not only frequency-dependent but also complex.

Formula (5.15) implies viscous structural damping. If in the direct analysis material structural damping is to be used (like in SASSI), then the expression would be slightly different in the damping part:

$$D_{str} = -\omega^2 M(\omega); \quad M(\omega) = M_{str} + \sum_{j=1}^{N}(S_j^T S_j)(\frac{\omega^2}{\Omega_j^2 - \omega^2 + 2i\lambda_j \Omega_j^2}). \quad (5.16)$$

Information about M_{str} and modal characteristics is obtained from the modal analysis of the detailed fixed-based structural model. This analysis is performed in the FEM general-purpose soft (e.g., ABAQUS is used by the author, but other programs can be used for the same purposes). To avoid mistakes, the output file of ABAQUS is automatically processed to get all the parameters. Then the terms are plotted over frequency (real and imaginary parts separately). The examples will be given below.

Equations (5.15, 5.16) enable the number of checks which is important for an analyst. First of all, for the low frequencies all diagonal terms of the dynamic inertia matrix must go to "rigid" real values directly calculated and printed out by ABAQUS (e.g., three first diagonal terms go to one and the same "rigid" mass). Second, peaks should occur at the natural frequencies also calculated and printed out by ABAQUS. Such checks help to find possible errors.

This condensation technology for the structure was first reported by Dr Tyapin in English in 2007 (see Tyapin (2007)). The same technology has been used in CLASSI for some time and is described in ASCE4-16 in the section C5-4 as "modal representation of structure". So, this is nothing unusual in it. The main advantage is that dynamic inertia describes the role of the structure in SSI in full (provided Rigid Base Assumption is accepted), so one can do without stick structural models in SSI at all. That means that the Rigid Floor Assumption implicitly used in stick models together with Rigid Base Assumption is no longer necessary.

5.5. Soil impedances and seismic loads: possible sources

Taking into account (5.15) and the link between seismic loads $F(\omega)$ and seismic displacements U_0 in the control point, one can rewrite the basic CAM equation (5.1):

$$[G(\omega) - \omega^2 M(\omega)] U_b(\omega) = B(\omega) U_0(\omega). \quad (5.17)$$

Here $B(\omega)$ is 6×3 complex matrix, $U_0(\omega)$ is a three-component vector. From (5.17) the resulting equation is obtained:

$$U_b(\omega) = \{[G(\omega) - \omega^2 M(\omega)]^{-1} B(\omega)\} U_0(\omega). \quad (5.18)$$

In practice, the 6×3 matrix in curved brackets in the right-hand part of (5.18) is calculated in the frequency domain, and then FFT is applied.

But to perform these calculations, one should get $G(\omega)$ and $B(\omega)$. Like a modal analysis of fixed-base structure, this may be done in different ways and with different software. It is not a part of CAM as a technology, though there is a certain author's practice described below.

5.1.1. The easiest way is to use formulae for soil springs and dashpots from ASCE4 Standards. It may be done if the rectangular or circular rigid base mat is resting on the surface of homogeneous half-space. The resulting matrix $G(\omega)$ is diagonal, the j-th diagonal element ($j = 1, ..., 6$) is described by

$$g_j(\omega) = k_j + i\omega c_j. \quad (5.19)$$

Here k_j and c_j are real frequency-independent values calculated according to the formulae given in the Standards. These formulae are approximate, but the uncertainty is not because of CAM: direct calculations without CAM with the same soil springs and dashpots should give the same result as CAM.

This approach needs no special verification, as direct simple formulae are used for impedances. Load matrix $B(\omega)$ will be discussed separately.

5.1.2. The second possible way is to use CLASSI software described in ASCE4-16. It may be used only for surface rigid base mats. Unlike the simplified formulae mentioned above in 5.5.1, this approach enables the complicated shape of the mat (not only circular or rectangular). Besides (and this is the most important advantage), horizontally-layered soil sites may be considered (and not only homogeneous ones, as in 5.5.1). Note that even for homogeneous sites CLASSI gives impedances different from those of 5.5.1

(especially in vertical and rotational directions). Impedance matrix $G(\omega)$ is no longer diagonal.

Special verification here is not needed, as CLASSI has passed through special verification procedure. The output of CLASSI (at least in the version of 1990-s used by the author) is directly that very 6 × 6 matrix $G(\omega)$ needed for CAM – no additional procedures are required.

One time CLASSI was actively used by the author, but nowadays SASSI is used instead, as described below.

5.1.3. Let us discuss the load matrix $B(\omega)$ participating in (5.17) – so far only for surface rigid basements and horizontally-layered sites. The common assumption about seismic excitation is that seismic wave in the absence of structures is propagating vertically. Horizontal boundaries of the soil layers do not spoil this vertical propagation. As a consequence, every horizontal plane in the soil (including free surface) is moving as a rigid body in three translational directions: two horizontal ones and one vertical. One can put a rigid weightless surface basement on the surface of the soil – nothing will change in the soil motion; base motion will be similar to the surface free-field motion $U_0(\omega)$. Like free-field surface, this moving base mat will be free of any forces. In order to get the fixed base required for $B(\omega)$, one should add to this picture the additional base motion opposite to the free-field motion. This additional base motion will cause the response of the soil – controlled by the impedance matrix and displacements of this motion. The resulting force acting on the base mat in this additional picture will be $F(\omega) = G(\omega) \times U_1(\omega)$. Here $U_1(\omega)$ is a 6D displacement of the base with the opposite sign, consisting of three components of $U_0(\omega)$ for translation and three zeroes for rotations. So, one can conclude that matrix $B(\omega)$ participating in (5.17) consists simply of the first three columns of the matrix $G(\omega)$. This is true for both approaches: 5.5.1 and 5.5.2.

5.1.4. The most universal software at the moment to get the impedance and load matrices is SASSI. The first version was transferred to Russia in the middle of 1990-s. Later on, the new version SASSI2000 was purchased (see Ostadan (2006)). SASSI methodology is also described in ASCE4-16. Like CLASSI it can treat horizontally-layered sites (even with local deviations from horizontal layering impossible for

CLASSI – e.g., the improved soil in the limited volume under the base mat, described in Chapter 7 of this book). Like CLASSI it can also treat the arbitrary shape of the base mat. Unlike CLASSI it can treat also the embedded basements. In practice for the embedded basements, there is a separation of the soil from the embedded side walls in the upper part – this is also treated in SASSI.

The main problem with SASSI in obtaining the impedances is that SASSI (at least in the two versions mentioned above and available at the moment) does not (unlike CLASSI) directly calculate and print out the 6×6 matrix $G(\omega)$ needed for CAM – some additional procedures are needed. They need special verification even though SASSI itself has passed through the required obligatory verification.

There are two main ways to obtain impedance and load matrices with SASSI.

5.1.4.1. The first way may be called "straightforward". One should model rigid weightless basement as a very stiff structure in SASSI, apply unit harmonic forces along all 6 DOFs one by one using MOTOR module of SASSI, and calculate 6D response of the basement to each of these forces. That will be flexibility complex matrix 6×6. The inverse matrix will be the impedance matrix $G(\omega)$. Then one should obtain the 6D responses of the same rigid weightless base to the 3 seismic waves, producing unit displacements along 3 DOFs in the free-field control point. That will be foundation input matrix $T(\omega)$ of size 6×3. Product of the impedance matrix and foundation input matrix gives seismic load matrix: $B(\omega) = G(\omega) \times T(\omega)$.

This straightforward approach may be implemented using conventional SASSI versions.

5.1.4.2. The alternative approach was developed some years ago, first published in 2005 in SMiRT papers by the author (see A. Tyapin (2005)). Later on, almost the same formulae appeared in the paper of J. Johnson et al (2010). It is referred to in ASCE4-16. This approach may be called "condensation" approach. Looking at SASSI, we see that first the nodal impedance matrix $D_s(\omega)$ is obtained there for the set of the "interaction" nodes. This matrix is also complex and frequency-dependent, but the size is $3N \times 3N$, where N is the number of nodes. The idea is to "condense" this huge matrix to the integral impedance matrix $G(\omega)$ and to the load matrix $B(\omega)$ directly, without modelling weightless basement, and without MOTOR module.

Let us consider several cases starting from the simplest one – surface rigid base. If all N interaction nodes are at the surface base and R is matrix $3N \times 6$ of rigid nodal translational displacements corresponding to the 6 unit "integral" rigid displacement of the base along all 6 DOFs, then $(-D_s \times R)$ is matrix of nodal interaction forces acting from the soil to the base in case of 6 unit integral rigid base displacements. To get the resulting integral forces from these nodal forces we are to multiply these nodal forces to R^T from the left:

$$-G = -R^T D_s R. \quad (5.20)$$

Thus, (5.20) is a formula for the condensation of "huge" matrix D_s into the 6×6 impedance matrix G.

Seismic waves in the simplest case described above (vertical waves in horizontally layered soil) will provide the same "rigid" displacement in all surface interaction nodes without structure. The appearance of the rigid weightless base at the surface will change nothing, so:

$$T = \begin{bmatrix} 1 & 0 & 0 \\ 0 & 1 & 0 \\ 0 & 0 & 1 \\ 0 & 0 & 0 \\ 0 & 0 & 0 \\ 0 & 0 & 0 \end{bmatrix}. \quad (5.21)$$

To get seismic load matrix $B(\omega)$ we are to multiply T by G from the left. Due to the special form (5.21) of T we will get $B(\omega)$ as the three first columns of G. This is the same as discussed above in section 5.3.

Now let us go to the second case – embedded rigid base with full contact at the bottom and side walls. Let the underground volume V be covered by interaction nodes. Some of these nodes are "internal", others are "boundary" ones. Here SASSI builds several "huge" impedance matrices of size $3N \times 3N$. The first one D_s (initial SASSI matrix) is still nodal impedance matrix linking all N nodes in the initial soil. It is obtained through the inversion of the flexibility matrix. But there appears another "huge" matrix of the same size – this is impedance matrix D_e of the excavated soil standing alone, obtained through conventional FEM modelling of the finite volume V without surrounding soil:

$$D_e = K_e - \omega^2 M_e. \tag{5.22}$$

Here K_e is a stiffness FEM matrix, M_e is an inertia FEM matrix, linking the same N nodes. Both matrices are obtained from 3D volume finite elements with 3 translational DOFs in each node.

Subtracting D_e from D_s we get another impedance nodal matrix linking the same nodes but for the "soil with an outcropped pit". If D_e and D_s are precise, all the terms of this matrix referring to the "internal" nodes in volume V would be zero (i.e., the "internal" nodes are no longer supported). In practice, this is not exactly the case, but residual terms are far less than the terms referring to the "boundary" nodes.

Now for the "soil with a pit" we have the case similar to the previous "surface" case: the bottom and the walls of the pit are "free surface". So, formula (5.20) is valid for the new nodal impedance matrix:

$$-G = -R^T (D_s - D_e) R. \tag{5.23}$$

We can go on with the similarity with "surface case" considering seismic loads. If seismic displacements at the free surface of the pit are U_e, to bring them back to zero we need nodal forces $(D_s - D_e) \times U_e$, and the resultants of these forces will be

$$B U_0 = R^T (D_s - D_e) U_e. \tag{5.24}$$

But to implement (5.24) we must separately solve the problem to obtain 3D wavefield U_e.

Luckily it may be shown that instead of (5.24) one can use another formula:

$$B U_0 = R^T D_s U_i. \tag{5.25}$$

Here U_i is that very 1D seismic displacement field in the initial soil (before the outcrop) we are using conventionally.

One more comment. Let us substitute (5.22) into (5.23):

$$G = R^T(D_s - D_e) R = R^T D_s R - R^T K_e R + \omega^2 R^T M_e R. \quad (5.26)$$

As K_e is a FEM stiffness matrix of the unsupported finite volume V, and R are rigid displacements, product $K_e \times R$ is zero. So, (5.26) becomes simpler:

$$G = R^T D_s R + \omega^2 R^T M_e R. \quad (5.27)$$

As M_e is a FEM mass matrix of the same volume, product $(R^T M_e R)$ is just a 6×6 rigid inertia matrix of this volume.

After that, we can once more clarify the physical meaning of (5.27). The first term $(R^T D_s R)$ gives us integral forces necessary to provide both (i) rigid motion of volume V, and (ii) corresponding motion of the surrounding soil. But impedance matrix G should describe only the second part, i.e., forces necessary to provide the motion of the surrounding soil only. That is why we are to account for V separately. Luckily we know forces necessary to provide rigid motion of the finite volume V – these are inertial forces. So, in (5.27) we subtract them from the total forces described by the first term.

Now let us verify the condensation procedure described above against the direct solution. The author uses a home-made version of SASSI without MOTOR module. Up to the development of nodal impedance matrix D_s everything is the same as in the conventional SASSI; after that equation (5.27) for integral impedances and equation (5.25) for integral loads are implemented.

The comparison performed especially for this verification will be as follows. First impedance matrix G will be calculated by condensation (5.27). The separate check will be made of the last term in (5.27) against the mass of the excavated soil. This check is not trivial as the condensation of mass matrix M_e is done in full with "huge" matrix. Load matrix B is obtained by condensation (5.25). Then the response transfer function matrix TF for the weightless rigid base will be calculated as

$$TF(\omega) = G^{-1}(\omega) B(\omega). \quad (5.28)$$

For the verification purpose, the same matrix *TF* will be calculated by conventional SASSI analysis with very light and very stiff embedded base modelled by 3D volume finite elements as "structure". The comparison with (5-28) will show the applicability of (5.27) and (5.25).

The sample soil is homogeneous half-space. Wave velocities: $V_s = 400$ m/s, $V_p = 1300$ m/s. Mass density 2.0 t/m^3. Internal damping is 4%.

Base size is 80 × 80 × 12 m. FEM mesh is 20 × 20 × 3 elements. Each element is a cube with 4 m sides. The total number of nodes is 1764.

Outcropped volume is $V = 80 \times 80 \times 12 = 76800$ m^3. The total mass of the excavated soil is 153600 tones.

First, the impedance matrix $G(\omega)$ was calculated for 11 frequencies (from approximately 0 to 10 Hz with a frequency step about 1 Hz). Equation (5.27) was used for the condensation. The second term in the right-hand part of (5.27) was calculated and printed out separately.

The highest circular frequency was 0.6289D+02 s^{-1}. Complex element (1, 1) of the second term was printed out as (0.60757D+09; -0.25315D+01). The exact value should be purely real and equal to (0.6289D+02)^2×153600 = 0.60751E9 (kN/m). Comparing these values one can see the accuracy of the mass condensation – it is excellent.

Does it make difference for the impedance matrix $G(\omega)$? Let us look at the resulting values of $G(\omega)$ calculated using (5.27). For the same frequency about 10 Hz element (1, 1) of $G(\omega)$ was printed out as (0.38074D+08; 0.58364D+09). We see that the second term in (5.27) discussed above is controlling the real part. Surely, this is for 10 Hz; for lower frequencies, the impact of the outcropped soil mass will be less significant (proportional to ω^2).

Complex element (1, 5) of the same 6 × 6 matrix linking horizontal motion to the rocking motion was printed out as (-0.36454D+10; 0.15561D+02). The exact value should be purely real and equal to the product of the previous value and (-6 m) – half of the embedment depth. This makes (-0.36451E+10) (kN). Once more the comparison shows the excellent result.

Now let us compare transfer functions from the free-field motion to the weightless rigid base motion computed for the centre of the base surface. The output from MOTION for X(X) TF, obtained through conventional SASSI analysis (i.e. without any condensation) is

```
VALUES OF TRANSFER FUNCTION NODE:   1544 DIRECTION:    X
IF     FREQ          RE               IM              ABS
 1    0.0305      0.9999E+00       0.4545E-05      0.9999E+00
33    1.0071      0.9498E+00       0.2858E-01      0.9502E+00
66    2.0142      0.8738E+00       0.1123E+00      0.8809E+00
99    3.0212      0.7920E+00       0.2008E+00      0.8171E+00
131   3.9978      0.6945E+00       0.2849E+00      0.7507E+00
164   5.0049      0.5795E+00       0.3703E+00      0.6877E+00
198   6.0425      0.4520E+00       0.4510E+00      0.6385E+00
230   7.0190      0.3268E+00       0.5138E+00      0.6090E+00
262   7.9956      0.1982E+00       0.5607E+00      0.5947E+00
295   9.0027      0.6465E-01       0.5899E+00      0.5934E+00
328  10.0098     -.6668E-01        0.5985E+00      0.6022E+00
```

Now let us compare it to the output from the condensation analysis using equations (5.25, 5.27, 5.28):

Frequency, Hz	Re	Im	Abs
0.0305	9.999E-01	-8.287E-07	9.999E-01
1.0071	9.498E-01	2.858E-02	9.502E-01
2.0142	8.738E-01	1.123E-01	8.810E-01
3.0212	7.920E-01	2.008E-01	8.171E-01
3.9978	6.945E-01	2.849E-01	7.507E-01
5.0049	5.795E-01	3.704E-01	6.878E-01
6.0425	4.520E-01	4.510E-01	6.385E-01
7.0190	3.268E-01	5.138E-01	6.090E-01
7.9956	1.982E-01	5.606E-01	5.946E-01
9.0027	6.465E-02	5.899E-01	5.934E-01
10.0098	-6.668E-02	5.984E-01	6.021E-01

As we see from the comparison, the accuracy of the condensation procedure is excellent.

To compare rocking we should take vertical TF Z(X) calculated in the corner of the base surface and divide it by half of the horizontal size (80/2 = 40 m). Here is the result of the conventional analysis for TF Z(X) calculated in the corner of the base surface:

```
VALUES OF TRANSFER FUNCTION NODE:   1764 DIRECTION:    Z
IF     FREQ            RE              IM              ABS
1     0.0305       -.6038E-05      0.4214E-06       0.6053E-05
33    1.0071       -.2188E-02      -.1652E-02       0.2742E-02
66    2.0142       -.1941E-01      -.2772E-02       0.1961E-01
99    3.0212       -.4176E-01      0.1653E-01       0.4492E-01
131   3.9978       -.4802E-01      0.4335E-01       0.6469E-01
164   5.0049       -.4307E-01      0.6269E-01       0.7606E-01
198   6.0425       -.3628E-01      0.7075E-01       0.7951E-01
230   7.0190       -.3303E-01      0.7023E-01       0.7761E-01
262   7.9956       -.3384E-01      0.6551E-01       0.7374E-01
295   9.0027       -.3784E-01      0.5835E-01       0.6955E-01
328   10.0098      -.4421E-01      0.5022E-01       0.6690E-01
```

Next comes the same result divided by 40 m to get rocking angles:

Frequency, Hz	Re	Im	Abs
0.0305	-1.510E-07	1.054E-08	1.513E-07
1.0071	-5.470E-05	-4.130E-05	6.855E-05
2.0142	-4.853E-04	-6.930E-05	4.903E-04
3.0212	-1.044E-03	4.133E-04	1.123E-03
3.9978	-1.201E-03	1.084E-03	1.617E-03
5.0049	-1.077E-03	1.567E-03	1.902E-03
6.0425	-9.070E-04	1.769E-03	1.988E-03
7.0190	-8.258E-04	1.756E-03	1.940E-03
7.9956	-8.460E-04	1.638E-03	1.844E-03
9.0027	-9.460E-04	1.459E-03	1.739E-03
10.0098	-1.105E-03	1.256E-03	1.673E-03

Now let us compare this result to the rocking TF YY(X) calculated by condensation using (5.25, 5.27, 5.28). The signs are opposite due to the sign rules for rocking angles.

Frequency, Hz	Re	Im	Abs
0.0305	-8.272E-08	-3.077E-08	8.825E-08
1.0071	5.482E-05	4.129E-05	6.863E-05
2.0142	4.855E-04	6.953E-05	4.904E-04
3.0212	1.044E-03	-4.134E-04	1.123E-03
3.9978	1.201E-03	-1.084E-03	1.617E-03
5.0049	1.077E-03	-1.567E-03	1.901E-03
6.0425	9.070E-04	-1.769E-03	1.988E-03
7.0190	8.256E-04	-1.756E-03	1.940E-03
7.9956	8.459E-04	-1.638E-03	1.843E-03
9.0027	9.460E-04	-1.459E-03	1.739E-03
10.0098	1.105E-03	-1.255E-03	1.673E-03

As one can see, the accuracy of the condensation procedure is high. The conclusion is that the condensation procedure based on equations (5.27) and (5.25) is accurate as compared to the conventional SASSI approach (and "straightforward" SASSI approach to the impedance and load calculation). This condensation procedure uses different nodal matrices in (5.25) and (5.27) – the difference is in the mass of the outcropped soil.

5.6. Comparison of SASSI impedances obtained using condensation with CLASSI results

The verification in section 5.5.4.2 was performed for the CAM variant of SASSI against conventional SASSI. Let us look at another comparison – the comparison of SASSI impedances (with condensation) with CLASSI impedances for the same surface basement. This time the soil will be layered.

The soil profile is composed of the soil layer 26 m thick and of the underlying flexible half-space. The rigid base is resting on the surface. It has quadratic shape with 30.6 m sides. Wave velocities in the half-space are $V_s = 800$ m/s and $V_p = 2100$ m/s. In the upper layer they are $V_s = 400$ m/s and $V_p = 1100$ m/s. Thus, the Poisson's ratio calculated out of these velocities is 0.4238 for the layer and 0.4151 for the half-space. The mass density of the soil is 2.0 t/m^3 both in the layer and in the half-space. Material damping is 0.05 for the layer and 0.02 for the half-space. This soil profile was chosen to study frequency-dependent impedances.

Impedances were obtained (i) by SASSI with condensation (5.27), and (ii) by CLASSI. For each of them two meshes were used: 8 × 8 and 16 × 16. Besides, the results for homogeneous half-space with the upper layer properties calculated by ASCE4-16 formulae are presented to demonstrate the influence of the soil layering versus homogeneous profile.

Figure 5.5 shows the comparison of (a) real parts and (b) imaginary parts of two different translational impedances – along OX and OZ (impedance along OY is similar to that along OX due to the quadratic shape of the mat).

Matching of SASSI and CLASSI results is good, though not excellent. In fact, basic mathematics in these two approaches is considerably different, so one should not expect the ideal matching. However, the results are very reasonable. It is interesting to note that the refinement of the mesh (from 8 × 8 to 16 × 16) shifts SASSI and CLASSI results in the opposite directions. One may conclude that the exact results lay somewhere in between SASSI_16 and CLASSI_16.

The goal of this comparison was to check the condensation procedure in SASSI. In CLASSI the impedance matrix is a part of original output; in SASSI this is not the case (special condensation procedure was developed by the author to obtain this matrix, as stated above). The conclusion is that this home-made procedure works well even for frequency-dependent impedances.

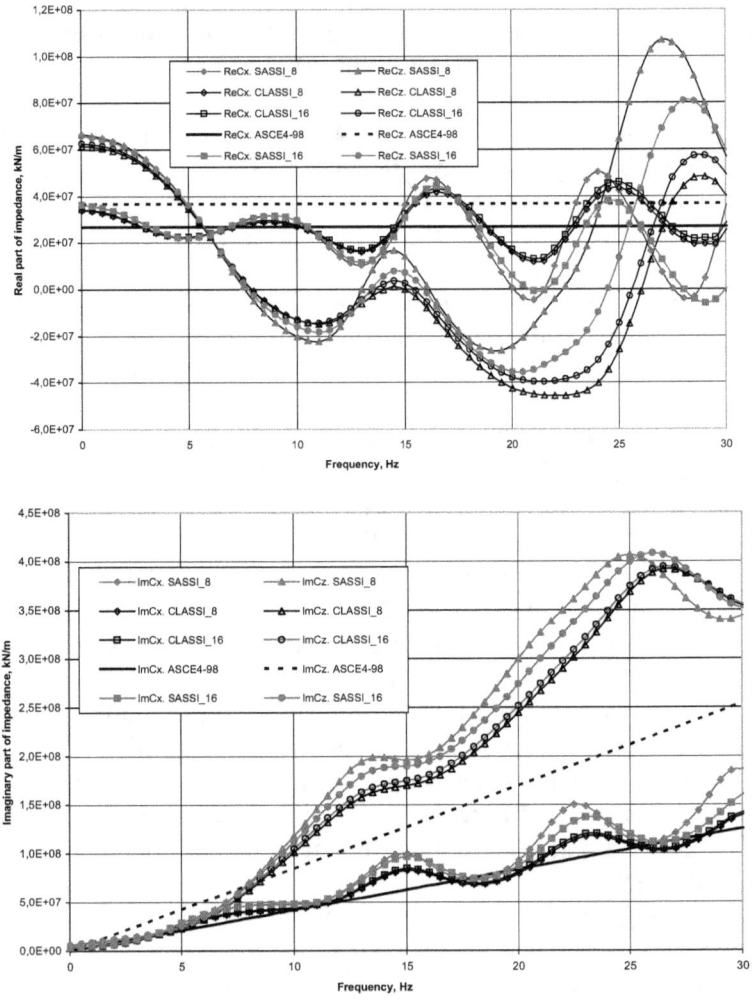

Figure 5.5. Real (top picture) and imaginary (bottom picture) parts of translational impedances

Comparison to the "ASCE formulae" results shows that the influence of the layering is significant, though the half-space boundary is rather deep (about one size of the mat). So, for the significantly layered sites simple formulae from ASCE4 cause significant errors.

5.7. Comparison of SASSI impedances obtained using condensation with ASCE4 results for almost homogeneous half-space

Another comparison was done during SSI analysis for almost homogeneous soil profile. Fig. 5.6 shows the comparison of horizontal impedances obtained by SASSI with condensation and by formulae of ASCE4-98 (they are repeated in ASCE4-16).

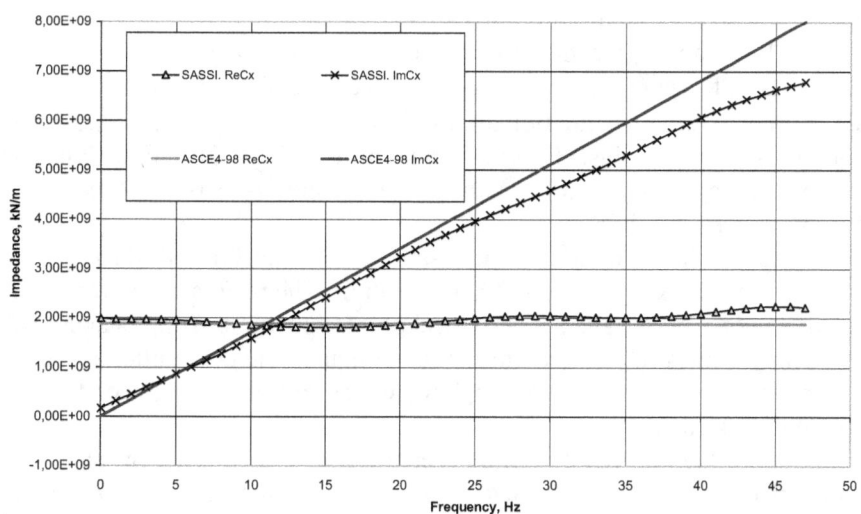

Figure 5.6. The comparison of horizontal impedances for almost homogeneous soil profile calculated by SASSI with condensation and by formulae from ASCE4-98

We see very good matching. Note that formulae of ASCE4-98 are the most accurate for horizontal impedances.

Let us complete this chapter with several conclusions.

In fact, the original CAM technology developed and used by the author and his team for the SSI analyses of structures with rigid basements contains three new issues.

1) The general SSI sub-structuring technology, enabling separate treatment of soil (impedance and load matrices) and structure (dynamic stiffness matrix developed for the fixed-base model). Combination of dynamic stiffness for soil and structure is performed in a very simple format. Seismic loads are also converted to the same format.

2) The condensation technology for the structure based on the modal analysis results obtained for the fixed-base structural model. This technology allows the further SSI analysis without stick structural models and rigid floors assumption (i.e. with very detailed FEM structural model), though the rigid base assumption is still used. The same technology is nowadays used in CLASSI and referred to in ASCE4-16.

3) The condensation technology for the soil using SASSI methodology but doing without structural modelling even for the underground part. The same technology was later developed by the U.S. specialists and referred to in ASCE4-16.

This chapter presented the verification issues on all three topics.

As to the general technology, this is a clear theory. The only issues appropriate for the verification are a) the solution of 6×6 algebraic linear equations, and b) Fast Fourier Transform (FFT). The first issue is resolved using Gauss direct method; the second issue is resolved using subroutines from SASSI.

As to the structural condensation, it is performed through the automatic processing of the ABAQUS output. The results in the format of the dynamic inertia have several checkpoints (position of the peaks, low-frequency values of the dynamic mass similar to the conventional inertia parameters printed out by ABAQUS), which are checked every time in convenient format.

As to the soil condensation, verification is performed by means of comparison of the results with conventional SASSI. The additional comparisons were made with CLASSI (for layered soil) and ASCE4-98 formulae (for homogeneous half-space).

The results of verification show, that CAM is accurate as mathematic and computational technology. The applicability of the physical assumptions (linearity of soil and structure, rigid base assumption) is to be validated separately.

CAM has been used since 2006 by the author and proved to be very effective SSI tool. However, the technology described in this chapter is just the first option of CAM. The second option of CAM (dealing with flexible base mats) needs separate discussion – it was not included in this book.

The author would like to add one more comment. Recently one of the counterparties required the demonstration of the CAM accuracy using SASSI2000 for the benchmark calculations. The idea was to compare the results for the rigid base mat in SASSI2000 and in CAM. The author expected to demonstrate perfect matching of the transfer functions and was astonished to find out that the results proved to be somewhat different. The example of the comparison is shown in *Fig. 5.7*. "Rigid" means SASSI2000 results.

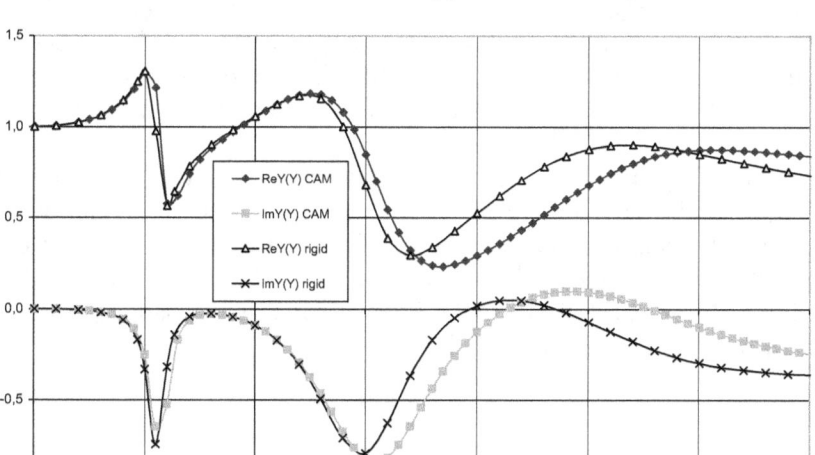

Figure 5.7. Comparison of the transfer functions Y(Y) to the response in the corner of the base mat (node 550) calculated by CAM and by SASSI2000 ("rigid")

The special investigation was carried out to find out the reason for this mismatching.

As described above, three programs participate in the calculations compared (besides simple algebraic program solving linear system 6×6 in CAM): (i) in CAM the impedances and loads are calculated by special version of SASSI; (ii) in CAM the dynamic inertia is calculated using ABAQUS; (iii) SASSI2000 is used for the comparison. The difference in the results may be caused either by the difference in the models used in these programs or by some mistakes in the home-made very simple program solving 6×6 linear systems in CAM.

Anyhow this case needs special investigation. Comparison of SASSI and SASSI2000 was performed above – matching was perfect.

Let us now compare SASSI2000 to ABAQUS. The geometry of the model from SASSI2000 was reproduced in ABAQUS in full (automatically in a special program), as well as masses, densities and spring parameters (stiffness and damping). However, the detailed investigation demonstrated at least two important differences between SASSI2000 and ABAQUS.

1) Mass matrices are developed differently in ABAQUS and SASSI2000. In ABAQUS they use consistent mass matrices. In SASSI they use averaged mass matrix – half consistent and half lumped, as mentioned in Chapter 3 (during the description of the G. Waas boundaries). This difference does not refer to the lumped mass matrices – they are treated in a similar way.

2) Stiffness matrices for shell elements are treated differently in ABAQUS and SASSI2000. However, springs are treated in a similar way.

Let us demonstrate the impact of these two factors one by one. First let us put very small mass density to all the shells, leaving them flexible. Both CAM and SASSI2000 results will change. *Fig. 5.8* demonstrates the results in node 550.

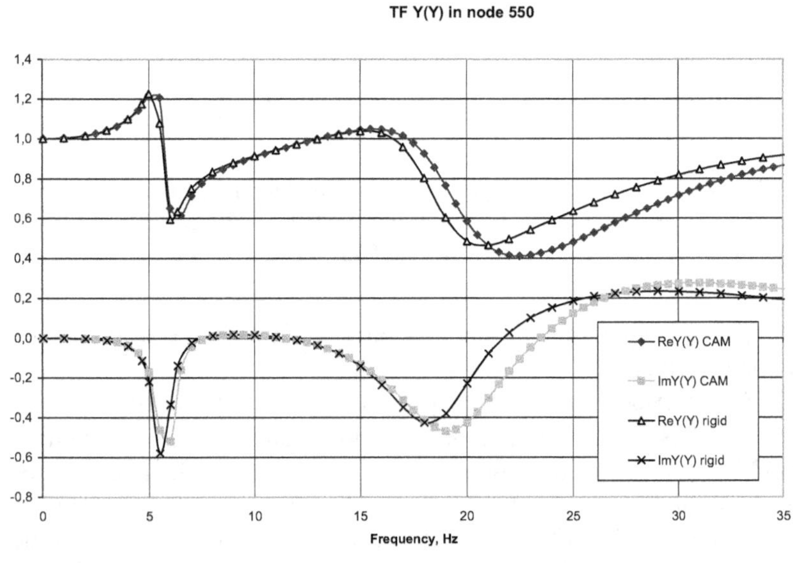

Figure 5.8. Comparison of the transfer functions Y(Y) to the response in the corner of the base mat (node 550) calculated by CAM and by SASSI2000 ("rigid") with weightless shells

We see that the difference is still there, though all curves shifted as compared to *Fig. 5.7*.

Now let us get rid of shell stiffness leaving only springs flexible – i.e. let us make all the shells very stiff. *Fig. 5.9* demonstrates the results in node 550.

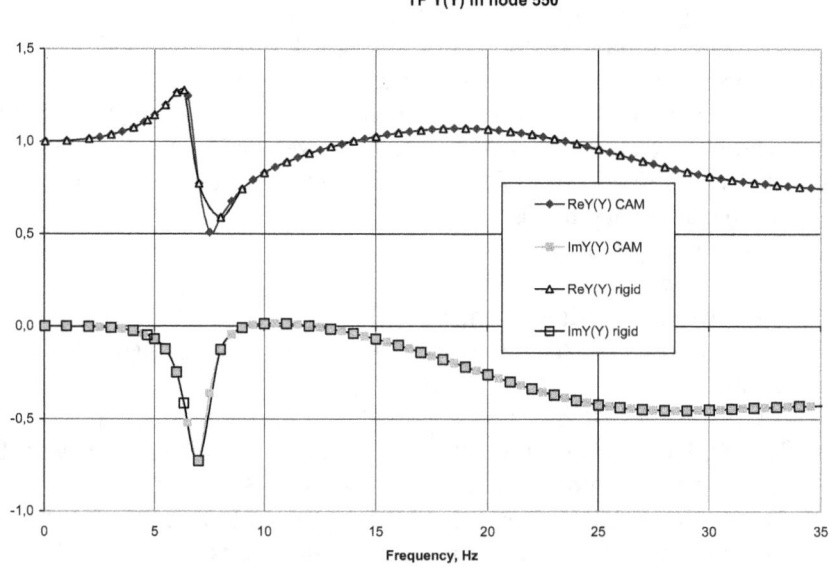

Figure 5.9. Comparison of the transfer functions Y(Y) to the response in the corner of the base mat (node 550) calculated by CAM and by SASSI2000 ("rigid") with weightless rigid shells

Here, at last, we see that perfect matching we were looking for from the very beginning. Some difference in curves in *Fig. 5.9* is caused by the EXCEL interpolation and different sets of frequencies used for the calculations in CAM and SASSI2000 (in CAM some intermediate frequencies were added with interpolated impedances and recalculated dynamic masses). But all the points calculated in both programs coincide perfectly.

This comparison demonstrates the accuracy of CAM. As described above, CAM does not work with particular elements (shells or springs, lumped or distributed masses, etc.) – it works with modal files obtained from ABAQUS. If these modal files are consistent with the models used in SASSI2000, then the results of CAM coincide with those of SASSI2000. We saw it in the last case with springs, weightless rigid beams and lumped masses. If the modal file from ABAQUS is inconsistent with the model used in SASSI, then the results are different. We saw it in the two previous cases. However, this difference has nothing to do with the accuracy of CAM – it is about the similarity of the models (shell elements in our case) in ABAQUS and SASSI2000.

The obvious preliminary condition for such a comparison is that SASSI2000 and CAM use the same model of the soil-structure system.

As to the ground part (the same soil profile was used both in CAM and in SASSI2000) this term was fulfilled.

However, in the structural part that proved to be not always the case. The geometry of the model initially developed in SASSI2000 was reproduces in full in ABAQUS. Several types of finite elements were used for the simplified model:

(i) lumped masses;
(ii) springs;
(iii) weightless rigid beams;
(iv) rigid shells (for the base mat), and flexible shells (for the walls and ceiling).

All the listed elements except shells are the same in ABAQUS and SASSI2000. However, shell elements are treated in a different way: both in mass matrices and in stiffness matrices. As a result of these differences, the initial comparison did not give the desirable matching. After making shell very stiff and weightless the results of SASSI2000 and CAM coincided: matching of all the transfer functions was perfect.

This situation enables another important conclusion. ABAQUS is a more advanced code than SASSI in terms of structural modelling. This is obvious – one should just compare the lists of the finite element types in both codes. On the other hand, SASSI2000 is more advanced in terms of soil-structure interaction (SSI). It means that even if a detailed structural model can be analyzed by SASSI, the results in the high-frequency range will be somewhat doubtful due to the primitive structural elements in the model. Therefore, the requirement to verify the design based on ABAQUS by the SASSI analysis of the detailed model is unreasonable. ABAQUS will give more trustable results for a structure, provided SSI is accounted for.

CAM is a technology which allows the combination of the best capacities of the two codes: SASSI for soil (without structure) and ABAQUS for structure (without soil). The only limitations are linearity and Rigid Base Assumption.

5.8. CAM and some of the SSI effects

CAM helps to get an additional insight into several important SSI effects. We will consider two of them: (i) principal difference between seismic response for homogeneous and layered soil profiles; and (ii) role of the embedment.

5.8.1. Two types of soil profiles

Let us compare two soil profiles discussed above in this Chapter: (i) horizontally-layered soil profile; and (ii) homogeneous soil profile.

For the layered profile we will consider the extreme case: a single homogeneous layer with thickness H, and shear wave velocity V_s underlain by the rigid half-space. Let us study horizontal impedance for the surface rigid base mat.

In Chapter 3 we showed that this layer has a special "critical" (or "opening") frequency

$$\omega_1 = \frac{2\pi V_s}{4H}. \qquad (3.29)$$

If there is no internal damping in the soil, this frequency corresponds to the resonance in two horizontal directions (as Rayleigh and Love waves have the same this special frequency). The resonant modes of the soil motion at this frequency (two modes in two vertical planes) do not depend on the horizontal coordinates; it means that every horizontal plane inside the layer, including free surface, moves as a rigid body. In fact, the wave field is described by the equation (1.9) from Chapter 1 where the wavelength λ is calculated for the shear wave. Without the internal damping in the soil the amplitude of resonance is arbitrary.

As a consequence, we can put a rigid weightless base mat at the surface of the layer, and it will move together with the soil without any moving force between soil and mat. On the other hand, we can treat this picture as a contact problem for getting horizontal impedance – at this frequency, it is zero.

Let us imagine the impedance curve in the frequency domain (like we saw in *Fig. 5.5*) for this case. For zero frequency ω there will be a certain static value of the real part; the imaginary part will be zero (without the internal material damping). For special "critical" layer frequency ω_1 given by (3.29) both real and imaginary parts will be zero. Between these two frequencies, the real part will continuously go down from the static value to zero. The imaginary part will stay zero – this is the consequence of the surface wave behaviour discussed in Chapter 3: all the surface waves (of both Rayleigh and Love types) in this frequency interval are "dying" and do not take energy from the moving base mat.

Now let us remember the basic CAM equation (5.17) and look at the combined stiffness in the left-hand part $[G(\omega) - \omega^2 M(\omega)]$. Suppose structure is rigid and centre of mass has zero height – it means that the dynamic inertia $M(\omega)$ in the horizontal direction is just a conventional mass. Then our combined stiffness in the frequency domain describes two crossing curves: $G(\omega)$ and parabola $\omega^2 M(\omega)$ as schematically shown in *Fig. 5.10*.

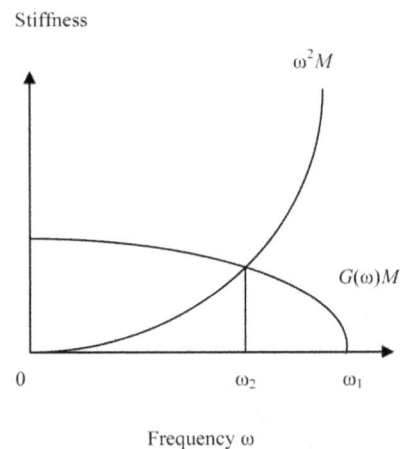

Figure 5.10. Scheme of two parts of the combined stiffness for soil layer on rigid half-space

No matter what was the static stiffness value $G(0)$ and what was structural mass M, two curves in *Fig. 5.10* cross at some frequency ω_2 between zero and ω_1. At this frequency, the combined stiffness $[G(\omega) - \omega^2 M]$ is zero, and we get from (5.17) the "undamped" resonance in the soil-structure system (i.e. the infinite peak of the corresponding transfer function $X(X)$ or $Y(Y)$).

Now let us take more real situation when the structure is flexible and centre of gravity has the non-zero height above the base mat. Let the internal damping in the structure be zero so far. The curve $\omega^2 M(\omega)$ is not a parabola any more, but it will still produce the undamped first resonance at some frequency below the layer frequency ω_1.

Let us make one step further and assume non-zero material damping both in soil and in structure. Now even when the real part of the combined stiffness is zero, there is still some imaginary part, so the first resonance will be damped. However, the frequency of this first resonance will be still below the layer frequency ω_1 (the more lightweight is the structure, the closer is the frequency of this resonance to the layer frequency ω_1). The main conclusion is that this resonance is always damped only by the internal damping (being several percents), so the peaks in the transfer functions are sharp. The physical reason is that in the low frequencies no "running" waves exist. "Wave damping" is switched off for the first resonances.

One more step further is to assume that the underlying half-space is not ideally rigid – even the rock has its finite wave velocities. In fact, we have already seen such a situation in section 5.6 in *Fig. 5.5*. The frequency, where real parts of the horizontal impedances crossed zero level, was then about 3 Hz. Below this frequency the imaginary parts of both horizontal and vertical resonances were small (though non-zero).

Such soil profiles may be called "considerably layered".

The alternative type is "almost homogeneous" soil profiles like that we studied in section 5.7 in *Fig. 5.6*. The real part of the horizontal impedance is almost constant over the frequency. Looking at *Fig. 5.10* we can see that parabola $\omega^2 M(\omega)$ will cross it but the crossing point may be shifted far to the right if the structure is lightweight.

There exist body waves (of Rayleigh and Love types) taking energy from moving base mat even for the low frequencies (without any threshold frequency, as we saw above) and even without the internal damping in the soil. So, every resonance is damped by the "wave damping". In practice both the internal damping and wave damping play role, but the wave damping is more important for the comparatively rigid structures (e.g., like nuclear structures).

Moreover, for the lightweight and low-frequency structures real resonance may "disappear". If we look at the dynamic inertia $M(\omega)$ in CAM (5.15) or (5.16) and compare it to the rigid mass M we see that dynamic inertia may be greater at low frequencies, but at high frequencies it is always less. So, in fact even a product $\omega^2 M(\omega)$ may be limited. It may happen so, that the curve $\omega^2 M(\omega)$ will never cross the curve $G(\omega)$ so, we will never see the real soil-structure resonances. But usually, for the low-frequency structures, the first resonances are caused by the structural (and not by the soil) flexibility. We will see it in Chapter 6.

In practice soil profiles are not the extreme cases; usually they are somewhere in between two extreme cases discussed above. But looking at the impedance curves one can indeed conclude whether soil layering is considerable in each particular case. Sometimes the answer can be obtained through the Fourier analysis of the microseismic motions (in response to transport, wind, etc). If the soil is considerably layered there can be seen that special frequency in the microseismic motions caused by different reasons.

Usually, colleagues ask about the depth we should look for the sharp layer boundaries. The answer is as follows. Having a particular structure and particular surface soil layers (more or less homogeneous) we can estimate the first frequency of this structure on homogeneous half-space with corresponding properties. Taking half of the first frequency we can estimate the wavelength in the soil corresponding to this half-frequency. A quarter of this wavelength gives a thickness of the layer having this very frequency as "critical" one. If there is no sharp boundary up to this depth, the soil profile may be treated as "almost homogeneous" – even the appearance of the boundary at the greater depth will not spoil the wave damping around the resonances.

5.8.2. Role of the embedment

Let us substitute (5.26) and (5.27) into (5.17). For the combined dynamic stiffness in the left-hand part of (5.17) we get

$$G(\omega) - \omega^2 M(\omega) = R^T D_s R - \omega^2 [M(\omega) - R^T M_e R] \qquad (5.29)$$

As we see, for the embedded structure the mass of the outcropped soil is subtracted from the mass of the structure. In some cases, the difference may be comparatively small (i.e. the mass of the structure substitutes the excavated soil). If we consider deeply embedded rigid structure with inertia matrix equal to that of the outcropped soil the difference is zero, and (5.17) is simply

$$[R^T D_s R] U_b = R^T D_s U_i. \qquad (5.30)$$

It means that RU_b is somewhat close to the U_i. In fact, the motion of the rigid embedded structure is a "rigid average" of the initial wave field U_i. This is a typical kinematical interaction. That is why specialists often say that for the surface structures inertial interaction plays the main role as compared to the kinematical interaction (as we saw in Section 4.2.1, in the simplest case kinematical interaction is absent). For the underground structures, as we see here, the opposite situation takes place: kinematical interaction prevails.

As usual, most often the situation is somewhere in between these extreme cases. We will see the example in Chapter 7.

Chapter 6. APPLICATION OF CAM

In this chapter, we will discuss two examples of the CAM application to the SSI analysis using Rigid Base Assumption.

6.1. Stiff structure

The first example refers to the NPP reactor building. The design of this particular block including both soil part and structure was later significantly changed, so at the moment the analysis presented in this section does not correspond to any particular building. However, the methodology used is valid; the author hopes that this will give a flavor of practical CAM implementation.

6.1.1. Site response analysis

Site response analysis (SRA) literally speaking is not a part of CAM, but it is the initial stage of the SSI analysis, as mentioned in Chapter 1. It starts from the soil profile # 0, i.e. the initial soil profile where field survey was carried out. However, seismologists prefer to give seismic excitation for the top of the soil profile with certain V_{s30}, i.e. with shear wave velocities V_s averaged over the upper 30 m of the profile. Actual soil profile #0 has different V_{s30} from that used by seismologists to give the initial seismic motion. That is why the first step is to cut the upper part or to add the upper part to the initial soil profile # 0 in order to get the required level of V_{s30} for the new soil profile # 1. A simple way to do this is as follows. If the required value is $V_{s30} = 1138$ m/s, then the time to cross these 30 m will be

$$t_{30} = H / V_s = 30 / 1138 = 0.026362 \ s. \quad (6.1)$$

In the multi-layered package this time will be the sum of times necessary to cross each layer:

$$t_{30} = \sum_i h_i / V_{si}. \quad (6.2)$$

In our case all the initial layers have similar thickness equal to 2 m. As a result, 16 layers will participate in summation (6.2): upper incomplete layer, 14 complete layers and lower incomplete layer. Total thickness of the 2 incomplete layers is equal to 2 m. The important conclusion is that t_{30} in (6.2) is a function of the TOG (top of grade) level of profile # 1, and it varies linearly between special points corresponding to the TOG falling into the border of each physical layer. Thus, after calculating t_{30} in these special points we can then use simple linear interpolation to find the desired TOG level of profile # 1, where t_{30} has the prescribed value (6.1).

Now let us discuss the lower boundary of the soil model. Let us find the layer where V_s crosses the value of 2000 m/s for the first time. Below this level we assume the homogeneous half-space with the same properties as in the lowest layer.

As a result, we now have the soil profile # 1, i.e. the soil profile where the initial seismic excitation was given by seismologists at TOG. It is shown in *Table 6.1* with low-strain properties.

Table 6.1

Soil Model of Profile #1 for low strains

Number of layer	Upper level, m	Layer thickness, m	Density, t/m^3	V_s, m/s	V_p, m/s	Soil type
1	3.220	0.503	2.42	560	1670	8
2	2.7	2	2.42	630	1840	8
3	0.7	2	2.42	710	2130	8
4	-1.3	2	2.42	760	2290	8
5	-3.3	2	2.42	860	2520	8
6	-5.3	2	2.42	1060	3090	8
7	-7.3	2	2.55	1180	3360	10
8	-9.3	2	2.55	1330	3590	10
9	-11.3	2	2.55	1420	3720	10
10	-13.3	2	2.55	1540	3900	10
11	-15.3	2	2.55	1690	4130	11
12	-17.3	2	2.55	1720	4170	11
13	-19.3	2	2.55	1730	4180	11
14	-21.3	2	2.55	1730	4170	11
15	-23.3	2	2.55	1720	4100	11
16	-25.3	2	2.55	1700	3960	11
17	-27.3	2	2.55	1700	3950	11
18	-29.3	2	2.55	1690	3920	11
19	-31.3	2	2.55	1610	3820	11
20	-33.3	2	2.55	1620	3820	11
21	-35.3	11.0	2.55	1620	3820	12
22	-46.3	11.0	2.55	1720	2950	12
23	-57.3	11.0	2.55	1870	3100	12
24	-68.3	11.7	2.55	1930	3700	12
26	-80	11	2.59	2280	4100	12
Half-space	-91	-	2.59	2280	4100	12

Now let us perform SHAKE calculations. Site response analysis (SRA) by SHAKE will give us the effective parameters of the soil layers accounting for the shear strains corresponding to the actual seismic excitation, as described in Chapter 1. This approximate method to account for the non-linear effects by means of equivalent linear iterations requires the so-called "degradation curves" – this is the second part of the input data. These curves are different for different soil types. Soil types for our profile are shown in the last column of the *Table 6.1*. In the *Table 6.2* there are comments about the four soil types used.

Table 6.2
Soil types used in the soil models

Soil type	Description
8	Gravel, gravel soil
10	Rock, depth 6 – 16 m from the surface
11	Rock, depth 16 – 37 m from the surface
12	Rock, depth 37 – 76 m from the surface

Degradation curves for these four soil types, got from the colleagues, are shown in *Fig. 6.1*.

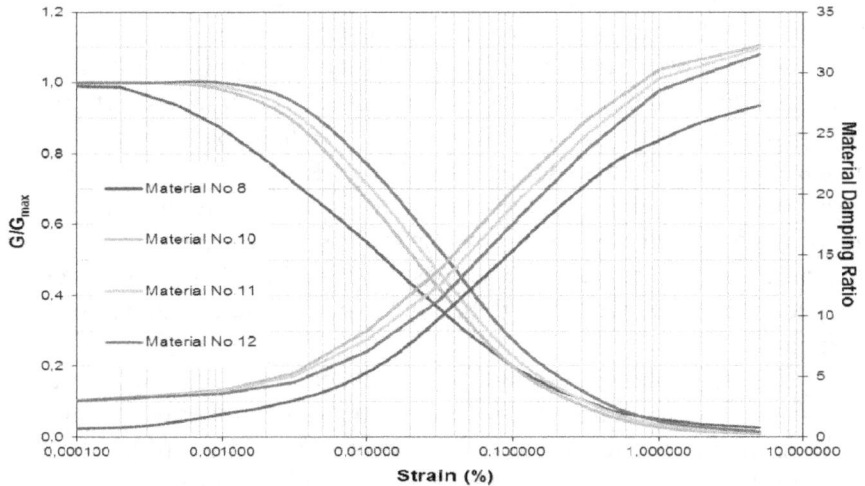

Figure 6.1. Degradation curves for different soil types

We see that all three rock types (materials 10—12) have more or less similar degradation curves, but gravel (soil type 8) is different.

Stiffness degradation for gravel starts at lower strains as compared to the rock.

SHAKE calculation, as described in Chapter 1, is a sequence of deconvolutions and convolutions. Deconvolution means a recalculation of the initial excitation time history downwards from the free surface of the profile # 1 to the outcropped surface of the underlying half-space. Convolution means a recalculation from the outcropped surface of the same half-space upwards to the free surface of profile # 2 (i.e. to the base level). Outcrop is a "virtual" procedure; nobody outcrops the half-space physically. It is just a math way to preserve the same seismic excitation (physically coming upwards) from the first soil profile to the second soil profile. It was discussed in details in Chapter 1.

Profile # 2 for one and the same structure, as mentioned above, may be different depending on the future soil-structure model. One can either consider the real embedment or not. We will model our building as a surface structure. It is conservative in our case and allowed by Standard ASCE4-98, as the ratio of the embedment (8.5 m) to the equivalent radius of the basement (40 m) is less than 0.3. Thus, profile #2 is similar to the profile #1 described in the *Table 6.1*, but without the upper layers above the base (in our case +1.0 m). So, our structure has a layer of gravel 8.3 m thick under the base (soil type 8) with V_s varying from 710 m/s to 1060 m/s. This will cause the important consequences.

As described in Chapter 1, deconvolution is performed twice. For the first run, a half-space with initial low-strain properties (from the *Table 6.1*) is used. For the second run, the half-space properties are manually changed to match the recalculated properties of the deepest layer obtained in the first deconvolution. The reason is that in SHAKE there is no degradation in the half-space. As a consequence, there may appear a contrast between the deepest layer and the half-space after the degradation in the layer, though before the degradation there was no such a contrast.

It may be shown that all the recalculated properties of the layers in the second deconvolution will stay the same as in the first deconvolution, in spite of the changes in the half-space properties. As a result, one can perform the second deconvolution linearly (i.e. without iterations) using the properties of the layers obtained in the first deconvolution after the degradation (i.e. after the iterations). Note that in the deconvolution procedure there is an additional averaging step between two vertical planes (as two horizontal time-histories are slightly different, the soil properties after the degradation are also slightly different in two vertical planes, so the averaging is performed). The half-space properties should be taken similar to the averaged properties of the deepest layer after the degradation. Then this second deconvolution may be combined in a single SHAKE run with the further convolution.

Convolution is performed three times. The first convolution is performed with profile # 2 (i.e. profile # 1 without upper layers above +1.0 m) as described earlier. For the second convolution, the additional very stiff layer is placed at the top of the profile # 2. Dead load from this additional layer is equal to the average dead load from the future structure. Mass of the structure is 344080 t; the area of the base is $83 \times 77 = 6391$ m^2. The same dead load is from the upper additional layer 10 m thick with a density 5.38382 t/m^3. The goal of this second deconvolution is to estimate the degradation in the upper soil layer right under the base (as in the first deconvolution there was almost no degradation in the upper soil layer due to the vicinity of the free surface). In other words, the second convolution is an attempt to estimate (approximately) the secondary soil nonlinearity in addition to the primary soil nonlinearity considered in the first convolution. Two convolutions result in different soil properties after the degradation in each layer. Note that in each convolution there is an additional averaging between two vertical planes (as previously in deconvolution). For the resulting effective soil model, the shear modules and damping coefficients for each layer of the profile # 2 got from these two convolutions are averaged with weights: 0.3 for the first convolution and 0.7 for the second one. This weighted average soil model will be used for the further calculations. The third convolution is performed using this very soil model – without iterations, just to get the resulting time-histories at the free surface of this model – and foundation input response spectra (FIRS) corresponding to these time-histories.

Now let us look at the results and compare low-strain profile # 0 with soil profile # 1 (after the deconvolution). Then we will compare three soil profiles # 2 (after two convolutions and weighted averaging, as described above).

Shear wave velocities along the depth for low strains in profile # 0 (V_{s0}) and for real strains in profile # 1 (V_{sel}) are shown in *Fig. 6.2*, shear wave velocities in profile # 2 – in *Fig. 6.3*, damping – in *Fig. 6.4*, primary wave velocities – in *Fig. 6.5*.

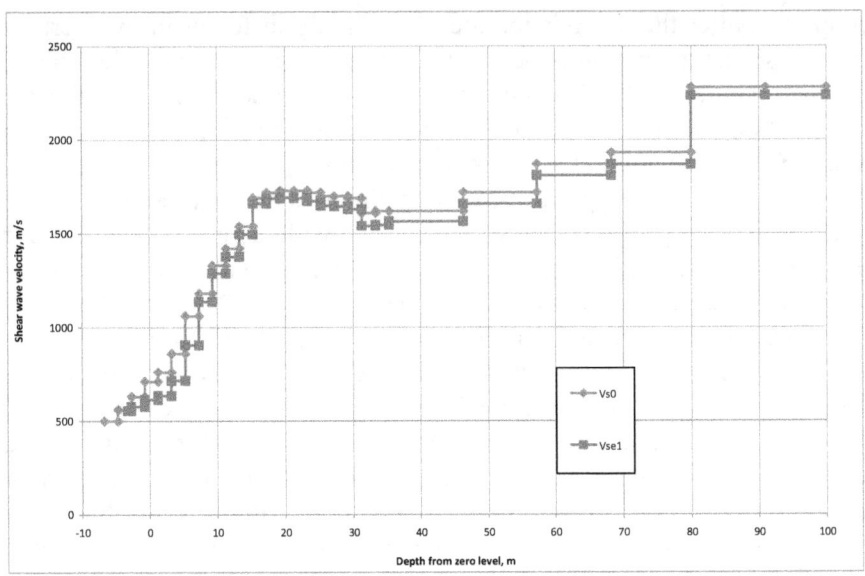

Figure 6.2. Shear wave velocities along the depth for low strains in profile # 0 (V_{s0}) and for real strains in profile # 1 (V_{se1})

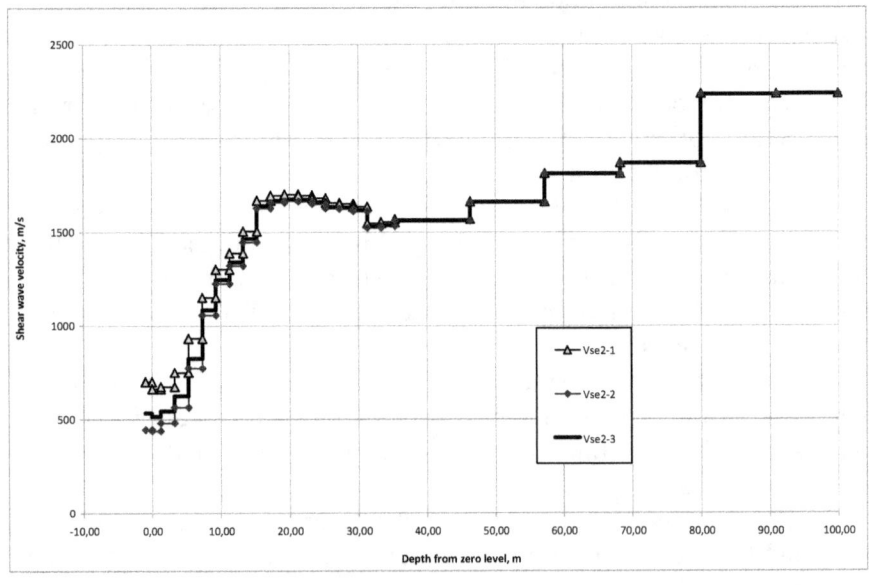

Figure 6.3. Shear wave velocities along the depth for real strains in profile # 2 after two convolutions (V_{se2}-1 and V_{se2}-2) and weighted averaging (V_{se2}-3)

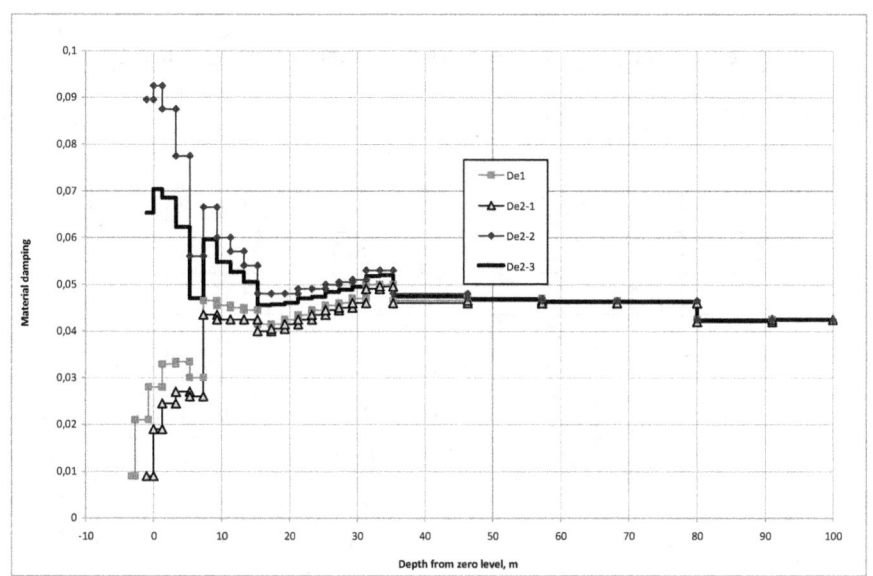

Figure 6.4. Damping coefficients for real strains in profile # 1(D_{e1}) and in profile # 2 after two convolutions (D_{e2}-1 and D_{e2}-2) and averaging (D_{e2}-3)

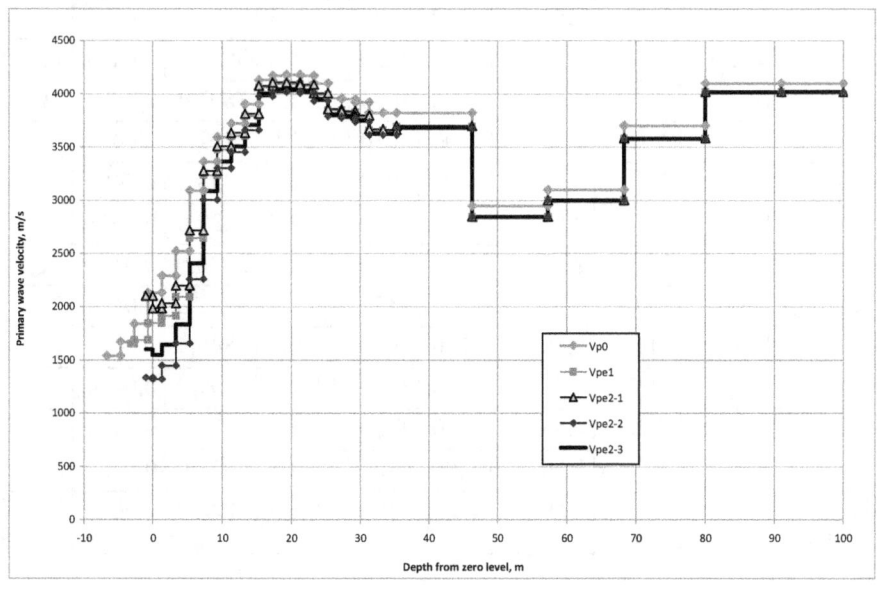

Figure 6.5. Primary wave velocities along the depth

The results for soil profile # 2 are given in *Table 6.3*.

Table 6.3
The resulting parameters of the soil model for "profile # 2"

Layer number	Upper level, m	Thickness, m	Density, t/m^3	V_{s0}, m/s	V_{p0}, m/s	V_s, m/s	V_p, m/s	D	Soil type
1	1.0	1	2.42	710	2130	534.3	1602.8	0.0654	8
2	0.0	1.3	2.42	710	2130	516.1	1548.4	0.0705	8
3	-1.3	2	2.42	760	2290	546.0	1645.3	0.0686	8
4	-3.3	2	2.42	860	2520	626.2	1834.9	0.0624	8
5	-5.3	2	2.42	1060	3090	825.3	2406.0	0.0470	8
6	-7.3	2	2.55	1180	3360	1084.6	3088.3	0.0596	10
7	-9.3	2	2.55	1330	3590	1245.9	3363.1	0.0548	10
8	-11.3	2	2.55	1420	3720	1338.8	3507.3	0.0527	10
9	-13.3	2	2.55	1540	3900	1463.0	3704.9	0.0506	10
10	-15.3	2	2.55	1690	4130	1639.4	4006.3	0.0456	11
11	-17.3	2	2.55	1720	4170	1668.1	4044.1	0.0458	11
12	-19.3	2	2.55	1730	4180	1675.6	4048.5	0.0461	11
13	-21.3	2	2.55	1730	4170	1672.4	4031.2	0.0471	11
14	-23.3	2	2.55	1720	4100	1658.8	3954.1	0.0474	11
15	-25.3	2	2.55	1700	3960	1634.5	3807.4	0.0484	11
16	-27.3	2	2.55	1700	3950	1631.6	3791.1	0.0489	11
17	-29.3	2	2.55	1690	3920	1618.1	3753.3	0.0495	11
18	-31.3	2	2.55	1610	3820	1529.5	3629.0	0.0518	11
19	-33.3	2	2.55	1620	3820	1537.7	3626.0	0.0520	11
20	-35.3	11.0	2.55	1620	3820	1561.4	3681.8	0.0474	12
21	-46.3	11.0	2.55	1720	2950	1659.0	2845.4	0.0469	12
22	-57.3	11.0	2.55	1870	3100	1809.6	2999.8	0.0464	12
23	-68.3	11.7	2.55	1930	3700	1866.1	3577.4	0.0464	12
24	-80	11	2.59	2280	4100	2233.3	4016.0	0.0424	12
Half-space	-91	-	2.59	2280	4100	2235.5	4020.0	0.0425	12

Let us compare the 2%-response spectra of the initial excitation with FIRS obtained after the third convolution. For three directions this comparison is shown in *Figures 6.6–6.8*.

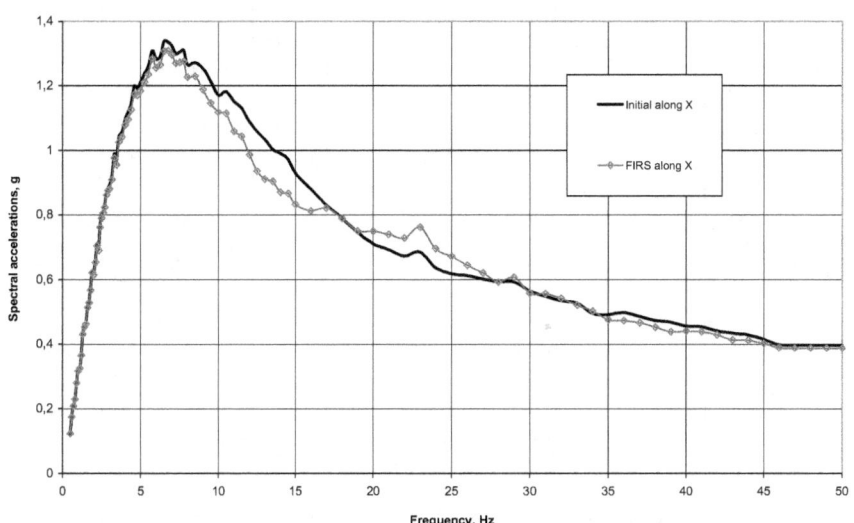

Figure 6.6. Comparison of RS (damping 2%) of the initial excitation and FIRS along X-axis

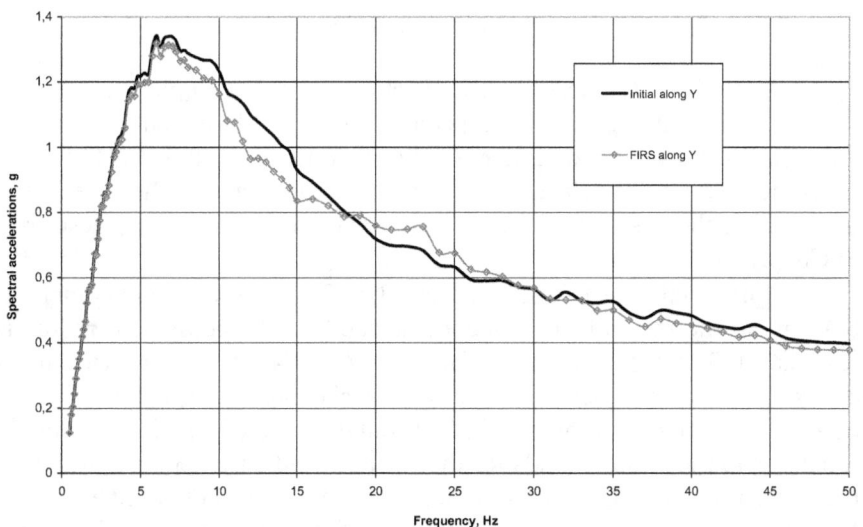

Figure 6.7. Comparison of RS (damping 2%) of the initial excitation and FIRS along Y-axis

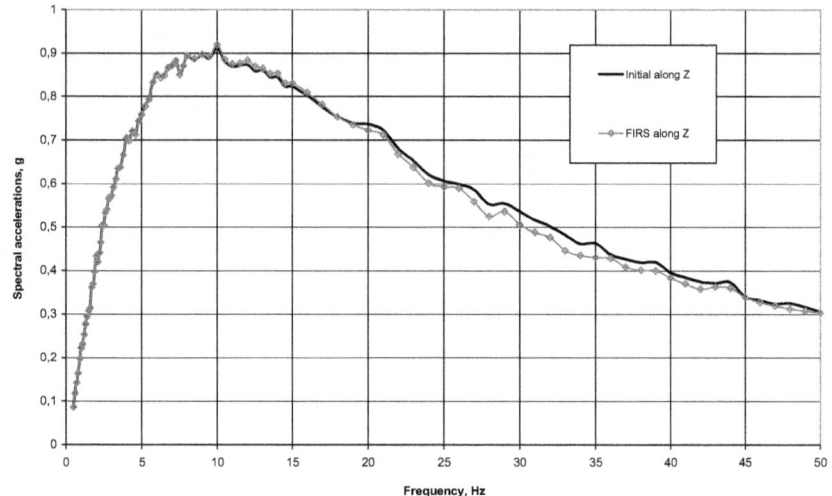

Figure 6.8. Comparison of RS (damping 2%) of the initial excitation and FIRS along Z-axis

We see that FIRS is almost similar to the initial RS. This is due to the small difference in TOG levels for soil profiles # 1 and # 2.

6.1.2. Soil impedances

After the SRA described in Section 6.1.1 is completed, the next stage is the calculation of the impedances for rigid basements resting on the soil profiles obtained earlier. At the same time, the transfer functions from the free field displacements to the forces impacting the fixed rigid base during the passage of the seismic wave are calculated, as described in Chapter 5.

Horizontal size of the base is 83 × 77 m. Actual embedment is 8.45 m, so the ratio of the embedment depth to the equivalent radius is less than 0.3. According to the Standard ASCE4-98, in our case one is allowed to consider our structure as a surface-based structure. For the case of vertical seismic waves in horizontally-layered media the transfer functions to the seismic loads for the surface rigid basement are similar to the corresponding terms of the impedance matrix, as shown in Chapter 4. In other words, the response force from the soil impacting rigid base moving harmonically with a unit amplitude along certain DOF without any seismic wave will be similar to the force impacting this base in case it is fixed, and there is a seismic wave causing unit displacement in the free field along the same DOF. As a result, one has to calculate just a 6 × 6 complex frequency-dependent impedance matrix.

This matrix is calculated using well-known computer code SASSI. The bottom of the base is divided into 20 × 20 = 400 rectangular finite elements with 441 contact nodes. Frequency is varied from about zero up to about 47 Hz; frequency step is about 1 Hz, so the total number of frequencies is 48. We say "about" because in SASSI all frequencies must be proportional to a certain frequency step controlled by the time step of the input time-history (0.004 s in our case) and Fourier number in FFT (8192 in our case).

The resulting impedance matrix due to the symmetry of the base is not fully populated. There are only two non-zero off-diagonal terms in the upper triangle of the symmetrical matrix, namely (1, 5) and (2, 4).

Figure 6.9 shows real and imaginary parts of the translational impedances. These are the first three diagonal terms (out of the total six ones).

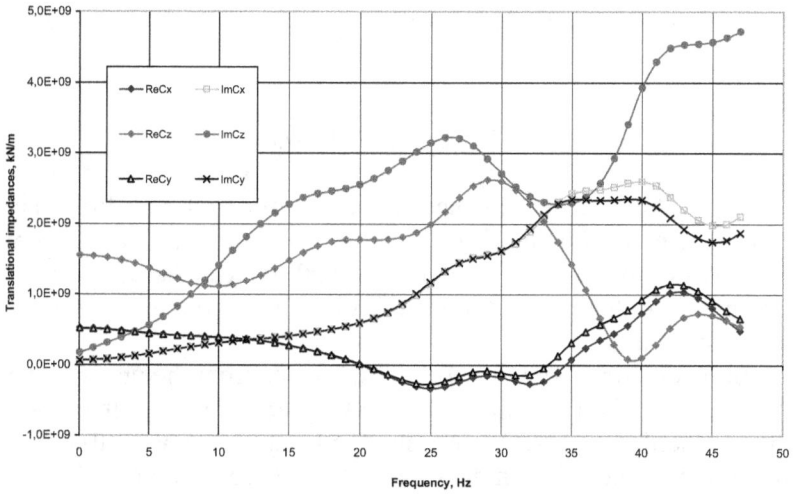

Figure 6.9. Real and imaginary parts of the translational impedances

Figure 6.10 shows real and imaginary parts of the rotational impedances for the same base. These are the last three diagonal terms (of the total six).

We see that both real and imaginary parts are far from straight lines prescribed by ASEC4-98. This is the result of the soil layering. Off-diagonal terms are not shown here (though they are calculated and used), because they are of minor importance for the surface basements.

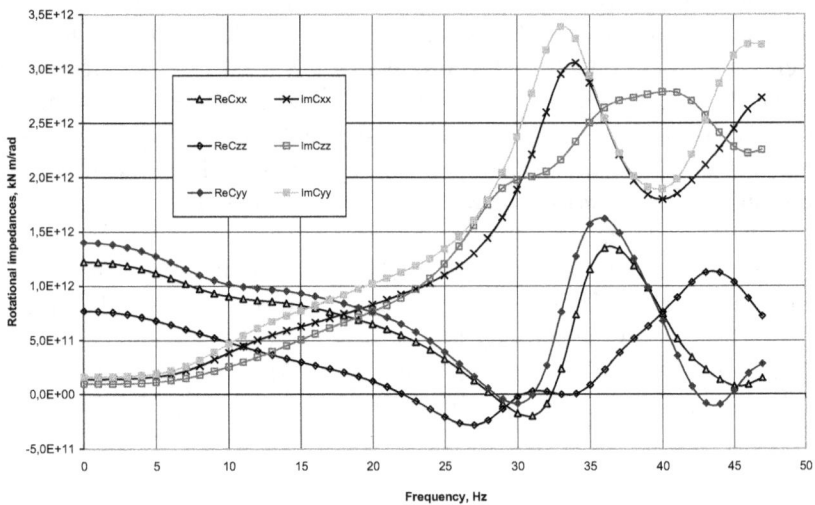

Figure 6.10. Real and imaginary parts of the rotational impedances

6.1.3. Dynamic inertia

Rigid soil-structure contact surface is impacted both from the soil and from the upper structure, as discussed in Chapter 5. Loading from the soil consists of the seismic loads impacting the fixed base, and also of the soil response to the base motion. Both these parts were calculated in the previous section.

In this section, we will consider the loads from the upper structure. They are controlled by the base motion and also by the so-called "dynamic inertia" matrix. As described in Chapter 5, this matrix depends on natural frequencies and modes of the fixed-base structural model.

The number of the fixed-base modes considered here is great: 1297 in the considered frequency range (up to 52.049 Hz). Let us calculate the accumulation of the relative modal mass along with frequency. Six curves (along each DOF) are shown in *Fig. 6.11*.

Note that the asymptotes are not equal 1.0 ; they are less. The reason is that the base itself with its considerable inertia does not participate in the fixed-base modes.

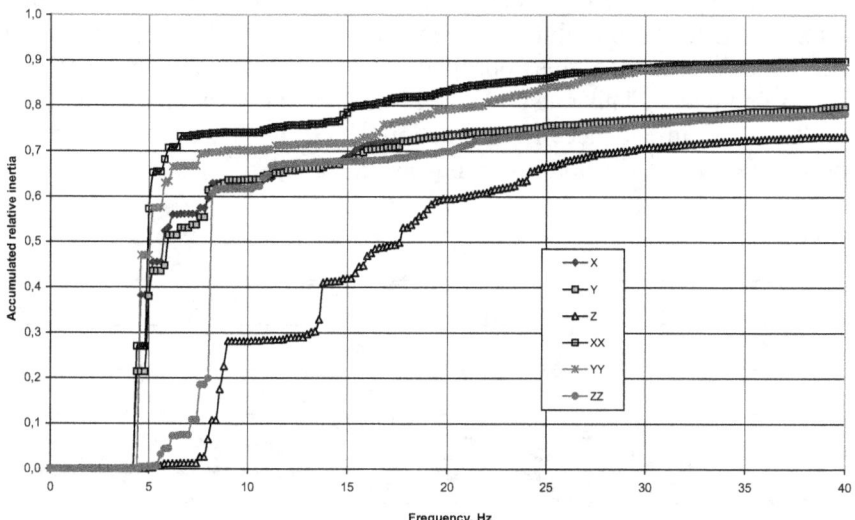

Figure 6.11. Accumulation of relative modal masses along six DOFs

Dynamic inertia is described by complex frequency-dependent matrix 6 × 6:

$$M(\omega) = M_0 + \sum_{j=1}^{2} \frac{\omega^2 S_{j,FB}^T S_{j,FB}}{\Omega_{j,FB}^2 + 2i\lambda_j \Omega_{j,FB}\omega - \omega^2}, \quad (6.3)$$

where M_0 – conventional "rigid" inertia matrix (real matrix 6 × 6); $\Omega_{j,FB}$ – natural frequency number j of the fixed-base structural model; $S_{j,FB}$ – line matrix 1 × 6 consisting of the six participation factors of the mode j along all six DOFs; λ_j – composite modal damping coefficient for the mode j calculated by the general FEM code (ABAQUS in our case) in the process of modal analysis.

For vanishing frequency, this matrix goes to the conventional real inertia matrix. The first three diagonal terms go to the conventional mass.

They (i.e. translational inertia along three axes) are shown in the *Fig. 6.12*.

Note that peaks in the curves correspond to the same frequencies where accumulated modal inertia in *Fig. 6.11* had steep rise.

In the further calculations, this dynamic inertia matrix will be used to calculate the motion of the contact surface.

Note that these results are sensitive to the coordinates – here they were shown in the coordinate system of the structural model created in ABAQUS. In our case, this coordinate center was at the upper surface of the basement slab. This must be taken into account when combining these results with impedance from section 6.1.2 – there the center of coordinates was at the bottom of the basement slab.

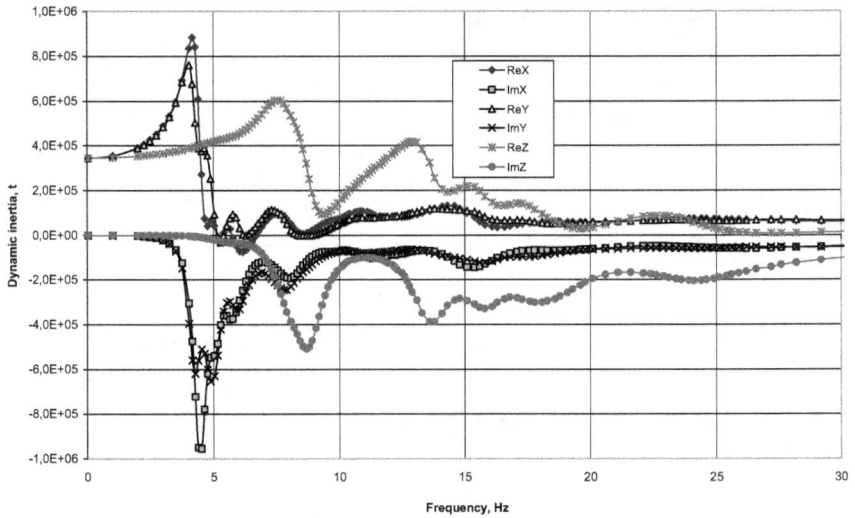

Figure 6.12. The first three diagonal terms of the dynamic inertia matrix

6.1.4. Transfer functions

Equation of motion for rigid contact surface is in fact just an equilibrium equation because this surface is weightless. Two parts of load coming from the soil (i.e. seismic load impacting the fixed base and the soil response to the base motion) are balanced by the load coming from the upper structure (i.e. the product of the dynamic inertia and base acceleration). This equation may be written as follows:

$$[D_{soil}(\omega) - \omega^2 M(\omega)] U(\omega) = D_{soil}(\omega) U_0, \qquad (6.4)$$

where D_{soil} – impedance matrix from section 6.1.2; $M(\omega)$ – dynamic inertia matrix from section 6.1.3.

Note once more that both matrices in (6.4) should be written in the same coordinate system. In our case this is a SASSI coordinate system with the centre at the base bottom. As the dynamic inertia matrix was developed in another coordinate system, it was additionally translated to the common "global" coordinate system similar to that of SASSI model.

As the right-hand part of (6.4) uses the free field motion U_0, the solution of (6.4) enables the calculation of the transfer functions from U_0 to the base motion U. This transfer function matrix is 6 × 3, as three rotational components of U_0 are set zeroes.

Standard ASCE4-98 required the variation in soil stiffness from the "medium" soil up and down certain times. In ASCE4-16 requirements are somewhat different, but we will describe the calculations performed following ASCE4-98. So, we get two additional profiles: "stiff" and "soft" ones. The coefficient of variation depends on the data volume, but should not be less than 1.5. Taking into account great volume of the field investigations, the coefficient of variation was assumed 1.5.

Scaling of the soil shear modules causes the change in impedances. If all stiffness in the system increase a^2 times, but masses and damping stay the same, the dynamic stiffness of the system will be described by a matrix D_1 instead of the initial matrix D_0:

$$D_1(\omega) = a^2 K_0 - \omega^2 M = a^2 \left[K_0 - (\omega/a)^2 M \right] = a^2 D_0(\omega/a). \quad (6.5)$$

"Double scaling" in (6.5) (i.e. scaling in values and scaling in frequency) enables obtaining the impedances for "stiff" and "soft" profiles directly from impedances for "medium" soil profile without the repetition of the SASSI calculations. However, in (6.4) these new impedance matrices will be combined with the same structural dynamic inertia matrix, so the resulting transfer functions will not be scaled.

Figure 6.13 shows the comparison of the absolute values of the transfer functions $X(X)$ for three different soils ("scaled" profiles).

Similar comparisons for the transfer functions $Y(Y)$ and $Z(Z)$ are shown in *Figures 6.14* and *6.15*.

We see that the first resonances are sensible to the soil properties: they are shifted in frequency when soil stiffness is scaled. In the corresponding response, soil deformation plays significant role. However, the higher resonances are not shifted – in the corresponding responses deformation of the building is more important than the deformation of the soil.

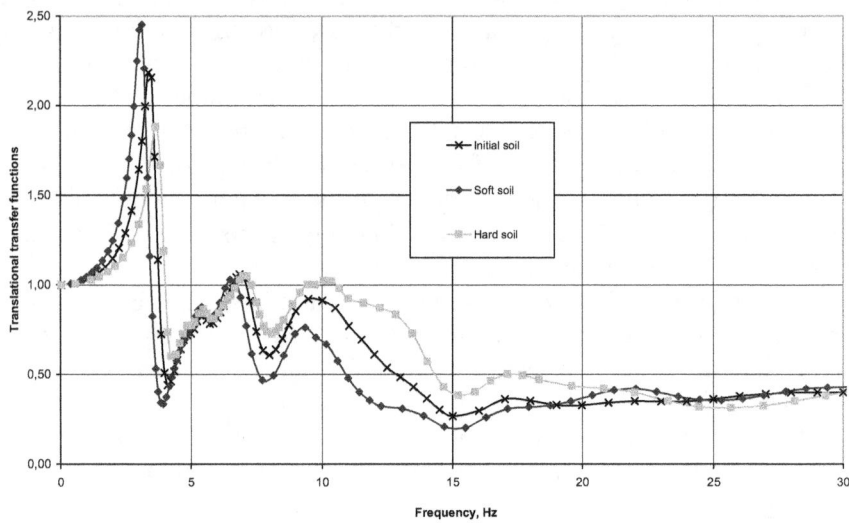

Figure 6.13. The comparison of the absolute values of the transfer functions X(X) for three different soils ("scaled" profiles)

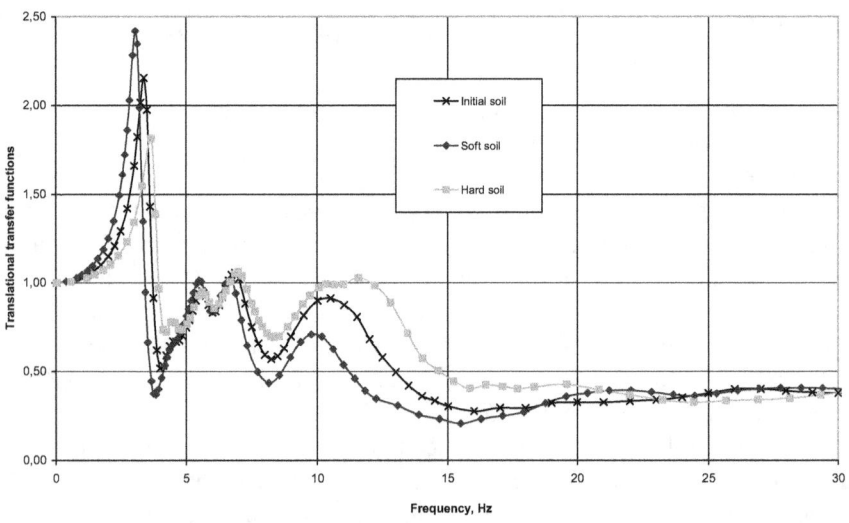

Figure 6.14. The comparison of the absolute values of the transfer functions Y(Y) for three different soils ("scaled" profiles)

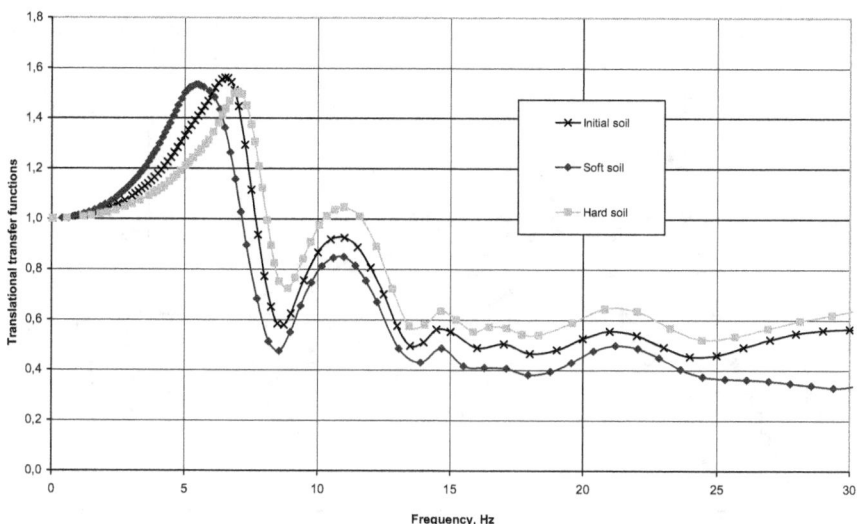

Figure 6.15. The comparison of the absolute values of the transfer functions Z(Z) for three different soils ("scaled" profiles)

6.1.5. Response spectra

After the transfer functions are obtained, one can calculate the six-component acceleration time-histories for the rigid base response. There are three ones (for three scaled soil profiles). Time-histories are calculated in the center of the basement slab bottom. For each component of each time-history the response spectrum (RS) is calculated (with 2% damping in oscillators).

Figures 6.16–6.18 show the comparison the RS along X, Y and Z for three scaled profiles. In addition to these three RS one more RS is shown – this is FIRS (i.e. RS at the free surface of the profile # 2), calculated in Section 6.1.1. It is denoted as Soil. Each RS is marked by a letter (M – initial medium soil; S – soft soil; H – hard soil). Spectral accelerations are given in SI unit system (i.e. in m/s^2) unlike section 6.1.1.

Figures 6.19–6.21 show the comparison the rotational RS around X, Y and Z axes for three scaled profiles.

Let us summarize the key features of the seismic response of the structure under consideration.

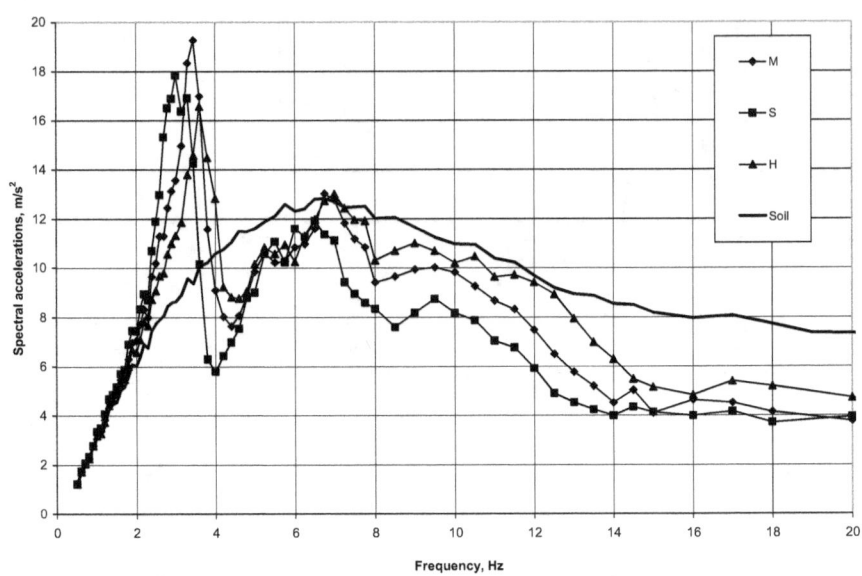

Figure 6.16. The comparison of the RS along X for three scaled profiles

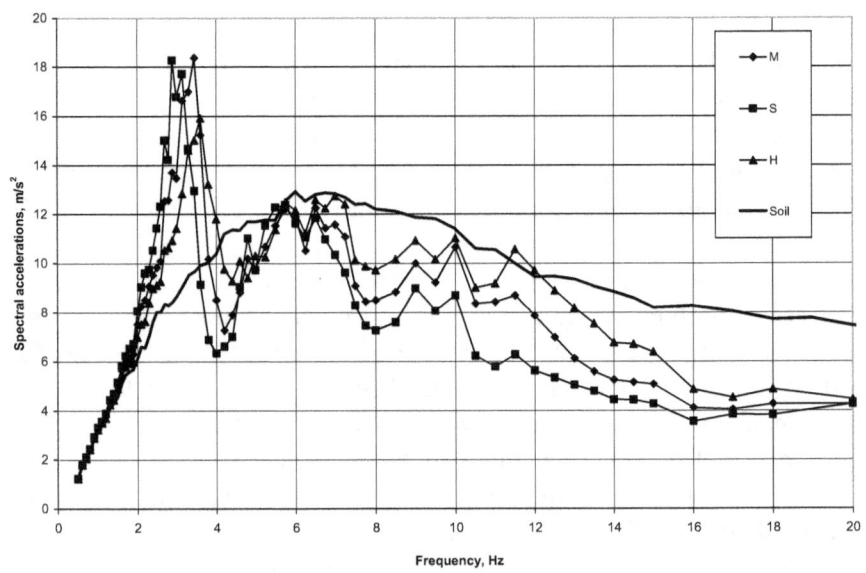

Figure 6.17. The comparison of the RS along Y for three scaled profiles

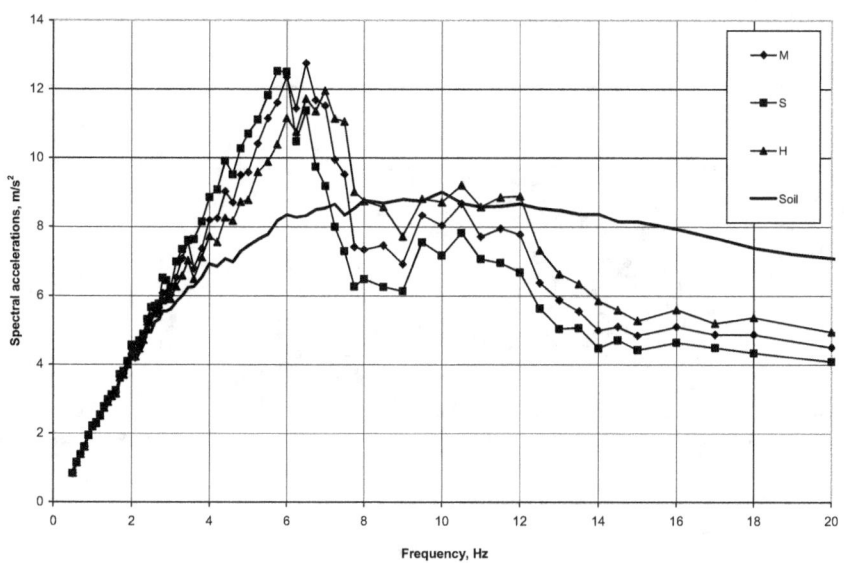

Figure 6.18. The comparison of the RS along Z for three scaled profiles

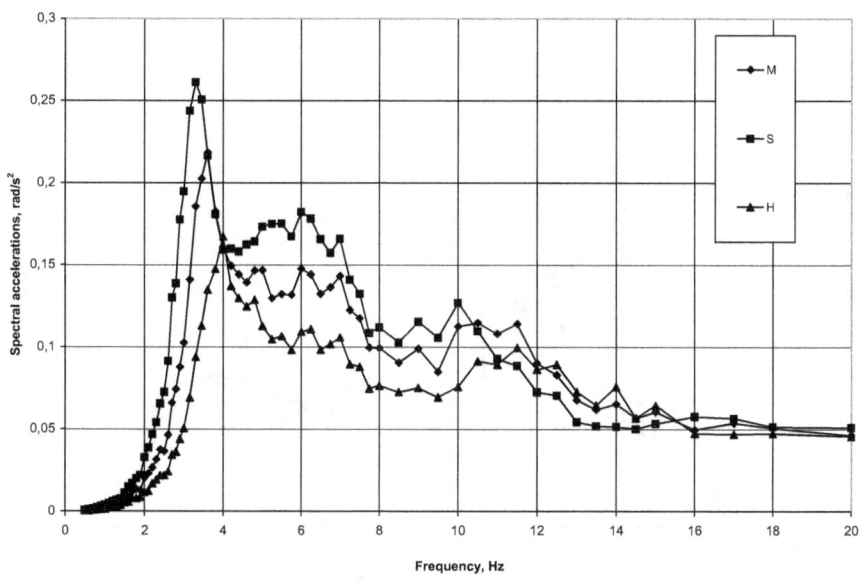

Figure 6.19. The comparison of the RS around X-axis for three scaled profiles

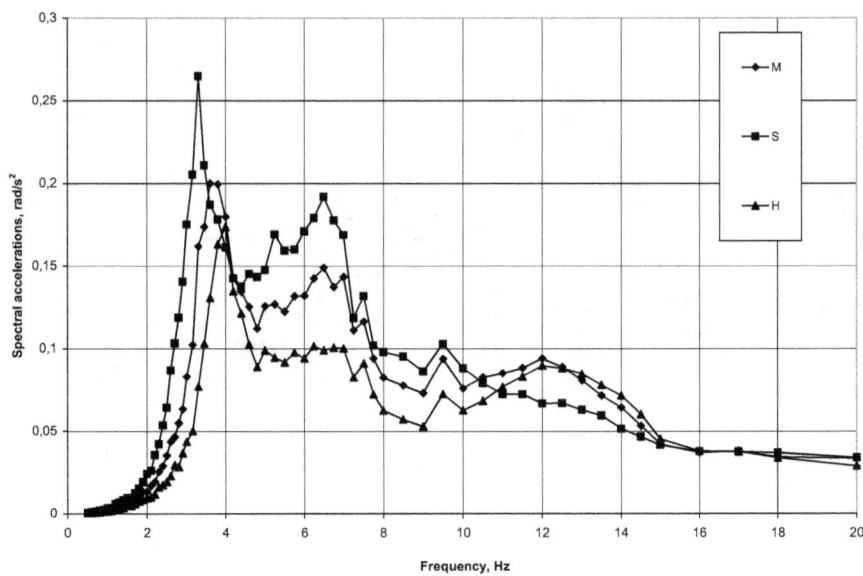

Figure 6.20. The comparison of the RS around Y-axis for three scaled profiles

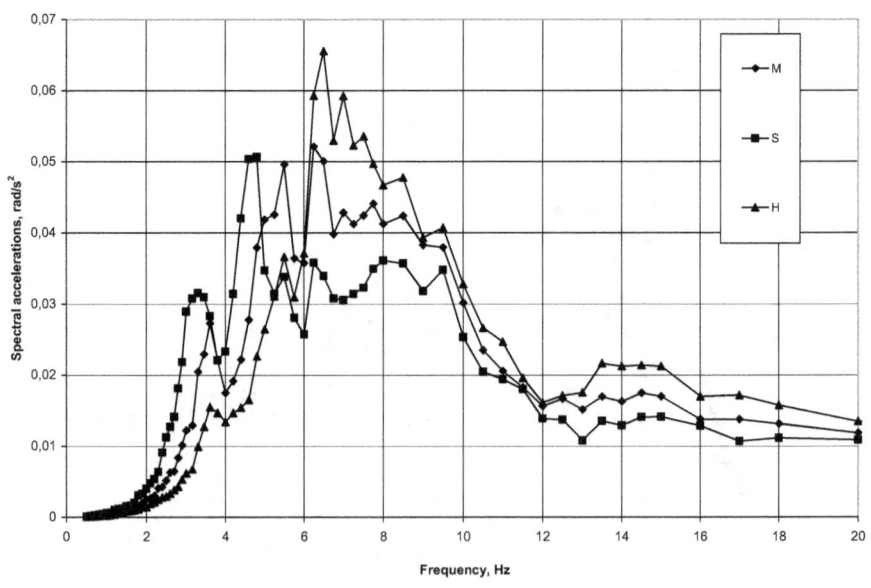

Figure 6.21. The comparison of the RS around Z-axis for three scaled profiles

The dominant frequencies of the fixed-base structure are comparable to the peak frequencies of the broad-band seismic excitation. Soil flexibility shifts dominant frequencies of the response to the lower frequencies as compared to the fixed-base frequencies. We see on *Fig. 6.16–6.18* that translational RS at the base for very low frequencies are similar to those of the excitation, then exceed excitation, and then fall below the excitation RS. Rocking RS have the same peak frequencies as horizontal RS in the same vertical plane.

6.2. High-rise building

Some time ago colleagues asked the author to apply CAM to the SSI analysis of the high-rise building. In this section, the author describes this case and compares it to the case described in the previous section.

6.2.1. Model description

The office building under consideration has 76 floors. It is 327 m high. The basement slab is 4 m thick and has a horizontal size 40 × 40 meters. All floors have the same horizontal size. Mass of the structure is 224804.6 t. Gravity center height is 144 m above the basement slab.

Fixed-base structural model was created by Victor Michailov in SCAD Office and then converted and analyzed in ABAQUS. The total number of nodes in the model was 214887; total number of DOFs – 1289322. The total number of finite elements made 245759. The first frequencies of the fixed-base model proved to be around 0.1 Hz. 7500 first modes were calculated; spectrum proved to be dense, and corresponding 7500 natural frequencies stood below 25.6 Hz.

Model is shown in *Fig. 6.22*.
The soil is modelled by homogeneous half-space with mass density 2.0 t/m³, shear wave velocity $Vs = 400$ m/s, primary wave velocity $V_p = 1300$ m/s and material soil damping 4%.

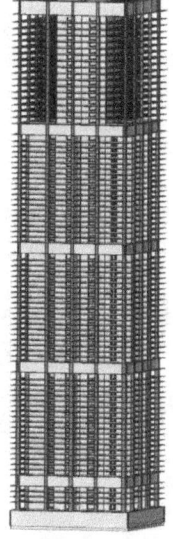

*Figure 6.22.
Model of the high-rise building under consideration*

Surely, this is a very simplified model: in the real world such a building has considerable underground part and pile foundation. But the goal here was to find the differences in seismic response between comparatively stiff structure described in the previous section and this low-frequency building.

6.2.2. Soil impedances

Soil impedances were calculated by SASSI. As shown above in Chapter 5, for the homogeneous half-space and surface rigid base mat, horizontal impedances are almost similar to the results of analytical calculations using well-known formulae from ASCE4. However, for the vertical impedances this is not so, and for rotational impedances the situation is also different. That is why SASSI results seem to be the best in this case.

Translational impedances are shown in *Fig. 6.23*. Two horizontal impedances are similar, as the mat has a quadratic shape. These are the first three diagonal terms of the impedance matrix.

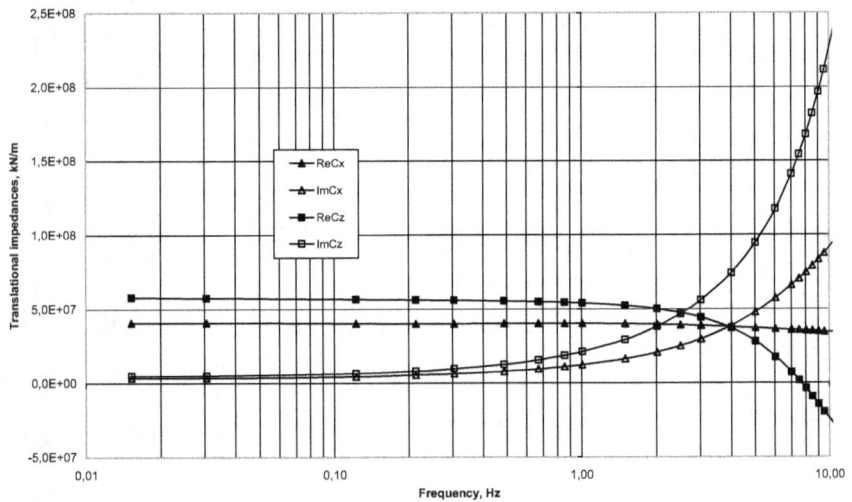

Figure 6.23. Horizontal and vertical translational impedances

Rotational impedances are shown in *Fig. 6.24*. Two rocking impedances are similar, as the mat has quadratic shape. These are the last three diagonal terms of the impedance matrix.

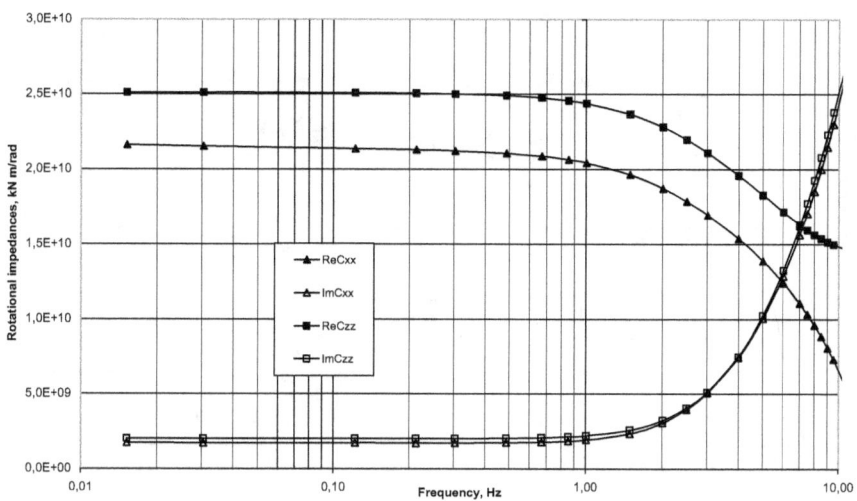

Figure 6.24. Rocking and torsional impedances

6.2.3. Dynamic inertia

Figure 6.25 shows the accumulation of relative modal masses along six DOFs for the fixed-base structural model shown in *Fig. 6.22*. XX and YY curves are almost similar; X and Y curves are slightly different. We see that rocking curves XX and YY practically come to 1.0. However, four other curves come to somewhat less value. This is because of the base mat, which does not participate in any fixed-base mode, though participates in total inertia (in the denominator for the relative modal mass).

The volume of the base mat makes $40 \times 40 \times 4 = 6400$ m^3. With the mass density of the concrete 2.75 t/m^3 it makes the mass of the base mat 17600 t, which is 7.83% of the total mass. As a consequence, even the full total number of the fixed-base modes can provide relative accumulated mass not more than $100 - 7.83 = 92.17\%$. At the frequency 25.6 Hz we already see along X and Y correspondingly 90.7 and 90.8%. The fastest accumulation occurs along rocking DOFs XX and YY; the slowest – along vertical direction Z. *Figure 6.26* shows dynamic inertia along vertical direction Z.

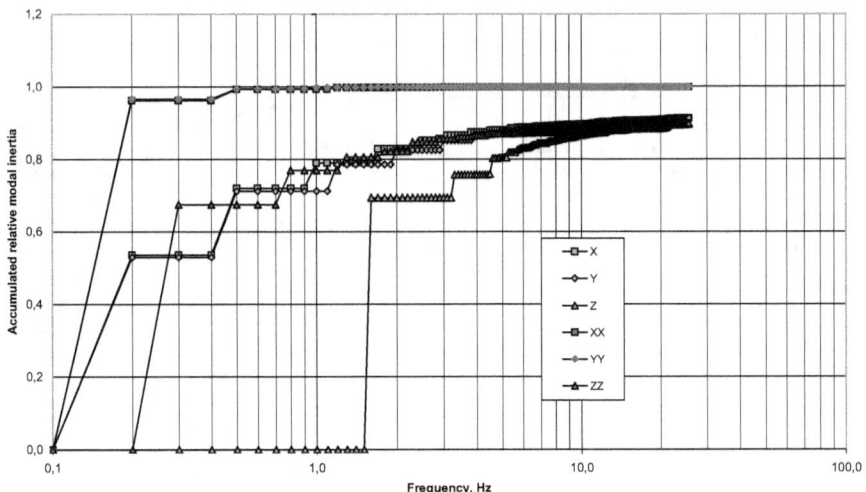

Figure 6.25. Accumulation of modal masses along 6 DOFs

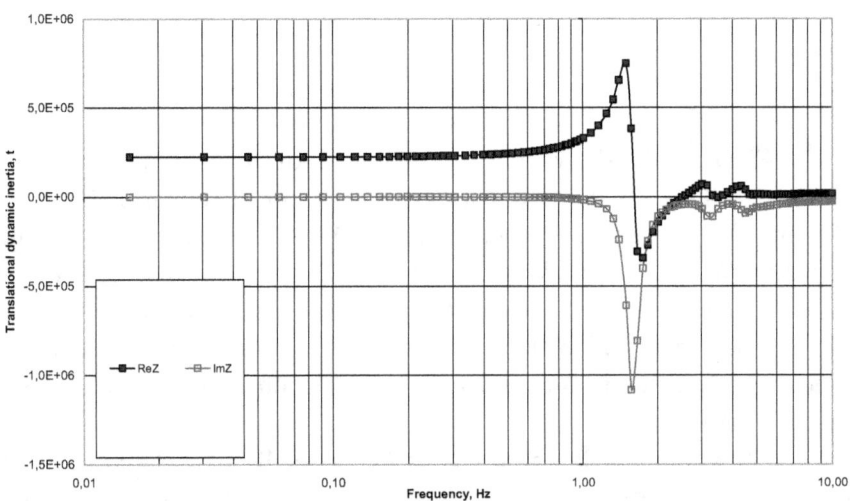

Figure 6.26. Dynamic inertia along the vertical Z axis

Comparing *Fig. 6.26* to *Fig. 6.12*, we see conventional behavior. For the very low frequencies complex dynamic inertia is almost real and close to the conventional mass. Natural frequencies are less for the high-rise building: we see the first peak at about 1.5 Hz (see also Z-curve in *Fig. 6.25*), then at 3.3 and 4.5 Hz there appear two next resonances, though of smaller amplitudes. After each resonance real part becomes smaller.

Figure 6.27 shows dynamic masses along two horizontal axes (they are almost similar). General picture looks very much the same, though natural frequencies are considerably less.

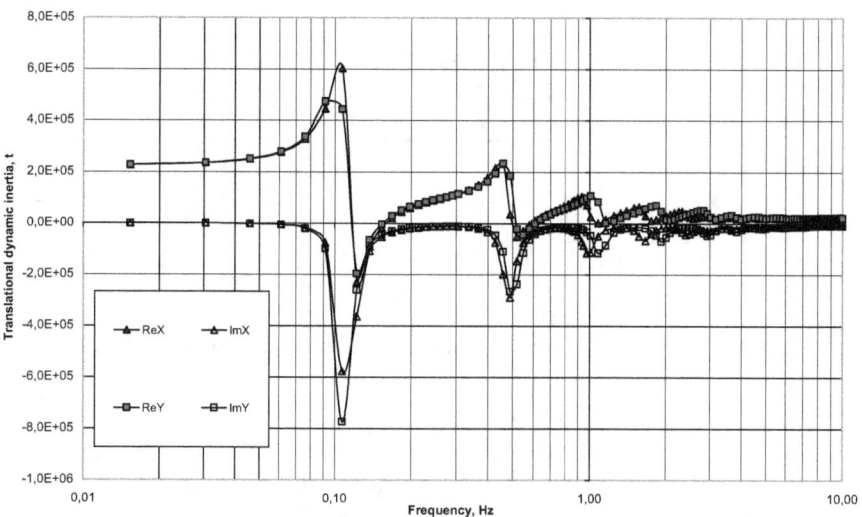

Figure 6.27. Dynamic inertia along horizontal X- and Y axes

By the way, such small natural frequencies cause some computational problems. In Fast Fourier Transform (FFT) transfer functions are calculated in *N* frequencies with a frequency step

$$\Delta f = (N \times \Delta t)^{-1}. \qquad (6.6)$$

In the present computer programs, *N* is maximum 8192. With conventional time step 0.004 s formula (6.6) gives frequency step 0.0305 Hz. This is more than enough for a detailed description of the conventional resonances like we saw in *Fig. 6.12*, but in *Fig. 6.27* this frequency step is too great to describe the first peaks at very low natural frequencies. That is why the author had to increase the time step two times – from 0.004 to 0.008 s, making a total duration 65.536 s. As the actual time-history has less duration, it was continued by zeroes.

Figure 6.28 shows rocking dynamic masses. As we see, the second resonances at 0.45 Hz are very small – the first resonances dominate. This is in line with *Fig. 6.25*.

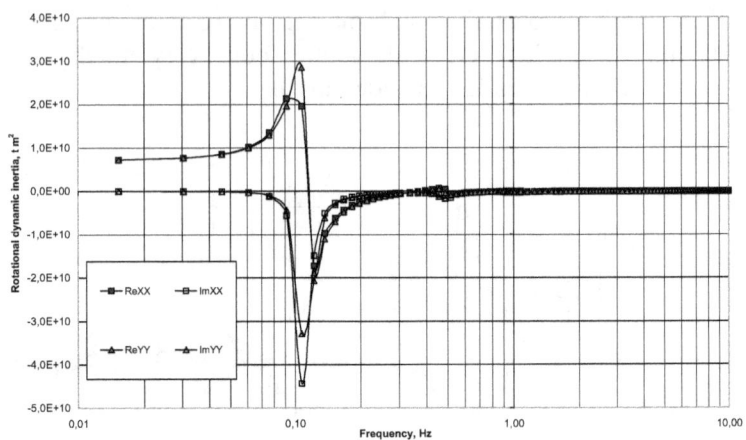

Figure 6.28. Dynamic rocking inertia around horizontal X- and Y axes

6.2.4. Transfer functions

The next step of CAM is to calculate the transfer functions from the free-field motion to the response motion of the rigid base. Following the same procedure, as described above, we get the transfer functions $X(X)$ and $YY(X)$ shown in *Figures 6.29* and *6.30*. Absolute values of the complex transfer functions are calculated for three soil cases (soil modules for the additional profiles were scaled 1.5 times up and down from those for the initial profile). In the second vertical plane (i.e. *OYZ*) the picture is the same.

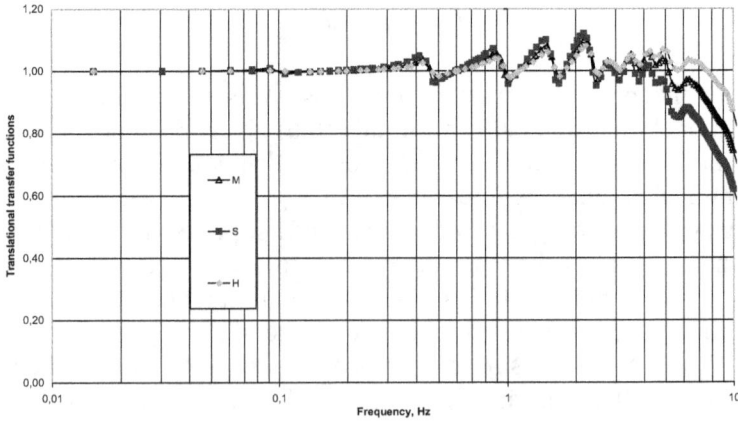

Figure 6.29. Absolute values of the transfer functions X(X) for three soil profiles

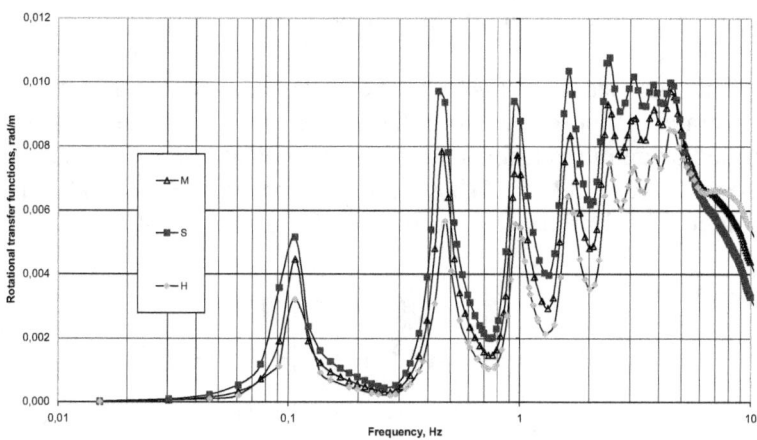

Figure 6.30. Absolute values of the transfer functions YY(X) for three soil profiles

We see that the amplitudes are increasing for the first five resonances with the increase of the natural frequencies. The most important resonance is the fifth one at about 2.4 Hz. Above the frequency 7 Hz the transfer functions in *Fig. 6.29* and *6.30* show no resonances – they become smooth. This is completely different from what we saw in *Fig. 6.13* and *6.14*.

However, if we look at the transfer functions in vertical direction $Z(Z)$ shown in *Fig. 6.31*, we see the traditional picture with dominant first resonance.

This principal difference in behaviour will be discussed below.

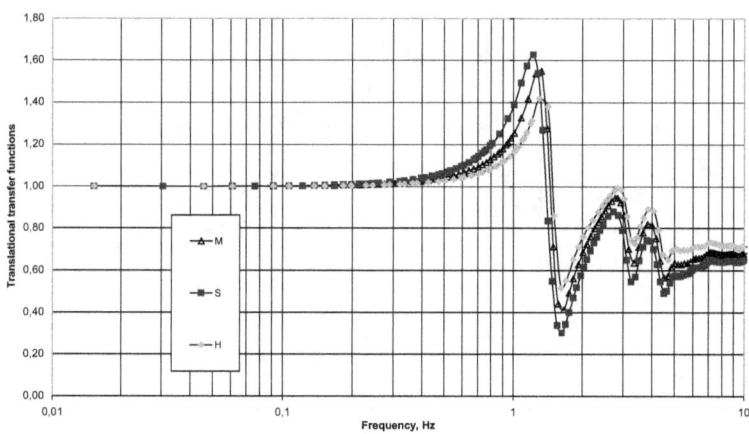

Figure 6.31. Absolute values of the transfer functions Z(Z) for three soil profiles

6.2.5. Response spectra

The next stage of CAM is the calculation of the response time-histories (and response spectra) in the center of the base mat. This stage is performed using the transfer functions described above and excitation time histories. *Figures 6.32–6.34* show response spectra (RS) with 7% damping along three axes for three soil profiles and RS for the free-field motion.

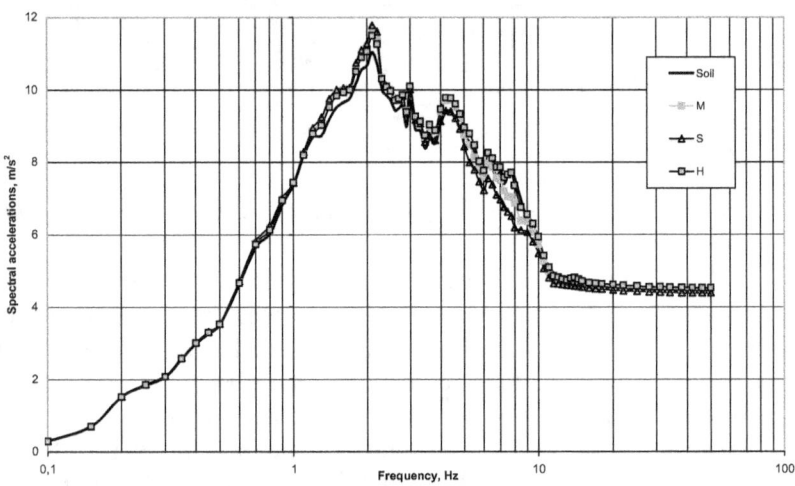

Figure 6.32. Response spectra with 7% damping along X

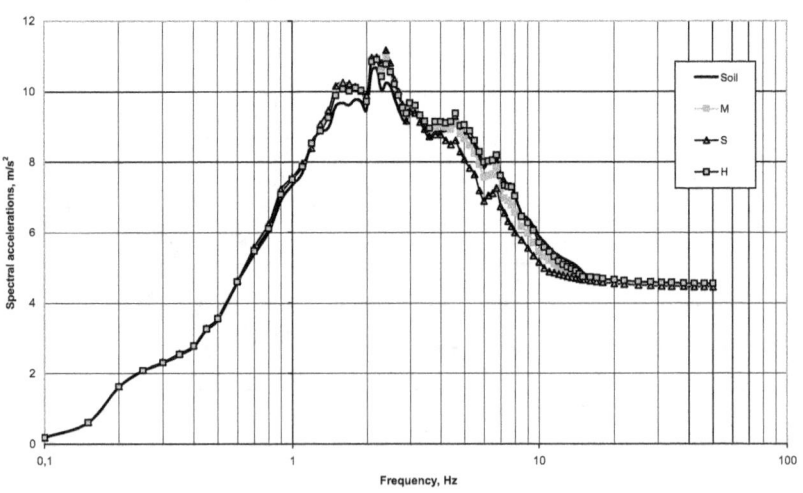

Figure 6.33. Response spectra with 7% damping along Y

Response spectra in the centre of the base mat in *Figures 6.32* and *6.33* are very close to the response spectra of the free-field motion. If not for vertical direction and rocking, one could conclude that SSI is of minor importance for the case considered.

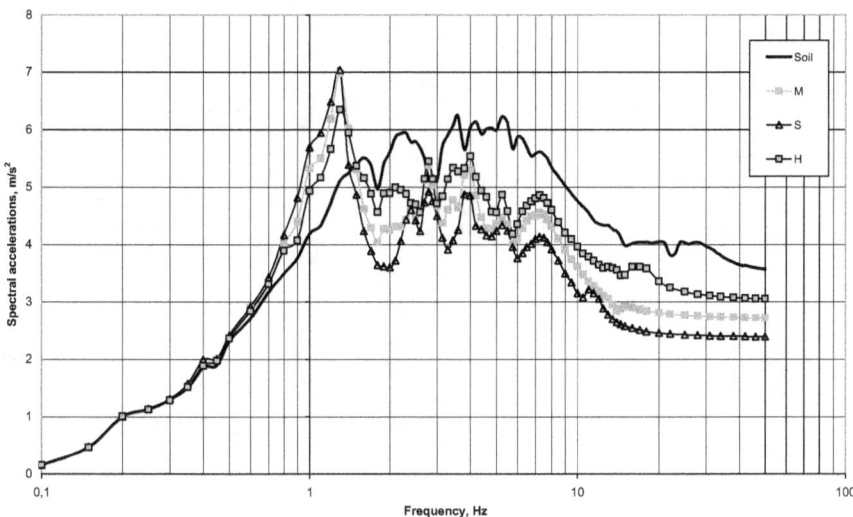

Figure 6.34. Response spectra with 7% damping along Z

In vertical direction we see in *Fig. 6.34* the picture very much like *Fig. 6.18*. At the very low frequencies all three RS at the base are practically similar to the free-field RS. Then we see the first resonance: RS at the base exceed the free-field RS. After the first resonance RS at the base go below the free-field RS.

Figures 6.35–6.37 show rocking and torsion of the rigid base around three axes for three soil profiles – RS with 7% damping.

Rotational RS cannot be compared to the free-field RS, as there no rocking or torsion at the surface of the soil in the free-field. However, to estimate the role of rotational response, one can multiply rotational accelerations by the half-size of the base mat (40/2 = 20 m) to get the contribution of the rotational response to the translational response at the edges and then compare the result to the translational accelerations we had before. For instance, at the frequency 2 Hz rocking around X-axis gives angular acceleration 0.1 rad/s^2, which makes vertical acceleration 2.0 m/s^2 at the edge of the base. Looking at *Fig. 6.34* we see that at 2 Hz this is a considerable contribution to the vertical response.

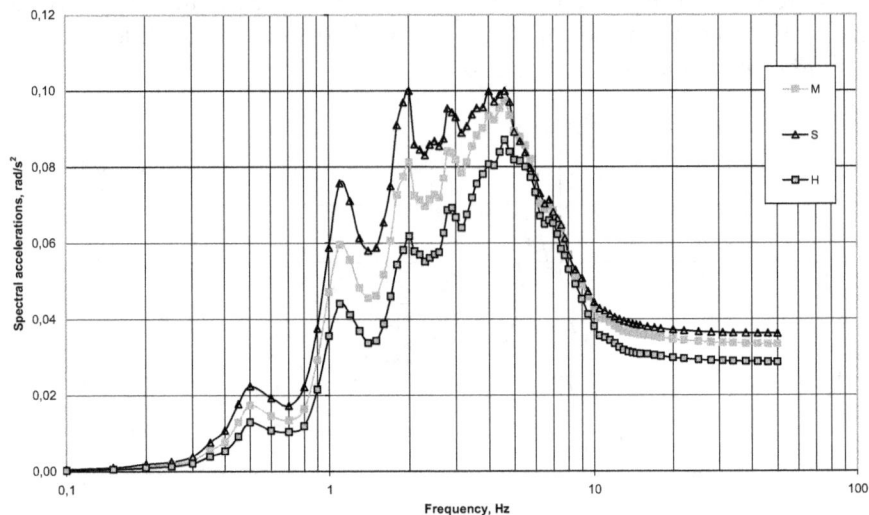

Figure 6.35. Response spectra with 7% damping around X

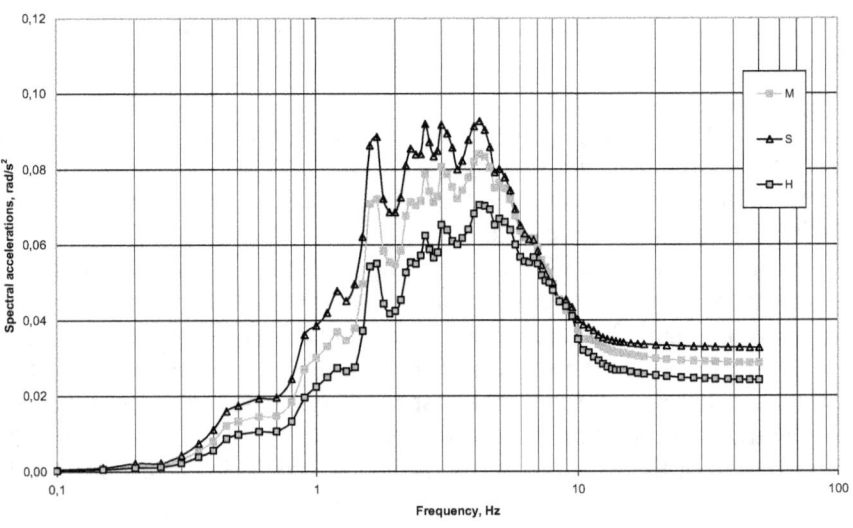

Figure 6.36. Response spectra with 7% damping around Y

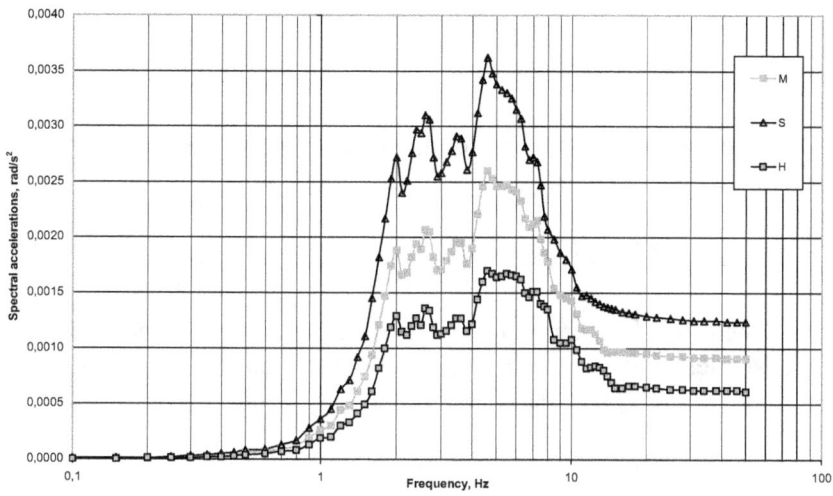

Figure 6.37. Response spectra with 7% damping around Z

On the contrary, the torsional response in *Fig. 6.37* is small.

So, the first conclusion is that the impact of SSI is different along different DOFs: minor along horizontal axes and around Z-axis; considerable along Z-axis and around X- and Y-axes.

6.2.6. The criterion for the SSI importance

Let us look at this situation from the point of view of criterion for the SSI importance set up in ASCE4. The authors of ASCE4 suggest obtaining natural frequencies of the two systems. The first system is the fixed-base model of the structure. In CAM it is analyzed anyhow; we performed this analysis and discussed the results in Section 6.2.3. The first natural frequencies for sway-rocking modes are 0.109 and 0.111 Hz; the first natural frequency of the vertical mode is 1.587 Hz.

The second system is the same model taking rigid and placed at the surface of homogeneous half-space. Practically instead of the half-space this model is placed on the soil springs described in the ASCE4. Let us calculate the first natural frequencies for this case, taking the medium soil with wave velocities V_p = 1300 and V_s = 400 m/s. First, we can calculate the Poisson's ratio v from

$$\frac{V_p^2}{V_s^2} = \frac{2-2\nu}{1-2\nu}. \tag{6.7}$$

It makes $\nu = 0.4477$, which is quite reasonable for saturated soils. Shear modulus is

$$G = \rho V_s^2 = 2\times(400)^2 = 0,32\times10^6 \text{ kPa}. \tag{6.8}$$

Then we will apply formulae for soil springs from ASCE4-98. Dimensionless coefficients for quadratic base mat ($B = L = 40$ m) are $\beta_x = 1.01$; $\beta_z = 2.17$; $\beta_\psi = 0.52$. Horizontal stiffness is

$$k_x = 2(1+\nu)\, G\beta_x \sqrt{BL} = 37,43\times10^6 \text{ kN/m}. \tag{6.9}$$

We can compare this value to the value of static stiffness calculated by SASSI: it was there 40.86E6 kN/m.
Vertical stiffness is

$$k_z = \frac{G}{(1-\nu)}\beta_z\sqrt{BL} = 50,29\times10^6 \text{ kN/m}. \tag{6.10}$$

We can compare this value to the value of static stiffness calculated by SASSI: it was there 57.9E6 kN/m.
Rocking stiffness is

$$k_\psi = \frac{G}{1-\nu}\beta_\psi BL^2 = 1.9282\times10^{10} \text{ kN}\times\text{m}. \tag{6.11}$$

We can compare this value to the value of static stiffness calculated by SASSI: it was there 2.16E10 kN m.
All three stiffness values calculated using ASCE4 formulae are somewhat less than SASSI static stiffness. But the difference is not dramatic. Besides, one should keep in mind that ASCE4 tries to estimate not static but effective stiffness, which is somewhat less than the static one.
Now let us estimate natural frequencies of rigid structure resting on these springs. The first will be vertical mode. Total mass of the structure is 0.2248E6 t; so

$$f_z = \frac{1}{2\pi}\sqrt{\frac{k_z}{m}} = 2.38 \text{ Hz.} \qquad (6.12)$$

ASCE4 suggests the comparison of this frequency to the dominant frequency of the fixed-base model. Along Z-axis it is 1.587 Hz. If the "rigid structure" frequency is two times (or more) higher than the "fixed-base" frequency, the SSI effects are considered insignificant. In our case we have ratio $2.38/1.587 = 1.5 < 2$. According to the ASCE4 criterion, the SSI effects cannot be neglected. And this is true – as we saw in Fig. 6.34, the difference between the free-field RS and RS at the base is really significant.

Now let us turn to the sway-rocking modes. First, we will estimate the so-called "partial" (or "uncoupled") natural frequencies. For the horizontal direction we can use (6.12) just changing vertical stiffness for the horizontal one:

$$f_x = \frac{1}{2\pi}\sqrt{\frac{k_x}{m}} = 2.05 \text{ Hz.} \qquad (6.13)$$

For the uncoupled rocking we can use a similar formula, but the inertia is described by rocking inertia moment given by ABAQUS in the process of modal analysis of the fixed-base model. In our case it is 6.9832E9 t m². So, we have

$$f_{yy} = \frac{1}{2\pi}\sqrt{\frac{k_\psi}{I_{yy}}} = 0.2644 \text{ } Hz. \qquad (6.14)$$

As we see, the uncoupled horizontal frequency (6.13) is more or less conventional (as compared to the nuclear building considered above), but rocking uncoupled frequency (6.14) is far less and quite unusual.

But this was a simplified approach neglecting the coupling between horizontal and rocking responses. There is no such coupling in the ASCE4 formulae for soil stiffness; however, there is such coupling in the inertia matrix. A non-diagonal element of this matrix coupling horizontal and rocking inertia is $M_{x,yy} = H_c\, m$, where m is total mass, and H_c is a height of the mass centre above the base mat. In our case it is 146.58 m. The first "coupled" natural frequency of sway-rocking mode should be obtained from the bi-quadratic equation

$$\det \begin{bmatrix} k_x - \omega^2 m & -\omega^2 M_{x,yy} \\ -\omega^2 M_{x,yy} & k_\psi - \omega^2 I_{yy} \end{bmatrix} = 0. \qquad (6.15)$$

Calculations give the first "coupled" frequency 0.26295 Hz. It is a bit less than (6.14) – the least one of the two "partial" frequencies. This is in line with general theory. Note that the first coupled frequency (0.26295 Hz) is very close to the "partial" rocking frequency (0.2644 Hz), but "partial" horizontal frequency (2.05 Hz) is eight times higher. It means that in the first coupled mode of the "rigid" structure on soil springs the rocking response will be manifested more than the horizontal motion of the base.

Let us return to the criterion of the SSI importance and compare our first "coupled" frequency to that of the fixed-base model in the same vertical plane: 0.26295/0.11179 = 2.352 > 2. According to the ASCE4 criterion, SSI effects are not significant for a sway-rocking response. This is in line with *Fig. 6.32* and *Fig. 6.33*. However, the difference with the threshold value is not so great (ratio is 2.35 versus 2.0); the threshold value 2.0 itself is empirical. That is why rocking in our case should not be fully neglected.

Let us provide the additional results, comparing maximal acceleration at the base with free-field accelerations. This comparison is shown in *Table 6.4*.

Table 6.4
Comparison of maximal accelerations

Soil variant	X	Y	Z	XX	YY	ZZ
Initial	4.4672	4.4764	2.7123	0.33152E-1	0.28545E-1	0.90462E-3
Soft	4.3615	4.4306	2.3787	0.35942E-1	0.32532E-1	0.12283E-2
Hard	4.5110	4.5362	3.0297	0.28479E-1	0.24027E-1	0.61282E-3
Rigid (free-field)	4.4136	4.5192	3.4364	0	0	0

We see that in terms of accelerations the rigid soil case (i.e. structural analysis without SSI) proved to be non-conservative almost everywhere (except vertical direction). However, the scale of non-conservatism is small.

One more comparison is about maximal integral forces under rigid base mat. It is shown in *Table 6.5*.

We see that in terms of forces the rigid soil case (i.e. structural analysis without SSI) proved to be conservative almost everywhere (with the exception of vertical force for hard soil). One more comment here: we see that the difference between soil cases is far greater in horizontal forces than horizontal accelerations. It is due to the rocking not visible at the base level in terms of horizontal accelerations, though impacting integral horizontal forces under the base.

Table 6.5
Comparison of maximal integral forces

Soil variant	X	Y	Z	XX	YY	ZZ
Initial	0.20713E6	0.24391E6	0.78674E6	0.10259E8	0.10500E8	0.68797E5
Soft	0.20232E6	0.23229E6	0.74783E6	0.91761E7	0.99954E7	0.66400E5
Hard	0.22761E6	0.25129E6	0.85553E6	0.10978E8	0.11307E8	0.70847E5
Rigid (free-field)	0.27400E6	0.26882E6	0.84750E6	0.11914E8	0.12147E8	0.72057E5

The conclusion about the ASCE4 criterion from this case is that it is reasonable, but should be applied separately for sway-rocking modes in two vertical planes and for the vertical modes. The results (in terms of the importance of the SSI effects) may be different in these separate cases. If in our case we simply compare lower frequencies (without attributing them to the modes), we make a conclusion about the insignificance of the SSI effects. This will be an error because we miss considerable SSI effect in a vertical direction.

The author should like to give additional comments to the ASCE4 criterion. In this criterion we see dynamic inertia of the structure (both conventional rigid inertia and flexibility described by the fixed-base frequencies and modes) and flexibility of the soil. In other words, only "inertial" SSI is considered. In practice we estimate how much is the difference between actual response motion of the base on one hand, and the response of the weightless base on the other hand. But there exists also "kinematical" SSI – it estimates how much is the difference between the response motion of the weightless rigid base and the free-field motion. In our case it does not matter – for vertical seismic waves in horizontally layered soil and for surface rigid base mat "kinematical" interaction is not manifested at all (see Chapter 4). This is in line with a simplified approach of the ASCE4 authors – they use soil stiffness for the surface rigid stamp. However, in the real world, nobody would erect such a building on soft soils without the underground part and piles. What can we say about the ASCE4 criterion in this case?

Fixed-base frequencies and modes will not change as compared to the previous case. However, soil stiffness (after accounting for the embedment and piles) will increase considerably. It means that in horizontal-sway directions (and probably in the vertical direction as well) the ASCE4 criterion will give the negative answer about the significance if the SSI effects. But in fact, this will be only the part of the answer – i.e. the answer only about the "inertial" interaction. In other words, it means that after we put in place piles and embedded basement, the further construction of the upper structure will not change the seismic response of the base. However, the second part of the answer is as follows: after we put in place piles and embedded basement (before the further construction), we already considerably changed the seismic response as compared to the free field – due to the piles and embedment, and not due to the inertia of this part. This is the "kinematical" interaction, not discussed in the ASCE4 criterion.

In other words, we come to the general conclusion that in case of rigid base mat the fixed-base seismic analysis is applicable in all cases, but the key question is about the excitation we put at this base (or alternatively use for the inertial loads). Three different situations may be listed. First, we can take this excitation directly from the free-field "control" motion – this is the conventional seismic fixed-base analysis without SSI still applicable in many cases for surface light structures on medium and hard soils. Second, we can calculate the seismic response of the underground part (including piles and embedded basement) without the upper structure. After that we will put this six-component response (different from the initial three-component free-field excitation due to the "kinematical" SSI) to the fixed base of the upper structure, neglecting the inertial SSI. It seems that for high-rise building considered above this approach may give reasonable results. Finally, the third situation (typical for the nuclear structures) is that both inertial SSI and kinematical SSI are important. Then the full version of CAM shall be used.

6.2.7. Specific of the low-frequency building in SSI

Let us comment on several other differences between the behaviour of the high-rise building and the behaviour of the conventional nuclear structure.

The first peculiarity is a strange behaviour of the transfer functions: in *Fig. 6.29* we see almost no peak at the first frequency 0.1 Hz for $X(X)$, though in terms of dynamic inertia this mode is dominating (see. *Fig. 6.27*). This is completely different from the behaviour of the transfer function $Z(Z)$ in *Fig. 6.31* and all transfer functions in Section 6.1 for the nuclear structure.

The explanation can be found in the calculations presented above in (6.13–6.15). In fact, the participation of the certain DOF in the first mode is controlled by the real part of the difference $K_j - \omega^2 M_j(\omega)$, where index j could be x, or yy, or z. For the horizontal direction ($j = x$) soil stiffness K_x is equal to the total mass M multiplied by ω^2 at the frequency $f_x = 2.05$ Hz (6.13); so, at the frequency about 0.1 Hz soil stiffness K_x is far greater than $\omega^2 M$ (about 400 times). Surely, $\omega^2 M_j(\omega)$ at the frequency 0.1 Hz is also greater than $\omega^2 M$ due to the peak of $M(\omega)$ in *Fig. 6.27*, but this peak is only about three times greater than the static value. As a result, the real part of the difference $K_x - \omega^2 M_x(\omega)$ stays far from zero at the frequency of 0.1 Hz – so, we do not see the peak at 0.1 Hz in *Fig. 6.29*.

Similar logic can be applied to the rocking DOF yy. For this direction ($j = yy$) soil stiffness $K_{yy} = k_\psi$ is equal to the total inertia moment I_{yy} multiplied by ω^2 at the frequency $f_{yy} = 0.26$ Hz (6.14); so at the frequency about 0.1 Hz soil stiffness K_{yy} is greater than $\omega^2 I_{yy}$ about 7 times. Due to the peak in *Fig. 6.27*, $\omega^2 I_{yy}(\omega)$ at the frequency 0.1 Hz is also greater than $\omega^2 I_{yy}$, and this peak is about four times greater than the static value. As a result, the real part of the difference $K_{yy} - \omega^2 I_{yy}(\omega)$ is closer to zero and causes a peak at the frequency of 0.1 Hz in *Fig. 6.30*.

The general conclusion is that the first sway-rocking modes in terms of the base motion are more rocking than swaying for the high-rise building. For typical nuclear structure (Section 6.1) we see the opposite picture: usually at the first frequency horizontal base motion prevails over the rocking one.

The second difference in behaviour between high-rise and nuclear buildings is in the forces presented in *Table 6.5*. We see that maximal horizontal integral forces are considerably less than the vertical one, though maximal horizontal base accelerations in *Table 6.4* are greater than the vertical one. This effect has nothing to do with SSI: we see it also in the last lines of the tables, where there was no SSI in analysis at all.

The explanation here is in dynamic inertia. As discussed in Chapter 5, in the frequency domain the integral forces under the base $F(\omega)$ are the product of base accelerations $A(\omega)$ and dynamic inertia matrix $M(\omega)$:

$$F(\omega) = M(\omega)\, A(\omega). \tag{6.16}$$

So, in fact, dynamic inertia describes the transfer functions from the base accelerations to the integral forces under the base. Let us rewrite formula from Chapter 5 showing the contribution of "rigid" inertia M_0 and fixed-base modes:

$$M(\omega) = M_0 + \sum_{j=1}^{n} \frac{\omega^2}{\Omega_j^2 - \omega^2 + 2i\omega\Omega_j\gamma_j} S_j^T S_j. \tag{6.17}$$

Here Ω_j – natural frequency number j; γ_j – modal damping for this mode; S_j – a line of six participation factors for this mode (after the normalization by masses); n – total number of the modes accounted for; i – imaginary unit. Let us look at the dimensionless coefficient in the sum. When current frequency ω is far greater than natural frequency Ω_j, this coefficient tends to minus one. It means that matrix $S_j^T S_j$, modelling modal inertia corresponding to the mode number j, is subtracted from the "rigid" inertia matrix M_0. Physically it means that relative motions along this mode are in counter-phase with "rigid" motions along with the base.

It can be put in other words. Conventional "rigid" inertia matrix itself can be presented as a sum of "rigid" inertia matrix M_b, corresponding to the rigid base mat without the upper structure, and the sum of the modal inertia matrices representing the upper structure – the same as in (6.17):

$$M_0 = M_b + \sum_{j=1}^{N} S_j^T S_j. \tag{6.18}$$

Assuming the full set of N modes to be present, we can substitute (6.18) into (6.17) and get

$$M(\omega) = M_b + \sum_{j=1}^{N} \frac{\Omega_j^2 + 2i\Omega_j\omega\gamma_j}{\Omega_j^2 - \omega^2 + 2i\omega\Omega_j\gamma_j} S_j^T S_j. \tag{6.19}$$

Once more let us look at the dimensionless coefficient in the sum. When current frequency ω is zero, this coefficient is equal unity, and we go to (6.17) and (6.18). When current frequency ω is far greater than natural frequency Ω_j, this coefficient tends to zero: at high frequencies the upper structure "disappears" from the dynamic inertia – mode by mode.

Along with the increase in the frequency ω each mode j comes through a certain evolution. It starts from the plain participation in the total mass at $\omega = 0$. Then up to $\omega = \Omega_j$ the contribution of this mode increases from unity up to approximately $(1 + 4\gamma_j^2)^{1/2}/(2\gamma_j)$. This value for 7% damping is about 7.21 and does not depend on j. For the frequencies ω above the frequency Ω_j the contribution of this mode falls down. For instance, for our first mode with natural frequency $\Omega_1 = 0.11$ Hz this coefficient at the frequency 2 Hz is

$$\frac{\Omega_j^2 + 2i\Omega_j \omega \gamma_j}{\Omega_j^2 - \omega^2 + 2i\Omega_j \omega \gamma_j} = \frac{0,0121 + 0,0308i}{-3,9879 + 0,0308i}. \quad (6.20)$$

The absolute value of (6.20) is about 0.008 – a significant drop from 7.21!

Now let us return to (6.16). Each of the two terms in the right-hand part has its peaks. For small frequencies ω the accelerations $A(\omega)$ are small. At the frequencies ω of the most intensive horizontal response (about 2 Hz, as shown in *Fig. 6.32* and *Fig. 6.33*) all lower modes "have gone" taking away their considerable modal inertia (see *Fig. 6.25*). As a result, the contribution of the lower modes to the integral forces proved to be small, though their contribution into the total inertia in static ($\omega = 0$) was dominating.

To have deeper insight let us look at the phases. *Figures 6.38* and *6.39* present the same transfer functions as *Figures 6.29* and *6.30*; however, this time real and imaginary parts are shown separately.

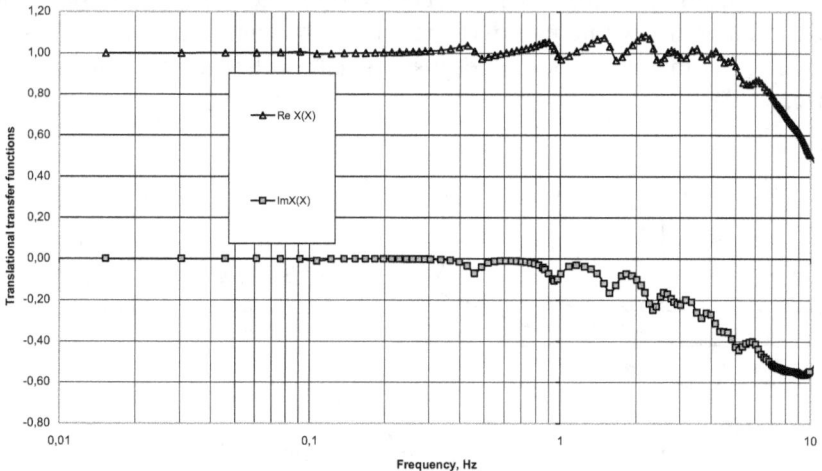

Figure 6.38. Real and imaginary parts of the transfer function from the free-field motion to the base response motion along X

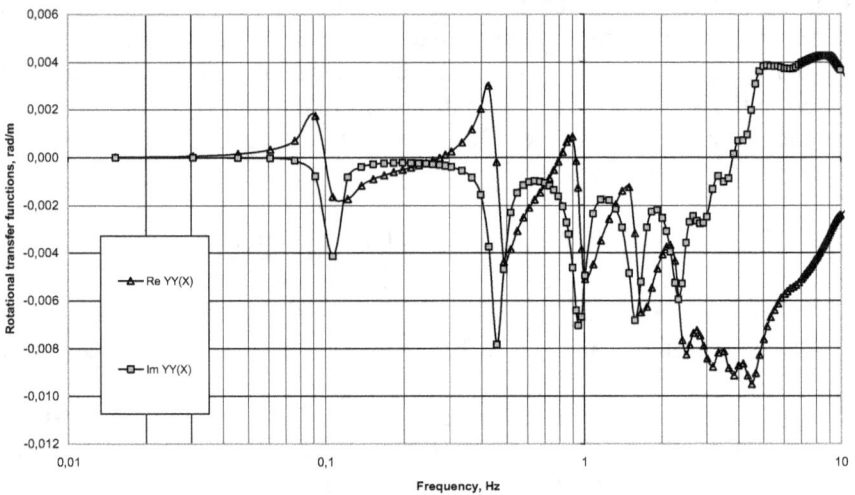

Figure 6.39. Real and imaginary parts of the transfer function from the free-field motion to the base response rocking motion around Y axis

Around 2 Hz, where the most intensive motions take place, the transfer function $X(X)$ in *Fig. 6.38* is almost real with positive real part. At the same frequency the transfer function $YY(X)$ in *Fig. 6.39* is complex with negative real part. It means that the real motion of the base will be as shown in *Fig. 6.40*.

It seems that for our high-rise building the base excitation is not able to move the whole massive upper part; the base and lower floors are moving, but the upper floors get just a small portion of motion from the base.

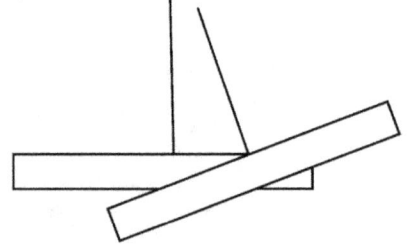

Figure 6.40. Schematic combination of horizontal and rocking motions at the base

Let us now estimate the role of the rocking soil flexibility as compared to the role of the horizontal soil flexibility. To do this, we will artificially increase rocking stiffness a million times (practically forbidding rocking response at the base). Let us take integral response forces under the base for the initial soil and fixed base from *Table 6.5* and add in *Table 6.6* the new line with constrained (i.e. fixed) rocking and free horizontal response.

Table 6.6
Comparison of integral forces under the base

Variant	X	Y	Z	XX	YY	ZZ
Initial	0.20713E6	0.24391E6	0.78674E6	0.10259E8	0.10500E8	0.68797E5
Fixed rocking	0.27911E6	0.26218E6	0.78691E6	0.11908E8	0.12399E8	0.73972E5
Fixed-base	0.27400E6	0.26882E6	0.84750E6	0.11914E8	0.12147E8	0.72057E5

We see that the results without base rocking are almost similar to those with a fixed base. The only exception is a vertical force, where fixed rocking gives the results similar to the initial soil – this is reasonable because rocking does not impact vertical force for our symmetrical structure (so, fixation of rocking DOFs changes nothing in terms of resultant vertical force). The conclusion is that all the decrease of the integral horizontal and rocking forces in SSI (see the first line of *Table 6.6*) as compared to the fixed-base analysis (i.e. without SSI; see the last line of the *Table 6.6*) is due to the rocking soil flexibility, and not due to the horizontal one. This conclusion is in line with previous calculations of the first natural frequencies. However, piles and embedment will increase rocking stiffness of the soil considerably, so in the real world this conclusion should be additionally validated.

Chapter 7. COMPLICATED SOIL ENVIRONMENT

7.1. Impedance/load calculation

In the above-considered cases, the contact surface was placed at the border between the rigid basement and the initial soil. Let us call this case "plain soil environment". Often one deals with another case: rigid basement is surrounded with a finite volume of "modified soil", different from the initial soil. Let us call this case "complicated soil environment". It was briefly mentioned in Chapter 4, but in this chapter we will study it in detail. In this case there are two surfaces: S_1 – the border of the rigid basement, and S_2 – the external border of the modified soil. This is illustrated in *Fig. 7.1*.

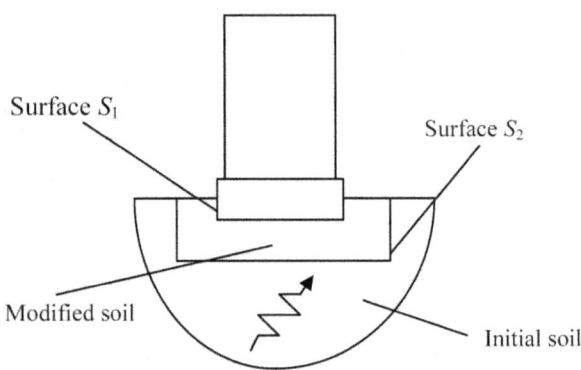

Figure 7.1. "Complicated soil environment"

Let us consider the contact problem number j for complex soil environment with "empty" content of the basement: surface S_1 gets "rigid" displacements $e_j(x)$ along DOF number j in the modified foundation, and surface S_2 gets some non-rigid response displacements $d_j(x, \omega)$. No external forces are applied at the surface S_2; loads $q_j(x, \omega)$ are applied only at the surface S_1. This is the first set of loads/displacements for the future implementation of the reciprocity theorem. It is illustrated on *Fig. 7.2*.

The second set of loads/displacements for the future implementation of the reciprocity theorem is taken from the "stopped seismic wave" in the same soil foundation (i.e. with "empty" content inside S_1 and modified soil between S_1 and S_2). "Stopped" seismic wave was described in Section 2.1 in the primary superposition shown in *Fig. 2.1*. Now we apply the basic superposition twice. For the first time we use surface S_2 as surface Q in Section 2.1 (see *Fig. 2.1*). As a result, we get some seismic load $L(x, \omega)$ at this surface fully substituting the seismic wave for the whole volume inside the surface S_2. Practically we go from the initial "problem A" to the "problem A_2", as was shown in *Fig. 2.1 – L* now has the meaning of *F* in *Fig. 2.1*).

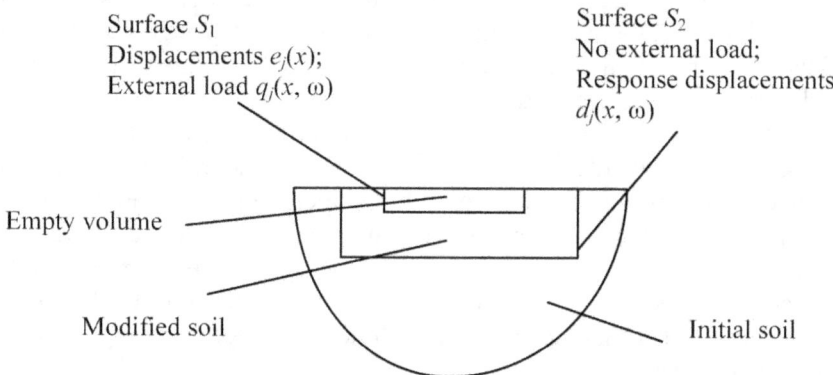

Figure 7.2. The first set of loads/displacements for the reciprocity theorem

For the second time the seismic wave inside surface S_2 (already substituted by the wave caused by L) is stopped at the surface S_1. This surface S_1 is fixed, so we have there certain external loads equal to the seismic loads $F(x, \omega)$ with opposite sign to fix it. It is illustrated on *Fig. 7.3*.

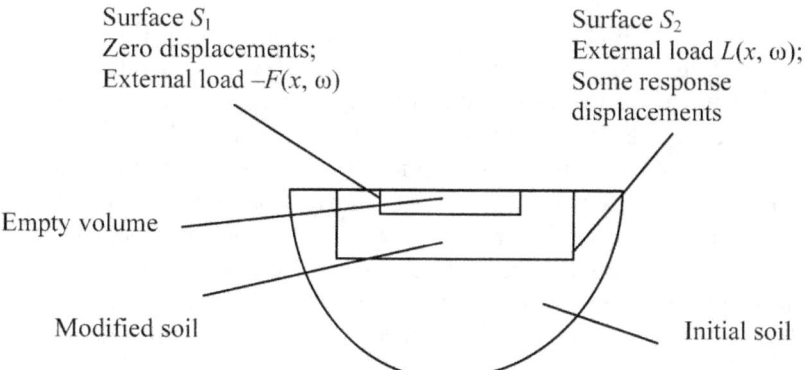

Figure 7.3. The second set of loads/displacements for the reciprocity theorem

Here comes the Reciprocity Theorem in the Frequency Domain (see Nowacki (1975)). It may be given as follows. Let us consider one and the same linear body with two sets of loads acting at the same surface. These two loads provide two corresponding displacement fields at this surface. The theorem states that the integral over this surface of the first load multiplied by the second displacement is equal to the integral of the second load multiplied by the first displacement. This theorem is well-known in static's where a load multiplied by displacement means work; however, it can be extended to the frequency domain where both load and displacement are complex and frequency-dependent. In the case of the mesh model the reciprocity theorem usually means just symmetry of the nodal impedance matrix.

In our case the body under consideration is shown in *Fig. 7.2*. The surface under consideration in the reciprocity theorem includes both surface S_1 and surface S_2. According to the reciprocity theorem we should multiply loads by displacements and integrate over surfaces S_1 and S_2. Loads from the first set (see *Fig. 7.2*) multiplied by displacements from the second set (see *Fig. 7.3*) give zero at S_1 due to the zero displacements (in the second set) and give zero at S_2 due to the zero loads (in the first set). The total sum is zero.

Loads from the second set multiplied by displacements from the first set give non-zero expressions at both surfaces S_1 and S_2. According to the reciprocity theorem total sum must be zero; so we can conclude that

$$\int_{S_1} F(x,\omega) e_j(x) \, dS_1 = \int_{S_2} L(x,\omega) d_j(x,\omega) \, dS_2. \qquad (7.1)$$

In the left-hand part of (7.1) we find the integral seismic load applied to the fixed rigid contact surface S_1 (i.e. to the rigid base in *Fig. 7.2*) in the complicated soil environment during the seismic event. This is the integral seismic load necessary for CAM. In the right-hand part of (7.1) we find the distributed seismic load $L(x, \omega)$ multiplied by non-rigid response displacements $d_j(x, \omega)$. As shown above in Section 2.2, the distributed seismic load $L(x, \omega)$ at surface S_2 does not depend on the content of the internal part (inside S_2) – it can be calculated from the "combined wave" problem for the initial soil (without modification and without structure) and contact surface S_2. This was discussed in Section 2.2.

However, to get displacements $d_j(x, \omega)$ one should solve contact problem number j for the modified soil foundation (see *Fig. 7.2*). Fortunately, it turns out that this problem should be solved anyhow – to get the integral impedances. So, no additional great efforts are needed for the load calculation as compared to the impedance calculation.

To obtain the integral impedances one should solve a set of contact problems for the external (to the surface S_1) modified foundation. We come to the same special modified soil foundation as in *Fig. 7.2*: the external part (out of S_2) is similar to the initial soil foundation; the intermediary part (between S_2 and S_1) is physically modified, and the internal part (inside S_1) is artificially modified to become "empty".

For this foundation, we solve a set of six contact problems (in case of N basements on the common foundation – $6N$ problems). In contact problem number j (see *Fig. 7.1*) we set "rigid" displacements $e_j(x)$ at the surface S_1 and obtain: *a*) response loads $-q_j(x, \omega)$ at the surface S_1, *b*) response displacements $d_j(x, \omega)$ at the surface S_2. After that, we get integral impedances

$$Q_{jk}(\omega) = \int_{S_1} q_j(x,\omega) e_k(x) \, dS_1. \quad (7.2)$$

As previously mentioned, to get the integral seismic load we solve the "combined wave problem" for the initial soil foundation and contact surface S_2, obtaining the distributed loads $L(x, \omega)$ as a result. Then we integrate these distributed loads with displacements $d_j(x, \omega)$ obtained above and get the integral loads as

$$P_j(\omega) = \int_{S_2} L(x,\omega) \, d_j(x,\omega) \, dS_2. \quad (7.3)$$

In this meshless (i.e. continuous) approach we work only with two surfaces: S_1 and S_2.

Now let us turn to the mesh approach (for finite volumes mesh approach is usually FEM, but for the infinite foundation it is not so, see SASSI; that is why the author prefers "mesh" instead of "FEM"). The important statement is that for a nodal set the modification of the soil may be modeled by means of changing the nodal impedance matrix. For example, to get "empty" finite volume inside the surface S_1 one should subtract nodal impedance matrix obtained for this finite volume (taken alone) from the nodal impedance matrix for the same set of nodes, but in the infinite soil foundation. To "replace" the outcropped soil in the finite volume by another soil one should simply add the nodal impedance matrix of the new soil (in the same finite volume) to the result of subtraction:

$$G_{modified} = G_{initial} - G_{outcropped} + G_{new}. \quad (7.4)$$

This approach is used in SASSI.

Let surfaces S_1 and S_2 be covered with two corresponding nodal sets N_1 and N_2. Then the matrix analogue of (7.2) is

$$Q = E^{T} G_{modified} E. \quad (7.5)$$

In (7.5) only the nodal set N_1 is used, and impedance matrix $G_{modified}$ is derived for this set only.

Now let us extend this set – add the nodes outside the surface S_1 with some response displacements obtained in the same contact problems for the modified soil. We shall work with extended impedance matrix $G_{modified}$ and extended nodal displacement vector D (combining displacements E in the nodal set N_1 and response displacements in all other nodes). However, in this extended sum no additional non-zero terms will appear, as in all the additional nodes the corresponding terms in $G_{modified} D$ are zero (these are in fact just equilibrium equations for additional nodes in the contact problem).

Now we shall further extend our nodal set – add the nodes inside surface S_1 with "rigid" nodal displacements $e_j(x)$. And here again, no additional non-zero terms will appear in the sum, as in all the additional nodes the corresponding lines and columns of the impedance matrix $G_{modified}$ are zero, because this volume is "empty" – guaranteed by appropriate usage of (7.4). So, for the impedance calculation we can use any extended nodal set we like (including "core" subset N_1) taking instead of (7.5) the modified equation

$$Q = D^{T} G_{modified} D \quad (7.6)$$

Now let us turn to the mesh analogue of (7.3). If we work with a nodal set N_2 and have U_0 as displacements in the seismic wave, we get ($G_{initial} U_0$) as mesh analogue of distributed load L, and further

$$P = D^{\mathrm{T}} G_{initial} U_0 \qquad (7.7)$$

Let us extend our nodal set – add nodes in the volume inside S_2. However, this volume is filled with initial soil (not modified as before). We extended summation in (7.7), but in all those additional nodes the corresponding terms in $G_{initial}U_0$ are zero, so no additional non-zero terms will appear in the extended sum (7.7).

Now looking at (7.6) and (7.7) we conclude that we can use for both formulae one and the same set of nodes, including (i) subset N_1 at the surface S_1; (ii) subset N_2 at the surface S_2; (iii) some nodes in the volume between S_1 and S_2 helping to model this volume by $3D$ finite elements; (iv) some nodes in the volume inside S_1 helping to model this volume by $3D$ finite elements. Matrix multiplication will cover all these nodes, though non-zero contribution in (7.6) will appear only from the nodes of subset N_1, and non-zero contribution in (7.7) will appear only from the nodes of subset N_2. Matrix D in (7.6) and (7.7) is one and the same. Matrices $G_{modified}$ and $G_{initial}$ are similar in size though different in values due to the different soil properties.

In practical calculations with SASSI it is convenient to start from $G_{modified}$, then after the solution of the contact problems calculate $(G_{modified}D)$. It will be used in (7.6) directly. Equation (7.7) may be rearranged using (7-4):

$$P = D^{\mathrm{T}} G_{modified} U_0 + D^{\mathrm{T}} (G_{outcropped} - G_{new}) U_0. \qquad (7.8)$$

The first term in the right-hand part of (7-8) is calculated as the product of $(G_{modified}D)^{\mathrm{T}}$ calculated above and U_0 calculated in conventional SASSI for the initial soil. As $G_{outcropped}$ and G_{new} are conventional FEM matrices for finite volume inside the surface S_2, it makes no principal difficulty to calculate (7.8).

The author has written his own version of SASSI to implement this approach. In addition to the "interaction nodes" set covering the whole underground volume, the author pointed up "rigid" subset of this full set as a part of the input. The solution in ANALYSIS after conventional creating nodal impedance matrix $G_{modified}$ is performed in two stages. First, for the contact problems, the DOFs corresponding to this rigid subset are additionally stiffened, and corresponding "rigid" loads E are applied. Full matrix D is the result of this stage, and $(G_{modified}D)$ is calculated. In the second stage only U_0 is calculated in a conventional manner, and then seismic load P is calculated using (7.8). Matrices Q (impedances) and P (loads) are the results of the SASSI run for each frequency.

In the SASSI calculations the greatest part of the computational resources is allocated to build the flexibility matrix and nodal impedance matrix $G_{initial}$. On the other hand, nodal set here can be almost arbitrary, as no finite elements are used at this stage. So, the most effective way to save computational resources is to minimize the SASSI nodal sets leaving just the "selected" nodes at the surfaces S_1 and S_2. For deeply embedded structures saving may be considerable.

However, one needs additional nodes inside both surfaces S_1 and S_2 to provide corresponding FEM calculations of $G_{outcropped}$ and G_{new}. To combine these matrices with $G_{initial}$ we have to condense impedance matrices $G_{outcropped}$ and G_{new} (better their difference) to these "selected" nodes. This can be done outside of SASSI, as both matrices are common FEM matrices.

It may seem that "complicated soil environment" is seldom met – only if certain soil volume is physically modified. However, it turns out that almost every embedded structure, in fact, should be analyzed in a "complicated soil environment" even if there is no physical modification of the adjacent soil.

Standard ASCE4-98 requires the consideration of the separation between soil and vertical embedded walls of the basement. To keep the linearity of the analysis, this Standard allows the implementation of the full soil-structure separation from the very beginning of seismic response for a half of the embedment depth, but not more than 6 m from the surface. The best way to account for this effect in the SASSI model is to consider the lower part of the actual basement as the underground basement, and to fill the upper part of the outcropped soil volume by a modified soil with "empty" properties (i.e. extremely light and flexible). Thus we come to the "complicated soil environment" illustrated in *Fig. 7-4*.

One can compare seismic load in this case with that in case of the full contact, using (7.7). Impedance matrix G is the same in both cases, as it refers to the initial soil. Free field displacements U_0 are also the same. Only displacements D are different in the upper part of embedded walls. In case of full contact they are "rigid"; in case of separation they are "non-rigid", as a response displacement at the free vertical surface to the kinematical excitation applied in the lower part in contact problems.

Let us draw the first conclusions.

A continuous and mesh formulae are developed for the case of the "complicated soil conditions" when the rigid basement is surrounded by the finite volume of the modified soil. Soil foundation is treated as a linear one with full contact with embedded basement (in case of separation this embedded basement starts at a certain depth). SSI is considered in the frequency domain following the SASSI ideology.

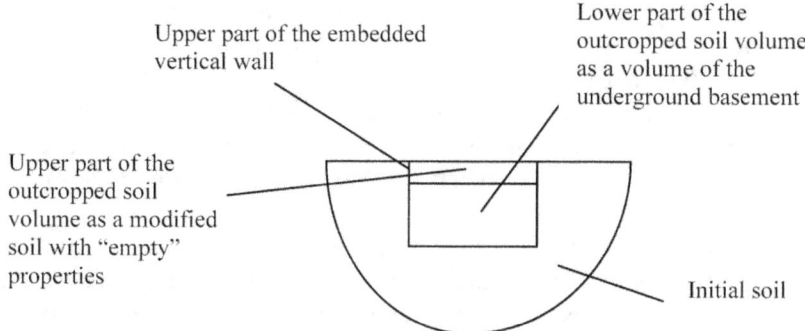

Figure 7.4. *"Complicated soil environment" as a tool to consider soil-structure separation in case of the embedded structure*

It turned out that principally only two surface integrals play a role: one over the contact surface at the basement, another one – at the boundary between modified soil and initial soil. These results are in good agreement with previously obtained mesh formulae.

That may help to save computational resources for deeply embedded structures if in SASSI one cuts the number of the interaction nodes to those at two surfaces. However, one should then condense FEM impedance matrices for the outcropped and substituting soils to these nodes.

Auxiliary contact problems must be solved to obtain integral impedances and integral seismic loads. Then the results in terms of the response displacements at the surface between the modified soil and the initial soil are used with free-field seismic motion in the initial soil.

The application field is rather wide, as "complicated soil environment" provides a tool to consider full separation between soil and vertical embedded walls (according to ASCE4-98).

7.2. Application to the soil upgrade case

Let us discuss the example of the intensive implementation of CAM for the complicated soil environment.

In a seismic design of heavy structures in soil sites, they often use "soil pillows" under the base mat. Inside the volume of the "pillow" the initial soil is either removed and substituted by another soil, or upgraded without outcropping. Different technologies of such an upgrade are available nowadays, but the result in mechanical terms is always one and the same – upgraded soil inside the "pillow" has properties substantially different from the initial soil. The upgrade can go in both directions: soft pillow in the hard surrounding soil and hard pillow in the soft surrounding soil. The first direction was studied for rock site and proved to be ineffective because the wave damping proved to be switched off. The second direction – i.e. a hard pillow in soft surrounding soil – is studied in this section.

Usually the main goal of the decision to create "soil pillow" is to withdraw the soil with unacceptable properties (e.g., liquefaction potential) or to decrease the settlement. However, the upgrade of the soil properties inevitably changes the seismic response. In this section, the effect of the depth and properties of the "soil pillow" on the structural seismic response is studied.

First, this effect is demonstrated using sample soil site and sample structure. Then the nature of the protective effect is studied closely. It turns out that kinematical soil-structure interaction plays a crucial role. Fortunately, soil pillow without structure may be often modelled by an infinite surface layer, enabling SHAKE calculations for layered sites and analytical solution for homogeneous sites. The results are compared to the SASSI results obtained for finite (in horizontal directions) soil pillow. Good matching makes the seismic protective effect trustable. The analytical solution enables a good understanding of the governing parameters.

7.2.1. Demonstration of the protective effect

Here is the description of the first sample structure considered. Rigid base mat 80.0×76.8 m is resting on the surface of the soil. "Soil pillow" in each horizontal direction extends 2.5 m beyond the base mat, so it is 85.0×81.8 m. For the convenience, it is assumed that the whole pillow is covered with a rigid base mat (actual inertia of the mat is preserved when the structural model is involved).

Initial soil is modelled by a set of 18 horizontal layers resting on a homogeneous half-space. The total thickness of the package is 90 m. Soil density is 2.0 t/m^3, material damping in the soil is 4%. Shear wave velocity V_s has a non-monotonous profile in the range from 499 to 585 m/s; primary wave velocities V_p are in the range from 1897 to 2145 m/s.

Upgraded soil in the "pillow" has properties considerably different from the initial soil. Shear wave velocity V_s is 1300 m/s, primary wave velocity V_p is 2400 m/s; mass density is 2.3 t/m^3; material damping falls to 2%.

Three variants of the pillow thickness are considered in this section. In the first variant (hereinafter it is called "medium") the thickness is 14.7 m. In the second variant (called "deep") the thickness is 18.7 m. In the third variant (called "shallow") the depth is 10.7 m. Soil pillow starts from the surface.

The seismic response is calculated using the first option of the CAM. The first step – SRA – is skipped in this case: soil degradation is not considered, time-history from the surface is not modified. Time-history is given with time step 0.004 s; duration is 30 s. Spectra will be shown below.

Impedances for rigid base mat resting on the flexible soil pillow are calculated by SASSI using methodology of the "complicated soil environment" (see the previous section). The upper structure is set by "rigid" inertia (mass is 374866 t, centre of gravity is 26.7858 m above the ground surface), and also by a set of natural frequencies and natural modes (described by their participation factors) calculated for the fixed-base detailed model in ABAQUS. The first natural fixed-base frequency is about 4.0 Hz. Modal damping coefficients calculated by ABAQUS are around 7%.

Having transfer functions and free-field motion one can use FFT to get the response of the base mat in the time domain. *Figure 7.5* shows the comparison of the response spectra along OX axis with 5% oscillator damping for different soils.

Soil modules were scaled two times as compared to the medium soil. Each curve in *Fig. 7.5* (except the last one corresponding to the initial free-field motion) is marked by a number (this is a number of the pillow thickness variant, see above) and letter (M – medium soil, S – soft soil, R – hard soil). In the first peaks the pillow thickness does not affect the response, but in the second peaks this effect is more pronounced. The worst variant in terms of the second spectral peaks is hard soil and shallow pillow. The best variant is soft soil and deep pillow.

As compared to the free-field spectrum, the response of the base mat is considerably less at the frequencies above 2.5 Hz. Near the frequency 5 Hz the decrease in spectral accelerations is doubled when the pillow thickness is changed from the shallow to the deep variant.

Figure 7.6 shows the response spectra along OZ axis.

There is a considerable difference in the seismic protective effect between horizontal and vertical directions. Pillow thickness does not affect the vertical response (unlike the soil modules variation).

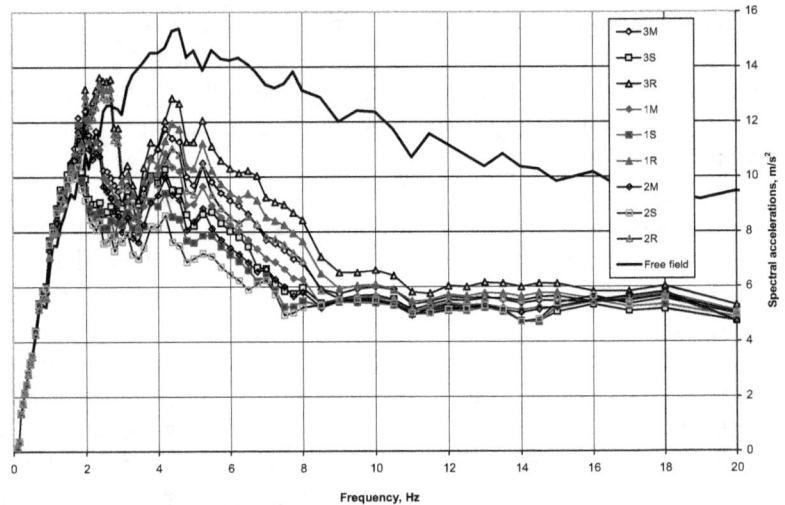

Figure 7.5. Comparison of RS along OX axis

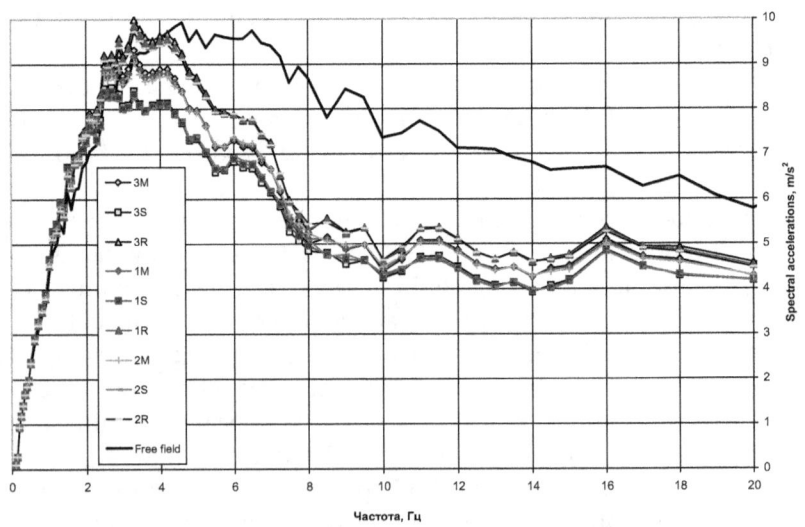

Figure 7.6. Comparison of RS along OZ axis

This was a demonstration of the seismic protective effect of hard "soil pillow" in the soft initial soil on the structural seismic response. The discovered effect enables the treatment of the "soil pillow" as an alternative kind of seismic base isolation. As compared to the conventional seismic base isolation this solution is much cheaper. Physical likeness with the mechanism of the conventional seismic base isolation is obvious: the first natural frequencies fall into the frequency range of the small spectral accelerations of seismic excitation. Besides, the effective damping increases (due to the wave damping in the soil). The relative displacements of the base mat increase, but unlike the conventional seismic base isolation they are not localized in the isolators, but instead they are distributed in the vicinity of the base. This may be favourable for the communications attached to the upper structure.

7.2.2. Role of kinematical interaction in the seismic protective effect of the soil pillow

It is well-known that SSI problem may be presented as a sequence of two separate problems: *a*) kinematical interaction, and *b*) inertial interaction. It was discussed in Chapter 2. The decrease in the seismic response noted above may be caused either by kinematical interaction, or by inertial interaction, or by both of them.

Without the "soil pillow" under the base mat, the response of the weightless surface rigid base mat to the vertically travelling waves in the horizontally-layered soil would be similar to the free-field motion at the surface. Thus, kinematical interaction would not affect seismic response at all. However, the upgrade of the soil in the "soil pillow" changes the situation. One should clarify how seismic response is changed after the soil upgrade, and how close is the resulting response of the weightless base mat to the resulting seismic response of the massive base mat under the massive upper structure obtained above. After this clarification, one can conclude whether the seismic protection effect of the soil pillow should be expected for relatively light structures (typical for civil engineering), or this effect should be expected only for heavy structures like the one considered above.

Figures 7.7 and *7.8* present the response spectra (5% damping in oscillators) in vertical and horizontal translational directions both for massive and weightless base mats as compared to the free-field motion. Variant 2 of the pillow thickness from the previous section is considered ("deep soil pillow"): thickness of the "pillow" is 18.7 m. Free-field RS and RS for massive base mat are taken from *Figures 7.5* and *7.6*. RS for the weightless base mat were calculated specially for this study.

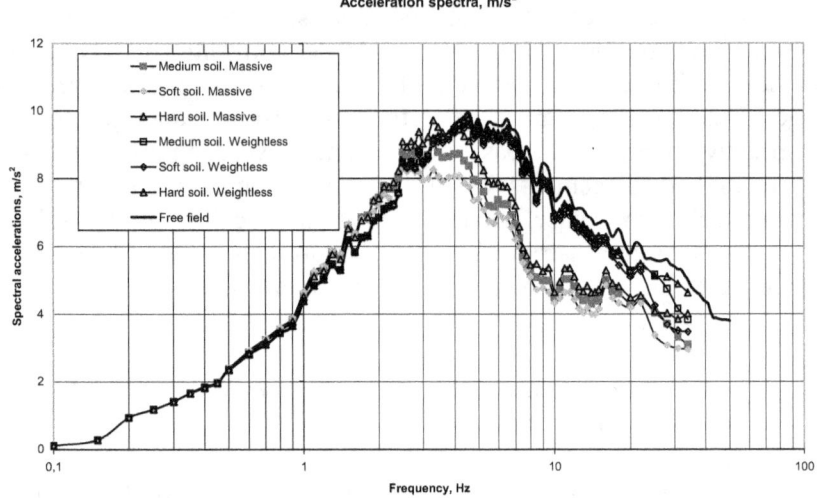

Figure 7.7. RS with 5% damping in oscillators: comparison of the free-field with the response in the centre of the base mat along the vertical axis Z

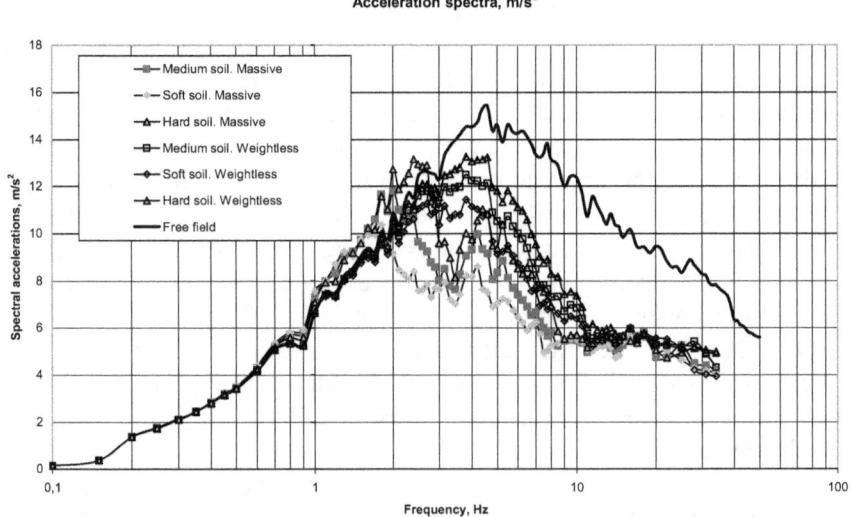

Figure 7.8. RS with 5% damping in oscillators: comparison of free field with response in the center of the base mat along horizontal axis X

Response spectra in *Fig. 7.7* for the weightless base mat for all three soil profiles are only slightly lower than the free-field RS. It means that a designer should not expect seismic protective effect from the "soil pillow" for the light structures in the vertical direction. The actual decrease in the seismic response for our sample structure in the frequency range above 3 Hz obtained above and shown in *Fig. 7.7* is explained in full by the great weight of the sample structure and not by kinematical interaction. One should expect that the response of a structure with smaller weight resting on the same base mat will be somewhere between RS for our sample structure and RS for weightless base mat (i.e. practically the free-field RS).

However, in *Fig. 7.8* one can see a completely different comparison. In the frequency range below about 2.5 Hz the response spectra for the weightless base mat are almost similar to the free-field like we saw in *Fig. 7.7* for vertical accelerations. However, for higher frequencies (especially above 4 Hz) the response spectra for horizontal accelerations go down from the free-field RS. They are still somewhat greater than the RS for the massive base mats under the massive upper structure, but closer to these spectra than to the free-field ones. It means that one should expect considerable seismic protective effect in the horizontal direction from our "soil pillow" even for the light civil structures on the same base mat. Roughly speaking, in the frequency range from 1 to 6 Hz about half of the actual decrease in spectral accelerations as compared to the free-field goes from kinematical interaction; another half goes from inertial interaction; for higher frequencies about 70–80% of the total decrease goes from kinematical interaction.

What is the reason for such a great difference between horizontal and vertical directions? The author believes that the main mechanism for the seismic protective effect of the "soil pillow" on the seismic response of the weightless base mat is a certain constraint put on the wave field in the initial soil. Hard "pillow" is somehow averaging the initial wave displacements over the thickness of the pillow. The controlling parameter for such a "constraining" effect is a ratio of the thickness to the wavelength. In the considered example shear wave velocity V_s near the surface for the medium soil is about 500 m/s. At the frequency 5 Hz wavelength in initial soil is 500/5 = 100 m, and the thickness of the pillow (about 20 m) makes one fifth of this wavelength. Primary wave velocity V_p near the surface is about 2000 m/s – it is four times V_s; the same ratio of the thickness to the wavelength (one to five) will appear for

V_p at the frequency four times greater than 5 Hz. And in fact at the frequency 20 Hz in *Fig. 7.7* we see greater deviation of the RS for the weightless base mat down from the free-field RS.

The same logic explains the difference in the RS deviations from the free-field RS between different soil profiles in *Fig. 7.8*. The softer is the soil, the less is the wavelength. The thickness of the pillow is one and the same for all cases; so, for the soft soil the same ratio of the pillow thickness to the wavelength is achieved at smaller frequencies. It corresponds to the results presented in *Fig. 7.8*.

This is for sure only a part of the explanation – the deviation in *Fig. 7.7* at the frequency 20 Hz is still smaller than in *Fig. 7.8* at the frequency 5 Hz. What is the reason? Let us additionally consider the transfer functions from the free-field motion to the response of the weightless base mat. They are shown in *Fig. 7.9*.

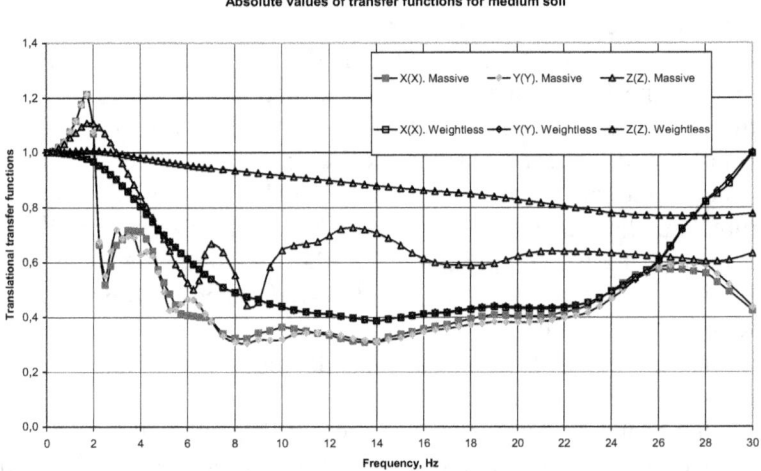

Figure 7.9. Absolute values of the transfer functions from the free-field motion to the response of the weightless base mat and massive base mat under the massive upper structure

We see the same difference: the absolute value of the transfer function $Z(Z)$ at 20 Hz is greater than the absolute values of $X(X)$ and $Y(Y)$ at 5 Hz. The author explains it as follows. As compared to the initial $V_s = 500$ m/s, in the "pillow" $V_s = 1300$ m/s is much greater (i.e. 2.6 times); so the "pillow" behaves as an almost rigid body. The same comparison for V_p gives different result: initial $V_p = 2000$ m/s, and in the "pillow" $V_p = 2400$ m/s (i.e., only 1.2 times greater). This hypothesis will be checked later on.

7.2.3. 1D modelling of the soil pillow

One can note that in *Fig. 7.9* the absolute values of the transfer functions $X(X)$ and $Y(Y)$ are practically similar though the two horizontal dimensions are slightly different (85 × 81.8 m). This fact causes the next question. In our case, the upgraded "soil pillow" was finite in horizontal directions. What if it were infinite in horizontal directions? In this case we have just a different upper soil layer. The response of the surface rigid weightless base mat is equal to the response of the free surface of such "modified" soil profile. It can be obtained using conventional SHAKE approach for the horizontally-layered soil and vertically propagating waves – much faster and easier than the response of the finite "soil pillow" requiring the SASSI analysis. The comparison of the results for the infinite pillow (SHAKE) and the rigid weightless basement resting on the finite pillow (SASSI) with free-field RS is shown in *Figures 7.10* and *7.11*.

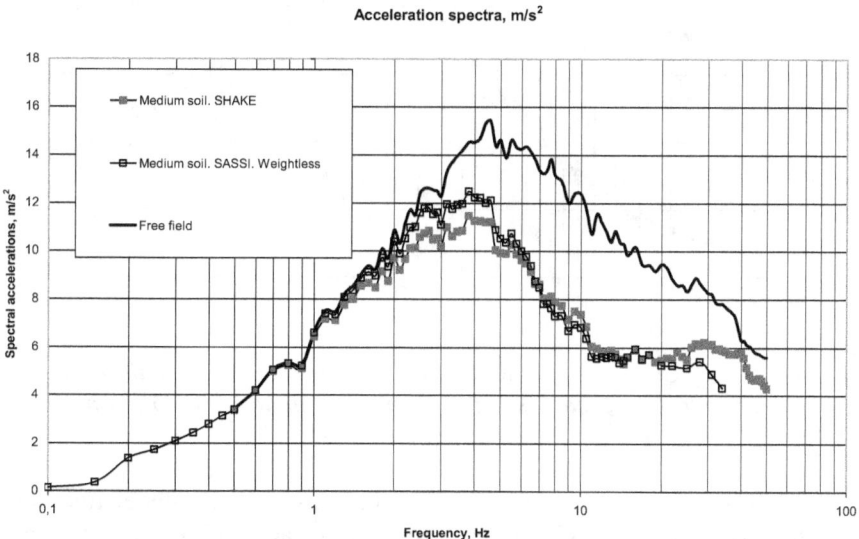

Figure 7.10. Comparison of RS (5% damping in oscillators) in the center of the weightless base mat resting on infinite and finite soil pillows with free field along an X axis

We see in *Fig. 7.10* that the main part of the protective effect (especially above 6 Hz) is well represented in the SHAKE model, i.e. for the infinite soil pillow. Finite size has a limited effect only.

In *Fig. 7.11* for the vertical accelerations one more curve is added. It is calculated by SHAKE for hypothetic soil profiles with artificially increased V_p = 5200 m/s in the "soil pillow".

As mentioned above, in terms of V_s the soil pillow is 1300 m/s and initial soil is 500 m/s, i.e. the ratio is 2.6. If we apply the same proportion to the initial V_p = 2000 m/s, we get hypothetical V_p for the soil pillow equal to 5200 m/s (and not 2400 m/s, as in our previous case). The resulting spectral reduction for the hypothetical soil profile at 20 Hz in the vertical direction in *Fig. 7.11* proved to be much closer to that in the horizontal direction at 5 Hz in *Fig. 7.10*.

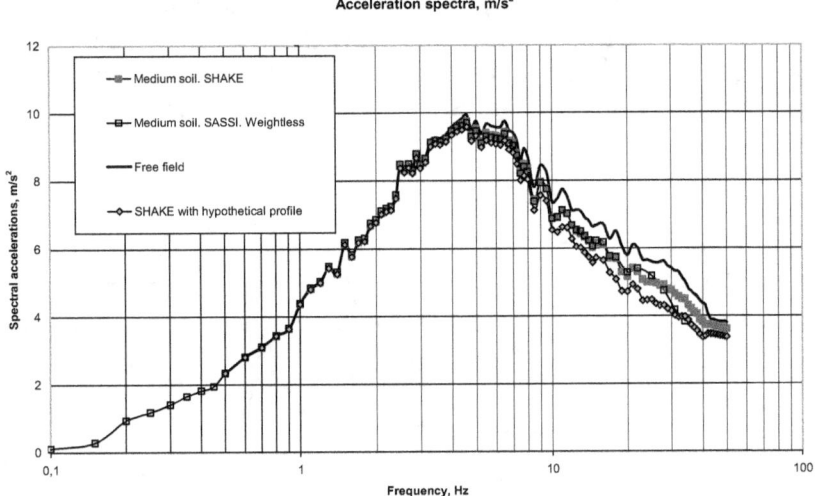

Figure 7.11. Comparison of RS (5% damping in oscillators) in the centre of the weightless base mat resting on infinite and finite soil pillows with free field along an Z axis

Let us consider the same problem in terms of the transfer functions analytically comparing: *a*) homogeneous half-space and *b*) the same half-space with the upper layer with upgraded properties. In the 1D wave propagation problem the transfer function from the free surface of the homogeneous half-space to the free surface of the upgraded layer is given by

$$TF = \frac{\cos a_1 + i \sin a_1}{\cos a_2 + b\, i \sin a_2}, \qquad (7.9)$$

$$a_j = \omega H / V_j, \quad V_j = V_j^0 \left(\sqrt{1-\delta_j^2} + i\delta_j \right), \qquad (7.10)$$

$$b = \frac{\rho_2}{\rho_1} \frac{V_2}{V_1}, \qquad (7.11)$$

where i – imaginary unit; ω – circular frequency; H – layer thickness; V_j – complex wave velocity accounting for the material damping with coefficient δ_j ($j = 1$ – for the half-space, $j = 2$ – for the layer); ρ_j – soil mass density ($j = 1$ – for the half-space, $j = 2$ – for the layer). If the layer has the same properties as the half-space, coefficient b in (7.11) becomes unit, values a_1 and a_2 in (7.10) become similar, and the resulting transfer function (7.9) becomes equal to unity, which is physically justified. One more physical check – for very small frequency ω both a numerator and denominator in (7.9) become real units, and the transfer function becomes unit, which is again physically justified. Formulae (7.9–7.11) are valid both for shear waves and for primary waves (surely, wave velocities are different for them).

Figure 7.12 shows the results of calculations using formulae (7.9–7.11) as compared to the previous results from *Fig. 7.9*. For each

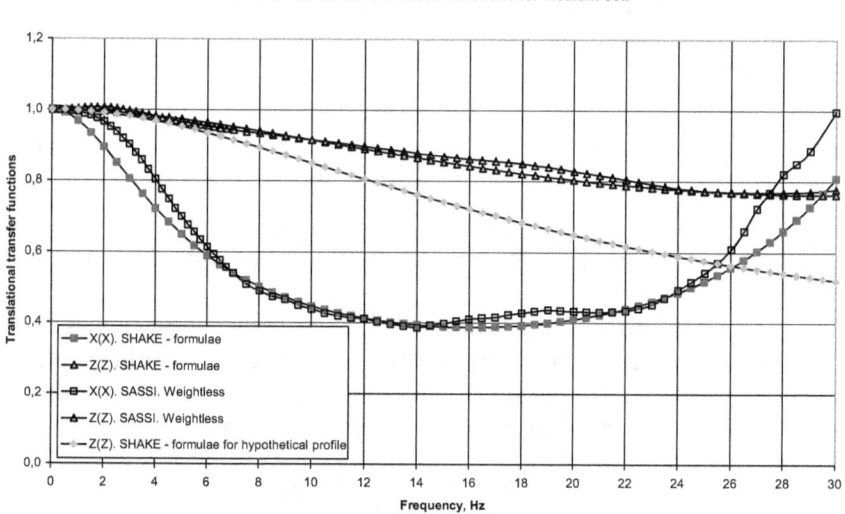

Figure 7.12. Absolute values of the transfer functions from free field motion to the response of the weightless base mat

direction (X and Z) one curve is taken from *Fig. 7.9*, another one is added using formulae (7.9–7.11). For the vertical direction, one more curve is added using formulae (7.9–7.11) for the hypothetical soil profile with $V_p = 5200$ m/s.

One can note a good agreement between analytical results (7.9–7.11) and previous results. As mentioned earlier, the substitution of the finite soil pillow by the infinite one in SHAKE caused some differences in curves below 6 Hz (remember *Fig. 7.10*) for horizontal directions. One should additionally note that the initial soil in SASSI was not completely homogeneous – the upper soil layer 5.7 m thick had V_s not 500, but 585 m/s. Below there was also some non-homogeneity in V_s not considered in formulae (7.9–7.11) – probably this is a reason for some deviations around 18 Hz.

The important note is that the curve for the hypothetical profile V_p at 20 Hz gives the same value as the curve for horizontal direction at 5 Hz – this is the proof of the author's hypothesis about the ratio of thickness to the wavelength promised earlier.

Let us now further develop formulae (7.9–7.11). What if the stiffness of the soil pillow increases infinitely? From equation (7.10) one concludes that a_2 will go to zero. So, the first term in the denominator in (7.9) will go to unity. What about the second term? Note that velocity ratio V_2/V_1, participating in (7.11), is equal to the ratio a_1/a_2. As a result, we see in the denominator the ratio $\sin(a_2)/a_2$, going to unity, when a_2 goes to zero. Finally, we come to the "limit" transfer function for the rigid layer:

$$TF_{\lim} = \frac{\cos a_1 + i \sin a_1}{1 + i a_1 (\rho_2 / \rho_1)}. \qquad (7.12)$$

Thus, the unlimited increase in the stiffness of the "soil pillow" will lead to a decrease in the transfer function limited by a certain "limit curve" (7.12).

And what will be the effect of an increase in the thickness of the "soil pillow"? For the moderate material damping the absolute value of numerator in (7.12) will be around unity, and the absolute value of denominator will depend on the imaginary part. We get

$$|TF_{\lim}| \approx \left[1 + H^2 (\rho_2 / \rho_1)^2 (\omega / V_1)^2 \right]^{-1/2}. \qquad (7.13)$$

Thus, the infinite increase in the thickness of the rigid "soil pillow" will lead to the infinite decrease in transfer function (it goes to zero).

Note that the last term in (7.13) can be expressed using wavelength $L(\omega) = 2\pi V_1/\omega$; then (7.13) can be modified to

$$\left|TF_{\lim}\right| \approx \left[1 + 4\pi^2 \left(H/L\right)^2 \left(\rho_2/\rho_1\right)^2\right]^{-1/2}. \tag{7.14}$$

Here one can clearly see the role of the ratio H/L – this very ratio was discussed above. Besides, one can estimate the "border" value of this ratio when it starts to play a role (the second term in (7.14) is then comparable to the unity). This value in our case (similar densities) is about 0.183 – i.e. near one fifth mentioned above.

The last comment is that the horizontal size of the pillow for successful 1D modelling should be great enough as compared to the pillow thickness to avoid considerable rocking of the pillow.

7.2.4. Effect of the soil pillow stiffness

The effect described above was used in the design of several NPP blocks. In the process, there were performed the feasibility studies. Let us look at the results.

Profiles of the shear wave velocity and internal damping in the initial soil are shown in *Fig. 7.13* and *Fig. 7.14*. They account for the soil degradation (A2H09 and A2H19 are two generated components of the excitation time-history).

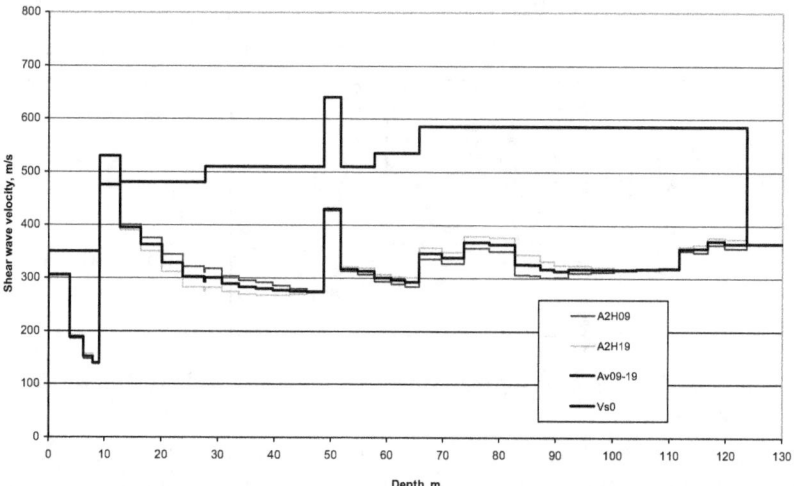

Figure 7.13. Initial soil profile: shear wave velocities V_s

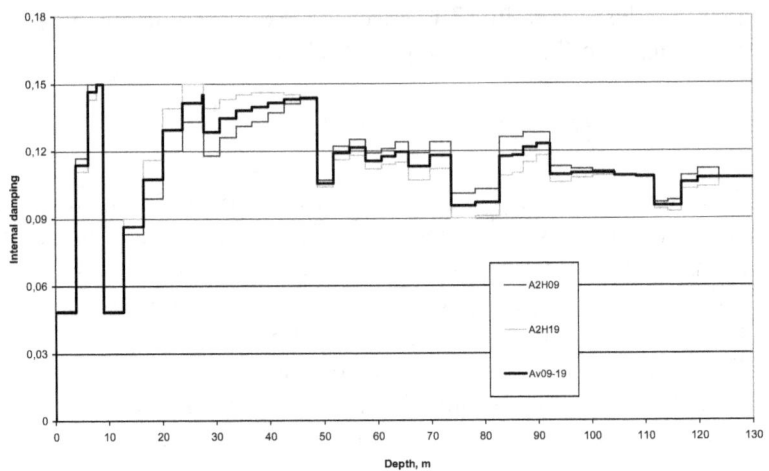

Figure 7.14. Initial soil profile: material damping D

"Soil pillow" is schematically shown in *Fig. 7.15*. Soil density in the pillow is less than in the previous study (only 2.15 t/m^3 this time). Base mat (before the extension) in horizontal plane is 80.0 × 76.8 = = 6144 m^2; equivalent radius is 44.22 m. The ratio of the actual embedment depth to this radius is 9.05/44.22 = 0.2046 < 0.3 – so, we are allowed to treat the base as surface one.

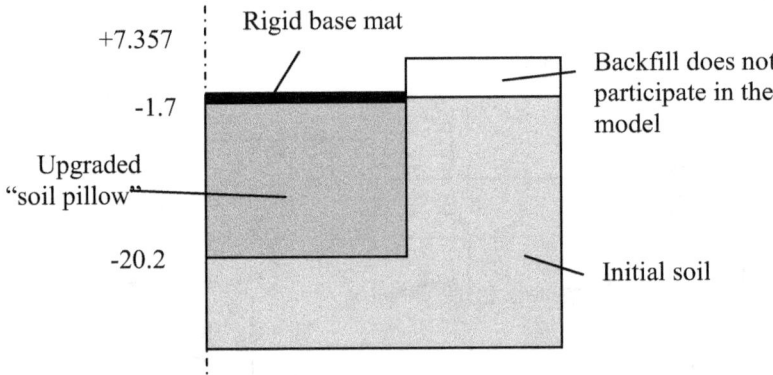

Figure 7.15. Scheme of the model with the upgraded "soil pillow"

The main goal of the study was to compare the results for different shear wave velocities V_s in the "soil pillow". *Figures 7.16* and *7.17* show translational and rotational impedances for different V_s. Four realistic values of V_s are compared to the unrealistic very high value $V_s = 13000$ m/s.

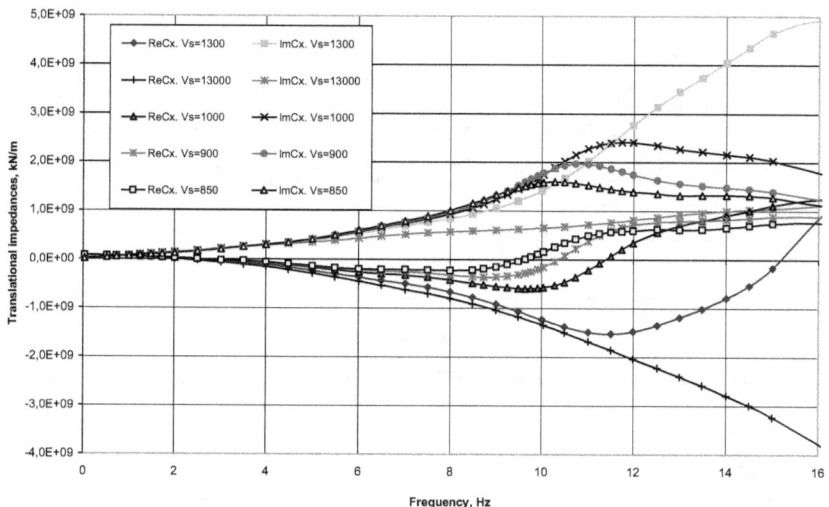

Figure 7.16. Translational impedances with upgraded "soil pillow"

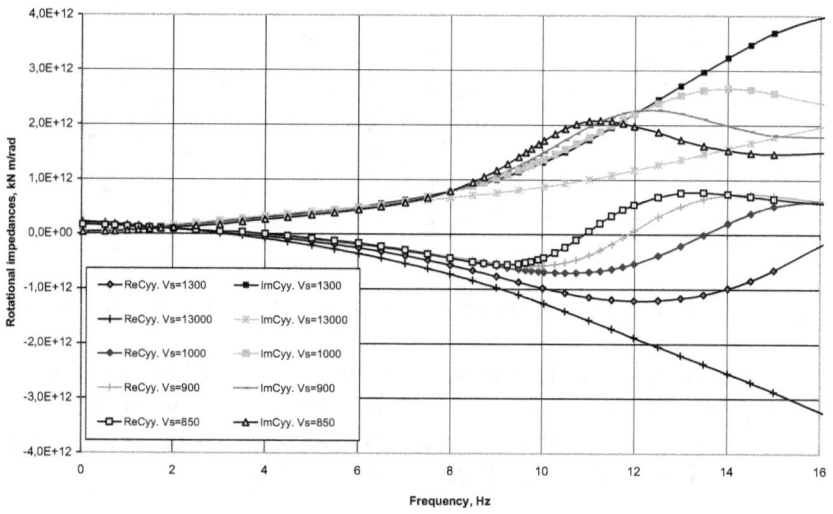

Figure 7.17. Rotational impedances with upgraded "soil pillow"

Figure 7.18 shows the transfer functions $X(X)$ for the weightless rigid base mat, and *Fig. 7.19* — the same under the structure.

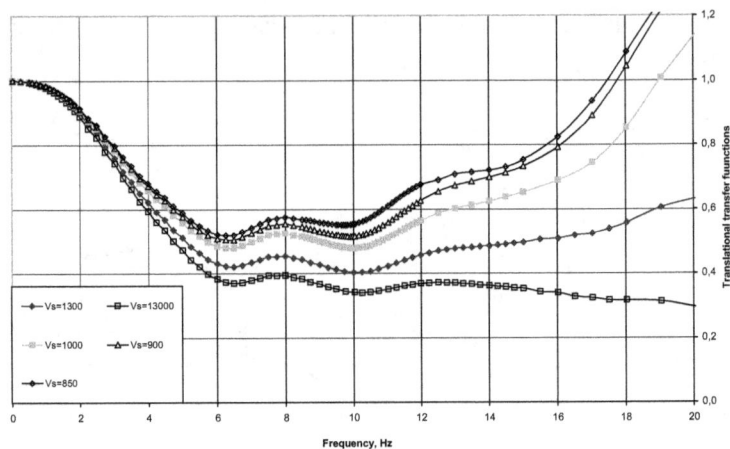

Figure 7.18. Transfer functions X(X) for the weightless rigid base mat

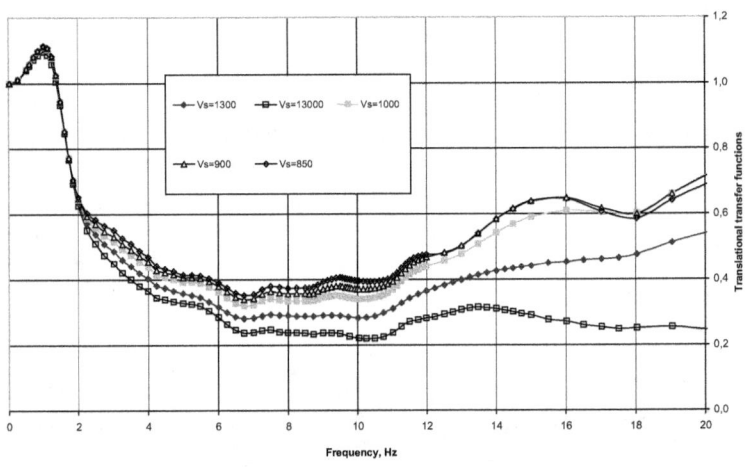

Figure 7.19. Transfer functions X(X) for the rigid base mat under the structure

As expected, the less is soil stiffness in the pillow, the less is a seismic protective effect. It is in line with theoretical conclusions of the previous section about the contrast between initial soil and upgraded one – the main driver of the whole effect.

7.2.5. Conclusions about soil upgrade

In soil sites with soft soils, the considerable reduction in structural seismic response may be achieved by upgrading the soil under the base mat in the finite volume of the so-called "soil-pillow". Hard "pillow" in the soft soil provides seismic protection.

Kinematical interaction plays the main role in the reduction of the effective seismic input in the sample case in horizontal directions. It means that the surface of the "soil pillow" gets smaller accelerations as compared to the free field – even without the upper structure. So, the "soil pillow" will protect even comparatively light civil structures in the horizontal direction. For heavy structures there appears the additional reduction at the overcritical frequencies due to the inertial interaction.

The second conclusion is that the protective effect does not depend significantly on the horizontal size of the "soil pillow" (though horizontal size should be large enough as compared to the thickness to avoid considerable rocking of the pillow). As a result, the protective effect in terms of kinematical soil-structure interaction may be estimated using 1D horizontally-layered soil models with the upper layer modelling soil pillow. In the simple case of the homogeneous initial soil, one can use the simple formulae, presented above and combining parameters of the initial and upgraded soils with a thickness of the "soil pillow".

The protective effect for weightless base mat (i.e., kinematical interaction) is controlled mainly by the ratio of the pillow thickness to the wavelength in the initial soil. The increase in the pillow stiffness leads to the limited reduction, while the increase in thickness leads to the unlimited reduction. However, for the great reduction, the thickness must be considerably greater than the wavelength.

In the vertical direction, unlike the horizontal one, the protective effect in the sample case is caused only by the great mass of the considered structure. Kinematical interaction in the vertical direction is of little importance – it does not change the motion at the surface of the "soil pillow", as compared to the free field. The first reason for that is that the primary wave velocity V_p is considerably greater than the shear wave velocity V_s; as a result, the ratio of thickness to the wave length at the same frequency is much smaller for the primary waves as compared to the secondary (shear) waves. The second reason is that for the shear waves the degree of the upgrade is considerably greater than for the primary waves (ratio of the upgraded velocity to the initial velocity is 2.6 for V_s versus 1.2 for V_p). The greater is the degree of the upgrade, the more pronounced is the response reduction effect.

The protective effect of the "soil pillow" enables partial control over seismic response in certain frequency range without conventional seismic isolation. The main condition for that is soft initial soil in the site.

CONCLUSIONS

The author hopes that his recommendations about Site Response Analysis (SRA) presented in Chapter 1 will be useful for the reader. It refers to the approximate treatment of the secondary non-linearity in the SHAKE calculation, and also to the "half-space tuning method".

The author tried to present a consistent picture of the Soil-Structure Interaction (SSI) analysis. Direct and impedance methods, in fact, have a common origin and may be treated as particular cases of one and the same "platform" approach based on primary and secondary superposition, as shown in Chapter 2. Platform models enable systematic classification of the SSI methods. The only assumption is the linearity of the soil outside certain selected volume.

For the direct approach described in Chapter 3 the key factors are non-reflecting boundaries and accurate excitation. Bottom boundaries are important if no rock is seen at the bottom. Nowadays intensive studies are performed in this field to account for the soil non-linearity. Meanwhile, the equivalent-linear approach is used.

For the impedance methods described in Chapter 4 the key factor is the representation of impedances and loads with regard to the frequency-dependence and interlinks between different directions. Impedance methods enable important simplifications in SSI analysis. However, every simplification is based on certain assumptions – these assumptions should be checked for the applicability case by case. For example, the Rigid Base Assumption (RBA) widely used in the impedance methods is not universal.

Combined asymptotic method (CAM) described in Chapter 5 is a powerful tool of the SSI analysis. The author tried to explain how this method helps not only to get final results but to estimate the intermediary results in a convenient format and understand main drivers of the SSI effect in consideration.

For this purpose the author presented in Chapters 6 and 7 several examples from his analytical practice. The author deals mostly with the nuclear structures, but in Chapter 6 a high-rise building is also considered. The whole SSI field of research historically was initiated by engineers from hydro- and nuclear industries, but nowadays some civil structures reach the parameters (first of all, mass) comparable to those special structures. So, SSI effects may be of importance not only in specific fields like NPP design.

The part of the CAM title – namely "asymptotic" – is not discussed in this book. The author decided to limit the scope by the so-called "first CAM option". This option is based on the rigid base assumption (RBA) and is mathematically rigorous. However, the reader should know that there exists also "the second CAM option", treating flexible base mats. Unlike the first CAM option, this option is approximate, but has "asymptotic" accuracy: the stiffer is the base mat, the more accurate are the results. The author hopes to present this option in the next book.

The author did not try to mention all the prominent contributions in the history of the SSI field. So, this book is not an encyclopedia – rather an author's view. Those who want to learn more about this field are invited to read the materials of the International Conferences on Structural Mechanics in Reactor Technology (SMiRT) held once in every two years since 1973. Substantial information is also in the ASCE4 Standards.

The author hopes that this book is useful for engineers and researchers. The response is welcome! The E-mail address of the author can be found in the Introduction.

REFERENCES

Birbraer A.N. (1998) Seismic Analysis of Structures. – Saint-Petersburg: Nauka, 1998 (in Russian)

Lysmer J., Kuhlemeyer R.L. (1969). Finite Dynamic Model for Infinite Media // J. of Engineering Mechanics Div., ASCE. – 1969. – V. 95. – EM4. – Pp. 859-877.

Lysmer J., Waas G. (1972). Shear waves in plane infinite structures // J. Eng. Mech. Div. ASCE. – V. 98. – EM1.– Pp. 85-105.

Lysmer J.P. et al. (1981). SASSI – A Computer System for Dynamic Soil-Structure Interaction Analysis. Report No. UCB IGT/81-02, University of California, Berkeley.

Seismic Analysis of Safety-Related Nuclear Structures and Commentary. ASCE4-98 (1999). Reston, Virginia, USA.

Seismic Analysis of Safety-Related Nuclear Structures and Commentary. ASCE4-16 (2017). Reston, Virginia, USA.

Johnson, J.J., et al. (2010). A hybrid method to develop SSI parameters for rigid embedded foundations of arbitrary shape. / 2010 ASME Pressure Vessel and Piping Conf., ASME, New York.

Lysmer J., Udaka T., Seed H.B., Hwang R. (1974) LUSH – a Computer Program for Complex Response Analysis of Soil-Structure Systems Rep. EERC 74-4. Berkeley, California.

Lysmer J., Udaka T., Tsai C.F., Seed H.B. (1975) FLUSH – A Computer Program for Approximate 3-D Analysis of Soil-Structure Interaction Problems. Report No.75-30. University of California, Berkeley.

Lysmer J. (1982) Seismic Site and Soil-Structure Interaction Analysis / In: Martins J.B. (ed.) Numerical Methods in Geomechanics. NATO Advanced Study Institutes Series. Series C. – Vol. 92. Springer, Dordrecht. https://doi.org//10.1007/978-94-009-7895-9_18 .

NUREG 1.208 (2007) A Performance-Based Approach to Define the Site-Specific Earthquake Ground Motion. U.S. NRC, Washington DC.

Nowacki W. (1975) Elasticity Theory. – Moscow, Mir (in Russian, translated from Polish)

Ostadan F. (2006), SASSI2000. A system for analysis of soil-structure interaction. Revision 2. Jan. 2006

Schnabel P.B., Lysmer J., Seed H.B. (1972) SHAKE – a Computer Program for Earthquake Response Analysis of Horizontally Layered Sites. Rep. EERC 72-12. Berkeley, California.

Tyapin A. (2005) Frequency-Dependent Springs in Seismic Analysis of Structures // SMiRT-18. Beijing, 7-12 August 2005. K06_5.

Tyapin A.G. (2007). The frequency-dependent elements in the code SASSI: A bridge between civil engineers and the soil-structure interaction specialists // *Nuclear engineering and design.* – 237. – Pp. 1300-1306.

Tyapin A.G. (2011). The effects of the base mat's flexibility on the structure's seismic response. Part II: platform solutions // SMiRT21. New Delhi. 6-11 November 2011. # 266.

Tyapin A. (2012). Soil-Structure Interaction, Earthquake Engineering, Halil Sezen (ed.). Chapter 6. – Pp. 145-178. Available from: http://www.intechopen.com/books/earthquake-engineering/soil-structure-interaction.

Tyapin A. (2015). Reciprocity theorem and seismic loads impacting rigid basement in complex soil environment // SMiRT23. 2015. Manchester, UK. Rep. 36.

Tyapin A.G. (2017). Effect of soil improvement on seismic response // SMiRT24 Busan, Korea, 20-25 August 2017. Rep. D5-S14-2.

Wolf J.P. (1985) Dynamic Soil-Structure Interaction. Prentice-Hall, Englewood Cliffs, NJ.

Alexander Georgievich **Tyapin**

SOIL-STRUCTURE INTERACTION IN SEISMIC ANALYSIS

Computer-aided page proof by *A.G. Tyapin*
Editor V.V. Cosmin

Signed for printing 5.03.2019. Format 60×90/16
Offset paper. Times type. Offset printing.
Conventional 12,5 printed sheets.

ASV Construction, Sweden,
Mardvagen 16 131 50 Saltsjo-Duvnas

www.ingramcontent.com/pod-product-compliance
Lightning Source LLC
Chambersburg PA
CBHW070831300426
44111CB00014B/2517